Quality Field Instruction in Social Work

Program Development and Maintenance

EDITED BY
Bradford W. Sheafor
Lowell E. Jenkins
Both of Colorado State University

Published in cooperation with the
Council on Social Work Education

Longman
New York & London

QUALITY FIELD INSTRUCTION IN SOCIAL WORK

Longman Inc., 19 West 44th Street, New York, N.Y. 10036
Associated companies, branches, and representatives
throughout the world.

Developmental Editor: Nicole Benevento
Editorial and Design Supervisor: Frances Althaus
Cover Design: Eileen Beirne
Manufacturing and Production Supervisor: Anne Musso

Library of Congress Cataloging in Publication Data

Main entry under title:

Quality field instruction in social work.

Bibliography: p.
Includes indexes.
1. Social work education—Addresses, essays,
lectures. 2. Field work (Educational method)—
Addresses, essays, lectures. 3. Social work
education—Curricula—Addresses, essays, lectures.
I. Sheafor, Bradford W. II. Jenkins, Lowell E.
HVll.03 1982   361.3'07   81-14250
ISBN 0-582-28346-9   AACR2   .

Manufactured in the United States of America
9 8 7 6 5 4 3 2 1

Dedicated to

Nadine,
Perry, Brandon, Laura
Christopher, Sheryl, and Sara

Barbara,
Shelly, Elizabeth, and Jennifer

and

The thousands of field instructors
who give of their time, talents, and energy
to improve the quality of social work practice
through the instruction of students—
the next generation of social workers

Contents

Preface

The Council on Social Work Education (CSWE) has consistently supported the development of quality field instruction programs through accreditation standards at both the baccalaureate and master's levels and through publishing a significant amount of the available literature on this subject. Yet, field instruction programs of good quality have not typically developed. Recognizing this deficiency, the CSWE House of Delegates passed an ambitious directive in 1976 calling for social work education to begin substantive efforts to improve the quality of field instruction:

> ... CSWE should further develop and refine criteria and guidelines for the provision of field experiences. These criteria should cover the objectives, the obligations on the part of both the educational institutions and the practice setting, the content and demands to be made on the students, the criteria to employ in evaluating field experiences, and the interrelationship of the field experience and classroom work. It is recognized that implementation of this recommendation will require, ultimately, an intensive study of various field experience structures and their outcome, but, prior to such study, the basic issues and questions for research need further definition.*

To achieve greater quality in field instruction, practice and education each must have a sound understanding of the complexities of field teaching and a recognition of the resources required for a quality program. This book attempts to present a comprehensive view of the multiple dimensions of field instruction and to fill a significant gap in social work literature—the lack of a single volume providing an overview of the purpose, structure, and tasks required for student learning. It begins at the most general level and moves to the specifics of actually selecting learning assignments.

* "House of Delegates Acts on Structure and Quality, Practice, and Education Proposals," *Social Work Education Reporter*, Vol. 24, No. 2 (May, 1976), 12.

Several themes emerge as one reads through the chapters of this book. They seem particularly significant considering the great variation in the location, practice experience, and educational role and level of the authors.

First, field instruction is approached as a fully legitimate and re-spectable form of education. Although field instruction is too often re-legated to a second-class citizenship in higher education, the authors consistently reflect the view that it is as difficult as, and perhaps more demanding than, classroom instruction. Underlying many chapters is the perception that most schools and agencies do not allocate enough time and resources to support this complex task.

Second, field instruction is just that—instruction. The focus must be on the student and his or her growth and development as a compe-tent social work practitioner. While engaged in this educationally directed activity, the field instructor must be viewed by self and others as a teacher. To make this point, the familiar term "supervisor" is care-fully omitted as it implies a role in which the primary emphasis is on the administrative and accountability needs of an agency, with the growth and development of the worker or student as a secondary goal.

Third, field instruction provides a rare opportunity to experience individualized learning. This is not an argument for a one-to-one field instructor–student approach. In fact, it is argued that there are advan-tages to having groups of students assigned to a field instructor who can provide both individual and group instruction. Rather, it is recog-nition that field instruction offers a precious few months in a social work student's career when assignments can be controlled for the ex-press purpose of enhancing his or her development as a professional practitioner. The field instructor with a sound base in social work practice, knowledge of teaching-learning theory and approaches, and an accurate assessment of the learning needs of that student can pro-vide an unique opportunity for learning. Of course, the student must be prepared to make use of that opportunity.

Fourth, effective field instruction is marked by clarity of purpose. All parties engaged in the instructional process must be clear about the specific learning objectives of the activity and committed to their attain-ment. Included in this must be a common conception of social work. In this book social work is presented as a profession concerned with help-ing people prevent or resolve problems of social functioning (i.e., at the interface of person and environment). Although the practice of some social workers may deviate from this central thrust, the luxury of such variation cannot be afforded in the scarce time available for field instruction.

The fifth theme is that of the complex management problems associated with field instruction. There are many essential actors (i.e., school, agency, field instructor, student, and client), and the failure to make a meaningful commitment by any one can negate the work of the rest. Further, complex coordination and communication problems that plague field instruction are evident throughout the book.

Sixth, it is consistently recognized that each school must develop its own character. No standard set of guidelines can serve all programs. In fact, we avoided including examples of materials, fearing that some programs might adopt them without appropriately relating them to the school's unique character. An effort was made to suggest alternative approaches in each chapter in order to highlight the importance of schools selecting their own approach.

Seventh, although many social work field educators believe that instructional activity varies significantly in relation to MSW or BSW levels of instruction, practice setting, or geographic area, the authors almost universally found that the basic principles they identified were applicable to field instruction generally—and the specialized characteristics were of secondary importance. We would encourage those who can identify the differences to introduce their data into the literature.

Eighth, there is recognition that, as with any teaching endeavor, a certain degree of art is involved. The authors reflect a commitment to the enhancement of that art through the disciplined use of knowledge of teaching and learning processes, structure, and methods. The similarity to a process of planned change through engagement, assessment, planning, intervention, and evaluation appears with some regularity.

Last, a theme of regret appears. Regret that field instruction has not received the disciplined attention it deserves. Regret that experiential education has not truly developed academic credibility. Regret that research and scholarship to strengthen this form of teaching have been given relatively little attention. The other side of this regret is a challenge to correct the deficiencies and maximize the learning opportunities provided through high-quality field instruction programs.

Quality field instruction is difficult. In a professional field, "learning for doing" is the culmination of the student's academic experience, and the teacher's skill is reflected in the interaction of students with clients. Of the total curriculum, students most often consider this opportunity for direct contact with clients as the most valuable part of their professional education.

The focus of field instruction must be on the student. The task is more than serving clients or learning to do agency work, although those activities are important. It demands a carefully planned effort to enable students to draw consciously on their knowledge, values, skills, and life experiences to understand a human situation and helpfully intervene to improve it. It requires translating abstract knowledge and principles from classroom learning into practical applications. It also necessitates an understanding of self with the unique set of experiences, values, emotions, and capabilities that can be used to provide service. It requires a willingness and ability to understand the viewpoints of clients and the relationship of their needs and interests to the world around them. And, last, it means helping students become skillful in drawing on their own resources, as well as on the resources of the client-agency-community, to prevent or resolve problems in social functioning.

In field instruction the students are expected to begin the extremely difficult task of recognizing, understanding, and utilizing their total experience to engage competently in helping relationships. Yet, this experience must also be cast into the appropriate parameters of social work. The field instruction experience, then, must yield more than skilled helpers. It must also help to prepare committed professionals who function within the scope and expertise of social work, understand its expectations for ethical conduct, and plan to contribute to the improvement of the social work profession.

The authors of the chapters here prepared materials specifically for this publication. At times they were asked to give up presenting some favorite ideas about field instruction in order to add to the flow of the book and avoid repetition. At other times, they were pressured to meet deadlines and then wait long periods with little action. We are grateful for their tolerance, understanding, and willingness to live with our decisions.

We also wish to thank Karen Siefken, Gwynne Hallock, Nerena Parnell, and Carolyn Tressler who have typed, retyped, copied, collated, corresponded, and otherwise contributed to this venture.

Last, our thanks to our families whose love and support provided the strength and energy to complete this book.

Foreword

Quality Field Instruction in Social Work should become a landmark in the literature of field instruction. It is a comprehensive volume that provides a valuable historical perspective, acknowledging the past without tying field education to it, and incorporates new knowledge and perspectives without demanding a single model of field education that claims to serve all of social work education. In addition, it integrates what is well known about the delivery of field education with what is *not* so well known about the teaching-learning process in field education, and it effectively spans the gap between the general application of knowledge about learning and its specific application to field instruction needs.

The five parts of the book, taken together, address in depth all of the current complex issues on field education except, perhaps, some of the emerging legal concerns. They address what is, as well as what needs to be, and offer strategies and ideas for how to get there. The authors emphasize the importance of a social work frame of reference to guide field instruction and to give the reader an undeniable set and orientation toward development of quality field education soundly based on contemporary ideas of adult learning. The annotated bibliography should make this book a valuable reference tool for contemporary concepts and theories relevant to field instruction, as well as a handbook for all those involved in field education.

Sheafor and Jenkins have selected contributors with a vast knowledge of field instruction, including both graduate and undergraduate faculty (which is a must for this type of endeavor), and from a variety of geographical areas. The contributors all draw specifically on constructs from skill development, learning theory, and a knowledge of social work education and practice.

The editors have succeeded in integrating new perspectives on field instruction, pointing to future horizons. In itself a step forward, *Quality Field Instruction in Social Work* also indicates areas where further research is needed.

Norma Berkowitz

Part I
THE CONTEXT OF FIELD INSTRUCTION

Teaching and learning are difficult and complex activities under the best conditions. They require an investment of considerable time and energy on the part of both the teacher and the learner. Yet, time and energy are not enough to insure that a student can become a competent social work practitioner at the conclusion of the period of instruction. Knowledgeable and skillful field education requires much more.

Part 1 provides a framework in which the field instructor and student can place this teaching-learning experience into perspective. The three chapters in this part examine the context in which social work field instruction occurs, pointing out some of the reasons why "learning for doing" is difficult for both teacher and student.

In Chapter 1, "An Overview of Social Work Field Instruction," Sheafor and Jenkins examine the place of field instruction in social work education. Their model of field instruction (Figure 1-1) serves to integrate the several factors involved in this activity and, in fact, is the conception that organizes this book. Of special note is Sheafor and Jenkins's discussion of three approaches to field instruction: the apprenticeship orientation, the academic approach, and the articulated approach. The implications of each approach are analyzed and then connected to the learning paradigm presented in Chapter 2 and the historical analysis of field instruction found in Chapter 3.

In Chapter 2, "The Role of Frames of Reference in Field Instruction," Gordon and Gordon present several important ideas which are themes of this book. They identify three forms of learning: learning to "know," learning to "understand," and learning to "do." This learning approach is rooted in biological theory and parallels other learning theories. The authors conclude that learning which progresses from "knowing" to "understanding" to "doing" represents an effective approach to field instruction. This theory also helps to identify the difficult task the field instructor faces in helping a student translate knowing and understanding acquired in classroom instruction and other life experiences into knowledge- and value-guided practice.

The social work frame of reference and the learning frame of reference come together in field instruction. Supported by a helpful case example, Gordon and Gordon discuss what happens when the field instructor and student engage the educational process from this dual perspective.

In the third chapter, "A History of Social Work Field Instruction: Apprenticeship to Instruction," Aase George provides a historical perspective on the emergence of field instruction as an essential part of social work education. She traces the use of an apprenticeship model used in training "friendly visitors" in the pre-1900 Charity Organization Societies through the present patterns in undergraduate and graduate social work education.

Woven into George's material is the consistent reiteration that it is not possible to isolate field education from the history of social work education as a whole. The reader will see the emergence of accreditation standards; the influential role of field placement agencies in social work education; the influence of Freudian, Rankian, and other schools of thought on field instruction; the development of method specialties (e.g., casework, group work, community organization) and their application to field education; and a review of major studies of social work education.

1

An Overview of
Social Work Field Instruction

Lowell E. Jenkins
Bradford W. Sheafor

> The social worker should strive to
> become and remain proficient in
> professional practice and the
> performance of professional functions.
>
> NASW "CODE OF ETHICS"

Professional education lies at the heart of the social work profession and serves as a base on which the profession's commitment to providing high-quality social services is built. The ability of social work to fulfill this commitment depends on building and maintaining sound social work education programs in our colleges and universities.

A vital part of social work education is field instruction. Field instruction is an experiential form of teaching and learning in which the social work student is helped to: (1) consciously bring selected knowledge to the practice situation; (2) develop competence in performing practice skills; (3) learn to practice within the framework of social work values and ethics; (4) develop a professional commitment to social work practice; (5) evolve a practice style consistent with personal strengths and capacities; and (6) develop the ability to work effectively within a social agency. When field education is carefully examined, one often finds that field instructors and students undervalue the importance of using a knowledge-guided and carefully planned approach to this activity.

From its inception, social work education has consistently embraced the position that classroom and field learning are both essential elements of professional education. Yet, social work education has been unable or unwilling to submit the field instruction process to disciplined evaluation and, therefore, it has not generated an adequate literature to become an appropriately creditable part of higher education. One result has been great variation in field instruction, with much of it embarrassingly low in quality.

To the casual observer the development of a quality field instruction program may appear simple. After all, if experienced practitioners are willing to instruct novice students, the transmission of knowledge, values, and skills should be direct and clear. Certainly the availability of experienced practitioners who can share in the instruction of the student is essential; but the effective use of this valuable time and effort requires careful planning, a clear understanding of experiential education, a sound curriculum, and a good working relationship between the school and agency. It also requires an educationally knowledgeable and skilled field instructor and a dedicated student. One quickly learns, upon becoming involved in field instruction, that the task is exceedingly difficult. Quality field instruction requires considerable time, energy, funds, and expertise.

THE IMPORTANCE OF FIELD INSTRUCTION

Field instruction is much more than a carryover from the historical apprenticeship approach to social work education. It has the specific purpose of linking classroom learning with practice activities so that the new social worker can effectively engage in knowledge- and value-guided practice. It is this linkage that helps to differentiate the professional helper from the volunteer or natural helper. Unlike many academic disciplines, however, the purpose of learning in social work is not just for the personal development of the student. Additionally, it has the specific goal of preparing social workers to help individuals, families, groups, organizations, and even communities prevent or resolve problems of social functioning. These clients (and client systems) deserve social workers who are well prepared to competently provide services.

Further, in the present structure of social work education, field instruction consumes a considerable amount of each student's time and energy—both at the baccalaureate and master's levels. In most master's programs, for example, students spend from one-third to one-half of the educational experience in field instruction. It is often the only opportunity for students to engage in closely supervised professional practice with a protected caseload, allowing for the development of their professional selves. It is the responsibility of all persons engaged in that educational process (i.e., faculty, field instructor, and student) to maximize the learning experience.

An overworked and often misused term of the early 1970s was *relevance*. How to make college algebra or elementary Latin "relevant"

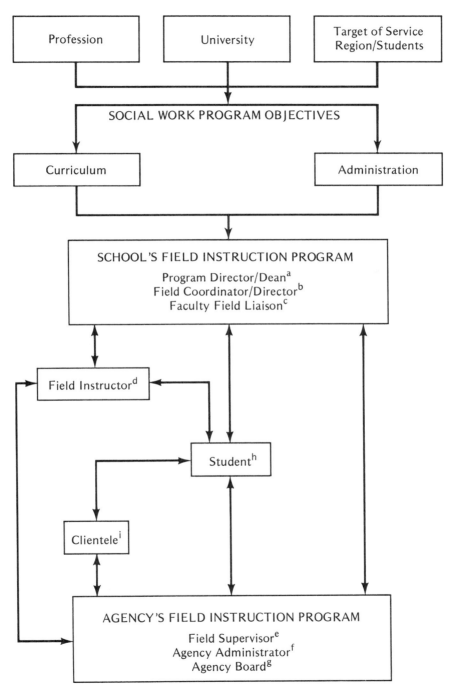

FIGURE 1.1   Field Instruction: A Comprehensive View. (*See note 2 at the end of this chapter for descriptions of the roles and responsibilities of the key participants.*)

perplexed and frustrated many educators. Social work education held the promise of greater relevance and has subsequently enjoyed considerable popularity. Relevance, in the best sense of the term, requires clear connection to concrete experiences. In social work education, that translates to a direct connection between practice needs and educational programs. Although social work education must never be limited to preparing students only for today's practice needs, educators and practitioners must constantly strive to build meaningful communication links that can help education stay attuned to developments in practice. It is evident that an appropriate place to begin strengthening these relationships is where the shared activity of practice and education most commonly occurs—in field instruction. It is there that schools and social agencies must collaboratively confront the task of preparing the student to conduct competent professional practice. It is also in field instruction that the match between educational objectives and the needs of practice becomes most clearly evident.

FIELD INSTRUCTION: A COMPREHENSIVE OVERVIEW[1]

The important place of field instruction in social work education is evidenced by the fact that it touches most aspects of the educational experience. Figure 1-1 depicts the many factors which must be considered when one takes a comprehensive view of field instruction.[2] It guides the following discussion of the field instruction process.

Sources of Sanction

For a social work program to develop to its maximum, sanction and support must be received from three sources: the college or university in which it is located, the profession of social work, and the students and/or region identified as the social work program's target of service.

First, it is essential that the program derive its purpose from the special mission of the *college or university* in which it is located. That mission will suggest an educational thrust or approach which will move the social work program in certain directions and constrain it in others. Although the clarity of that mission may be blurred at times, one would reasonably expect somewhat different programs to develop in a major research university, a land-grant college, or a small church-related school.

Second, in addition to being knowledgeable of and responsive to the factors in higher education at the specific college or university where it is located, the social work program must also accommodate the expectations of the *social work profession*. Professional education cannot be isolated from the emerging trends and patterns in service delivery. The ivory-tower isolationism that characterizes some aspects of academia is out of place in social work education. The idea that schools must build structures to encourage the practice community to participate in program development not only makes good sense but also has been strongly supported by the Council on Social Work Education House of Delegates.

> Educational programs should demonstrate that they provide opportunities for meaningful and continuing participation by practitioners and other representatives from practice settings that would make possible a significant influence on policy decisions that would affect the educational program.[3]

Structured input into decisions does not, of course, assure responsiveness. Faculty must be committed to listening to and hearing the issues with which practice is concerned. Education has a leadership responsibility which requires anticipating the needs of the profession in order to prepare new practitioners with the necessary knowledge, values, and skills to meet the practice demands of today and of the next few years. At the same time, education must use its resources to evaluate practice effectiveness and generate helping approaches to effectively serve client needs.

A program's approach to the task of curriculum development is also partially constrained by the profession. This may be expressed informally through evolving conceptions of the profession, such as the balance of its caring, curing, or changing functions;[4] the relationship of generalist to specialist approaches; and the relative emphasis placed on micro-, mezzo-, and macro-service levels. Further, through the National Association of Social Workers, such helpful but constraining factors as standards of practice, BSW and ACSW examinations, and standards for the conduct of ethical practice are explicated. Knowledge relevant to these factors must be transmitted to students. Finally, the Council on Social Work Education's standards for accreditation loom as another factor which brings greater comparability and quality to educational programs but also limits the autonomy of individual schools.

The profession, then, expects the schools to produce a graduate who is prepared to meet the practice expectations of social work. In this context, knowledge for the sake of knowledge is nothing, while knowledge for immediate use is everything. The schools, therefore, must develop and negotiate a curriculum that is responsive to both the academic tradition and the orientation of a particular university, as well as meets the needs of the social work profession for practitioners with particular skills.

Third, as opposed to technical training, professional education requires the preparation of people for autonomous practice—with the ability to make accurate judgments and to draw on a range of knowledge, values, and skills to help clients resolve problems in social functioning. Social workers must know why as well as what they are doing. They will be involved in complex interpersonal relations and must know themselves and their impact on the process, as well as understand the client or client group and its environment. Curriculum planning must accommodate the *development of the student* as well as prepare the student to understand and work with clients. Thus the particular strengths and limitations of the students who enter a program will have impact on its design. It is evident that the *uniqueness of the region or service area* where students are expected to practice will also influence some aspects of a curriculum.

Program Objectives

The social work program must bring together the three factors outlined above and develop its own program objectives. This activity shapes the program. Program objectives define the commitment of the school to specific goals such as providing baccalaureate and/or master's level education, preparing for practice or for additional educational levels, emphasizing on-campus or off-campus instruction, emphasizing classroom or experiential learning, and centering on human diversity issues and content or on another area of the curriculum. The program objectives also determine the general thrust of how the school's resources of faculty and staff, time, space, and money will be used. Thus, based on the program objectives, both curriculum and administrative structures are used as tools for achieving the program's goals.

Curriculum Development and Planning

Social work education has several factors that complicate curriculum-building efforts. Three major areas are evident. First, time, or the lack of it, is a major factor in social work education. Preparing the student for disciplined application of knowledge in practice acts which can be directed toward a range of client systems requires considerable time. Competition for the student's time between the classroom and the field instruction area has been a continuing problem.

Second, social work education is confronted with an ever-changing knowledge, value, and skill base. Educators and practitioners are increasingly engaged in research and knowledge building, yielding new information to incorporate into curricula. Basic knowledge that potentially affects the direction of social work practice must be gleaned from this new material, and new content that suits the special needs of specific programs must be sorted out.

Finally, social work is a profession with tremendous breadth. A profession which works at the interface of people and their environment inevitably will be confronted with issues on the scope of material to require of students. It is important to recognize that deciding what content is to be selected from the range of potential material can be frustrating and time-consuming. The selection of learning tasks and content, and the provision of adequate depth of material to meet practice demands, is often constrained by the interest and competence of a program's faculty.

Curriculum planners also need to specify their approach to the teaching-learning encounter. William Gordon and Margaret Schutz Gordon's knowing-understanding-doing paradigm[5] is helpful in clarifying the process of taking in theory or conceptual formulations, incorporating them into one's own practice style, and applying them in an objective and effective way. Their paradigm is comparable to other learning theories outlined by Bruner[6] and Kindelsperger.[7] This paradigm is briefly explained as follows: *Knowing* is the knowledge taken in and memorized, information stored but not applied; *understanding* is the use of stored concepts to explain specific situations; *doing* is the application of these concepts to real-life situations. Thus skill development in its broadest sense requires that the students have the opportunity to experience knowing, understanding, and doing through a planned, sequenced curriculum. Whether it be the Gordon-Gordon paradigm or some other learning theory, sound curriculum planning must identify the assumptions the school makes about how students learn.

Once assumptions are made about student learning, the social work program must develop objectives for each curriculum area. Typically these curriculum areas are labeled social welfare policy and services, human behavior and the social environment, human diversity, social work practice, social work research, and field instruction. These broad objectives are then translated into the learning objectives of a series of courses. In the variety of issues that must be resolved at this level if a school is to have an adequately integrated curriculum, one key issue concerns the function of field instruction. Is it to be viewed as an integral part of the curriculum where clearly specified content is taught, or is it a culminating experience where the student applies the classroom content? The answer to that question will affect the timing and number of courses used for field instruction, the demands placed on the field instructor to be knowledgeable about the content of classroom courses, and even the decision to use a block or concurrent structure for field instruction.

Program Administration

The implementation of a sound curriculum requires substantial administrative support. Adequate funds and staff must be provided for the program. A governance structure should allow for the full participation of faculty, students, and practice community. Space and other supports must be available in the form of offices, clerical staff, supplies, classrooms, and field settings for students to adequately perform their learning assignments.

A faculty incorporating a range of competencies and knowledge is obviously of importance. A cadre of new faculty members may flounder without experienced help in curriculum planning and development; likewise, a seasoned faculty may have difficulty changing perspectives and incorporating new content without the infusion of new blood. It is essential that the faculty commit themselves to giving time, effort, and thought to constructive curriculum development or the program is doomed to failure—or at least to less than optimum performance.

The two key administrators for field instruction in any school are the dean or program director and the field director or coordinator. These people are critical to the linkage of the program to the community, and their knowledge and support of field education is essential to making it a quality experience. The willingness of the dean or program director to commit the necessary resources of time, money, space, and energy to field instruction is prerequisite to building a sound program. Leadership at that level sets a tone for both the school's faculty and the agency field instructors, and it influences their willingness to view field instruction as a serious form of social work education.

Unquestionably one of the most taxing jobs in social work education is that of field director or coordinator. A person in that position must give leadership within the school to develop a sound field curriculum and compete with other interests to secure the necessary resources to implement it. The position demands that the coordinator develop good relationships within the social service delivery network, select and train a cadre of competent field instructors, understand the educational needs of the students and match them with field instructors, assign faculty members to serve as liaisons with the agencies, and evaluate student and field instructor performance. The skills with which these tasks are performed ultimately become pivotal factors in the overall quality of field instruction.

Implementation of the Field Instruction Program

The most well-designed curriculum, even when coupled with solid administrative support, is of little value if the implementation of the field instruction program breaks down. The lower half of Figure 1-1 identifies the several parties that are critical to any successful field instruction program. Inadequacy of commitment, support, or ability from any of these key contributors can have serious consequences for field learning.

The Agency. The social agency in which the placement occurs also plays a significant role. The agency must be committed to participating in the educational effort from its board down to its secretarial staff if the student is to have the maximum opportunity for learning. The agency must balance its commitment to offering a learning opportunity to the novice social worker with its charge to provide quality services to its clientele. The agency administrator is a central person who must free the necessary time of the field instructor to prepare for the role, provide space and equipment for the student to function as a professional social worker, and provide the supports of clerical staff, transportation, and equipment necessary to carry out responsible practice. For the agency, engaging in field instruction will not usually represent a cost-effective activity. The costs in most cases exceed the services rendered by the student. Yet, other benefits to the agency such as stimulation for the field instructor, direct contact with trends in social work education, recruitment of new staff, and fulfilling a commitment to enhance the quality of social services make the effort worthwhile.

The Field Instructor. The field instructor must also make a substantial investment in field instruction. Even though the agency should be expected to make time available for this educational activity, it often places a heavy load on the field instructor to arrange the necessary time to select assignments, teach the student, read the student's work, and participate in the school's varied activities for field instructors. Too often the agency does not even recognize this contribution when the field instructor is evaluated. To be a good field teacher takes time and energy which, when added to the tasks of an already busy social worker, call for special efforts. Linking the school and agency in the instructional process is a difficult task which requires knowledge of both the agency and the school. Further, the responsibility for individualizing the learning opportunities to best meet the needs of each student ultimately lies with the field instructor. Thus, skills in educational assessment as well as skill in teaching are required of the competent field instructor.

The Student. The student cannot be a passive learner in field instruction. Field instruction requires that the student actively participate in shaping the learning experience to meet his or her individual learning needs. Clearly the selection process is constrained by the learning objectives developed by the school and the service orientation and goals of the agency, yet there is considerable latitude for the student to negotiate an individualized learning experience. This negotiation frequently begins with the field director or coordinator when a placement is being planned and carries over into the daily decisions that the field instructor and student make concerning assignments. Field instruction is

often based on assumptions and expectations that the student is functioning as an adult learner who is willing and able to assume responsibility for the learning experience. For many students this is a new expectation for which they may not be prepared. Thus, field instruction
may place considerable strain on the students to develop a new sense
of responsibility for their own actions as well as for the welfare of
others through the provision of social services.

The Client. Finally, the client or client system cannot be ignored in the
process of field instruction. Careful planning by all parties is required
to assure that the quality of service to clients is not seriously compro-
mised for the sake of student learning. It is not uncommon for an agency
to develop a caseload of clients who can be passed from one student to
the next. At times the clients even take pride in their role in "teaching
the ropes" to new social workers. However, little attention has been
given in the field instruction literature to the rights and responsibilities
of the clients of students.[8]

Once the roles and responsibilities of each party in field instruction
are clear, considerable effort is still required to establish and maintain
linkages which facilitate the desired interaction of the parties. The process is fraught with issues which demand constant attention. The following material identifies eight critical relationships and some of the
common issues relevant to each.

1. *School-Agency.* The contract must clearly specify who calls
   which shots. It is often necessary to clarify this question of authority on issues such as protection of student learning vs.
   provision of agency service, selection and termination of field
   instructors, clarification of the role of the field consultant or
   liaison from the school, and identification of the range of learning tasks that are regularly faced in field instruction.
2. *Agency-Client.* Clients have a right to expect quality services
   when they seek help from a social agency. The agency potentially jeopardizes its reputation and its contract with clients if
   the student does not competently provide services. Issues related to adequate oversight of student work, quality-control
   mechanisms, right to nonservice, confidentiality, and so on,
   are common to the field instruction endeavor.
3. *Client-Student.* Although student interest in client services is
   rarely a problem, the student is by definition a novice seeking
   to learn appropriate helping techniques. That process will in-
   herently result in uneven performance. How to balance learning with service, and breadth with depth, often plagues this
   relationship.

4. *Student–Field Instructor.* In this relationship issues of participation in activities such as setting learning goals, selecting tasks, and determining utilization of time predominate. Balancing the role of teacher and supervisor places the field instructor in a difficult position, and the temptation of placing the school in the position of mutual enemy to unite student and field instructor frequently confronts this interaction.

5. *Field Instructor–School.* Issues concerning this relationship include the school's requirements of training for the field instructor role, type and amount of consultation from the school, grading, clarification of tasks to be performed, benefits from assuming field teaching responsibilities, payment, and participation in the school's governance.

6. *Field Instructor–Agency.* The field instructor is often caught between the school and agency in the field instruction process. Relative to the agency, the instructor faces the need to have time ensured for the instructional process and rewards such as salary increases and promotions reflecting the contribution he or she makes to student learning.

7. *School-Student.* Commonly found in this relationship are issues relating to clarity of expectation, methods of evaluation, temptation of faculty to use the student as a "spy on agency practice," and efforts to use the student as a change agent concerning the agency and its services.

8. *Student-Agency.* Finally, the student must regularly deal with overt or covert efforts from agency personnel to treat him or her as a source of free labor, as someone to perform routine tasks of a nonprofessional nature, and possibly as a "spy on the strange things they do at that school." In addition, the student will confront the issues commonly found when professionals work in bureaucratic structures (i.e., resistance to bureaucratic rules, rejection of bureaucratic standards, resistance to bureaucratic supervision, and conditional loyalty to the organization).[9]

The above is not an exhaustive treatment of the many linkage issues in field instruction. However, the examples given serve to illustrate the importance of all parties devoting considerable effort to resolve or minimize problems by maintaining positive working relationships.

NOTES ON THE NATURE OF FIELD LEARNING

Three approaches to experiential learning characterize social work field instruction: the apprenticeship, the academic, and the articulated orientations. Most schools operate with combinations or modifications of these approaches, or, too often, without specifying the approach used. To highlight the uniqueness of each approach, they are described here as they might be applied in their purest forms—as ideal formulations.

The Apprenticeship Approach

The apprenticeship approach was the first model used in social work education. The early-day friendly visitors were taught by observing an experienced person working with people and then emulating that practice with their own clients. The initiation of social work education under agency auspices (i.e., the New York Charity Organization Society) was a viable structure for using the apprenticeship model. Elements of this approach have been preserved in social work and may be seen in the supervision of new workers in an agency and in some approaches to the education of new persons for the profession. Using the Gordon-Gordon knowing-understanding-doing paradigm, we can describe the apprenticeship approach as placing primary emphasis on *doing* and from that activity deriving the necessary knowledge and understanding to support social work practice.

When we apply the apprentice model to social work education, we opt for an inductive approach to learning (i.e., helping students induce theory from practice examples). There are convincing arguments that effective work with people depends heavily on the helper's life experience which provides a background for understanding and empathizing with the human condition. It is not uncommon for employing agencies and graduate programs to use age or maturity as a factor in the selection process. The fundamental argument behind this position is that the student needs time to experience life beyond the "unnatural" college environment and to be in an independent living situation where one must take full responsibility for oneself. Although skills developed from that experience are important, often the additional experience of working directly with people is viewed as even more important.

When we apply the apprenticeship approach to curriculum design, we place a heavy emphasis on providing the student with a great deal of practice experience which begins early in the educational program. The effort is to get the students into contact with clients so that when the classroom provides theory, they will have a base of experience on which to apply that theory. Ideally, the classroom would aid the learning process by providing relevant theories at the time the student is ready for them. Unfortunately, outside of a tutorial arrangement, it is virtually impossible for classroom learning to match the experiential base of each student. The logical organization of content, as the classroom instructor views it, may not correspond to each student's readiness. It is the field instructor, provided that he or she has an adequate knowledge base, who is in the best position to teach at the student's pace.

If a school were to fully accept the apprenticeship approach, the curriculum would begin with a substantial practicum experience. Students would be given a block field placement to allow time to develop a solid experiential base to which they could then relate the underpinning knowledge. Although one might wonder about the responsibleness of an agency that makes its clients available for such a learning endeavor, the client risk is not too different with untrained workers or in concurrent class and field experiences which begin the first few weeks into a student's professional education. Our observations would, in fact, indicate that most schools—particularly at the graduate level—use a curriculum structure that partially reflects the apprenticeship approach.

Implementation of this model of field instruction depends heavily on the field agency providing the substance of the learning experience. It is the experience itself that has the greatest meaning for the student, and thus, the agency can be relatively free to determine the nature of that learning. From the school's perspective, the problems in the administration of any field program are significant, but the apprentice approach is much less time-consuming than other models of field instruction. The task primarily involves negotiation for good agency field instructors and adequate administrative support from the agency.

Difficult as those items are to negotiate, they do not require the constant maintenance needed in other educational approaches. Once the student is placed in a solid agency with a good field instructor, the school has little to do other than to put out grass fires. This approach involves a fairly limited investment of faculty resources in field instruction. Even the role of the faculty liaison to the agency is only to check on the student's progress to be sure that generally adequate development occurs. The primary responsibility for integration of class and field learning rests with the student and field instructor.

The Academic Approach

The second approach, the academic, places an emphasis on the student's cognitive development. Using the Gordon-Gordon learning paradigm, the emphasis now is placed on *knowing* and *understanding* with the *doing* viewed as providing examples for the learning that occurs in the classroom. With this approach, the student is expected to deduce a practice approach from classroom learning.

The academic approach is a central part of the fabric of higher education. Knowledge acquired for the sake of having that knowledge is valued in the educated person. If that knowledge has a practical application, it is a secondary gain which has increasingly been valued. The academic model characterizes the arena in which most baccalaureate social work programs operate (i.e., liberal arts colleges).

Experiential learning in the academic approach usually takes the form of a practicum; in teacher education, for example, the practicum is often tagged on as the last semester of the student's academic career. Some of the block-placement structures used by social work programs reflect adaptations of this approach. It represents a clear commitment by a school to prepare social workers capable of knowledge-directed practice.

Schools that use this educational model place a premium on selecting students with good cognitive ability. The "A" student from almost any major with little or no practice experience is an acceptable candidate for such schools. The tendency, when developing curriculum, at both bachelor's and master's levels, is to pack the early part of the experience with academic work and to delay or reduce field instruction as far as the market (i.e., students and practice community) will allow. This plan benefits the classroom instructors as it places little demand on them to coordinate their teaching with field instruction.

The difficulty with the academic approach rests with the student's need to try out the theoretical material while it is being presented. For many students, to store a large body of knowledge and draw on it as needed is a difficult task. Perhaps the common charge of irrelevant content is not unwarranted in these situations. At the same time, it is not uncommon for agencies to protest about the ivory-tower, inexperienced students who are dropped in their laps for field instruction. Yet, the proponents of this approach argue that having a good knowledge base and little practice experience is surely preferable to having both little knowledge *and* little experience when the quality of client service is risked for field instruction.

The academic model takes much of the pressure off of the field instructor. That instructor may feel somewhat threatened by the student who comes expecting the field instructor to show how the theory is applied—as promised by the classroom instructor. Otherwise, the paid faculty has assumed virtually the entire responsibility for the student's learning, and the field instructor essentially facilitates an experience where the students test out their knoweldge.

Once the placements are negotiated and the students assigned, the major maintenance task is to keep the field instructors informed of curriculum content. Mailing of the course outlines and an occasional meeting to discuss content should suffice. The faculty liaison becomes a prime resource for the student, as that person is presumed to be familiar with classroom content and should be able to help students with its application. The amount of time a school can expect to invest in faculty resources for this purpose would necessarily be greater than for the apprenticeship approach. However, once again, the primary responsibility for the integration of class and field learning rests with the student.

The Articulated Approach

Finally, the articulated approach is concerned with a planned relationship between cognitive and experiential learning. It calls for the faculty, the student, and the field instructor to share responsibility for the learning experience. In the Gordon-Gordon paradigm, the knowing, understanding, and doing would be of equal weight. The objective would be for the student to be fully aware of what is involved in a practice act, know why that intervention is selected, and be prepared to determine how the necessary helping techniques should be performed. Beyond that, the art of the student's individual practice style takes over.

The articulated approach has been a goal in social work education for some time. Yet, the reality of field instruction is that planned linkage between classroom and field content rarely occurs on paper and even more rarely in practice.

Application of the articulated model requires considerable planning. Both class and field learning must be developed with clear learning objectives which are carefully sequenced to allow their integration. This planning must have the full acceptance of the class and field faculty—a difficult if not impossible task in any but very small programs. To plan an articulated curriculum which is acceptable to the faculty members and is also attuned to the needs of the students and field agencies is even more difficult.

Yet the difficulty of the task is not a deterrent to the advocates of this position. They argue that its potential benefits make the effort worthwhile. It balances the premium placed on both cognitive ability and practice wisdom. The student can be neither all heart nor all head, and admission requirements should recognize this balance. It does not demand that the student be either an inductive or deductive learner but keeps knowledge development and practice close enough together in time to minimize these differences in learning style.

The structure of learning which the articulated approach requires begins with simple skill development at the time basic behavioral and practice theories are introduced. Perhaps the most appropriate learning sequence would be to begin with a laboratory experience in which fundamental helping skills are developed and the student is helped to develop self-confidence in using basic helping techniques. As more complex theoretical material is introduced in the classroom, the student might progress to a modified practicum or even a volunteer experience where these skillls are tested and refined—or the student might move directly from the lab to a full field experience. Throughout both the class and field experiences, the student starts with basic knowledge and simple tasks and gradually builds on that base. The close relationship between knowing and doing allows for a cycle of introduction to material, testing that in practice, reviewing the knowledge base, and integrating that into one's practice style. The concurrent structure of field placement is the most viable option to support this approach.

Agencies tend to prefer the articulated approach as it does not expect the student to provide service without an adequate knowledge base. Yet, it keeps the students directly involved in a service-giving capacity throughout the educational process and reduces the probability of graduating students who are cognitive giants and practice dwarfs. The cost to agencies is substantial as the agency field instructors, who become a real, if unpaid, part of the faculty, must commit considerable time. They must provide a substantial part of the educational task of articulation and inevitably must reduce their own service load to achieve the educational goals.

The cost to the school is also substantial. The field administrator must not only carry out the placement functions but must also constantly be engaged in curriculum-development activity to keep the expectations tuned to changes in the knowledge base and the direction of social work practice. The dissemination of information itself is a demanding task. There are also considerable costs to the school in faculty time if the field liaison is to play a significant role as a resource person or consultant for the field instructor on the field instruction endeavor. This requires regular and frequent contact where student progress can be reviewed and the field instructor can be helped to resolve any impediments to a good learning environment. To accomplish this integration requires time, effort, and commitment by both education and practice.

The greatest strength of the articulation approach is its focus on student learning. The faculty, the agency, and the field instructor join with the student to produce a practitioner capable of knowledge and value-guided practice. Its greatest limitation is the inordinate amount of planning and communication required to maintain an articulated plan. The cost of that activity, if it is done properly, is significantly more than for the apprentice and academic orientations.

SUMMARY

Which approach will best achieve quality field instruction? Clearly the approach selected should be a conscious choice. The school should examine the fit of that approach with the orientation of the college or university in which it is located and the political climate for introducing new approaches to field instruction. The school must also review the constraints on a field curriculum imposed by the profession and the characteristics of its student body. Further, it must consider the practice needs of the school's service area and the ability of the school and practice community to support the approach selected. Finally, a school must examine its ability to bring the necessary administrative resources to support the approach used and maintain the required linkage. A school's response to all of these factors must be a part of determining which approach to adopt.

All of higher education is concerned with the difficult task of providing instruction which will help students acquire knowledge and understanding. Disciplines that require students to translate that knowledge and understanding into practice activities have an even more difficult challenge. Social work field education faces that challenge. For a school to be clear about the approach it has selected for field instruction and the benefits and costs of that approach is a first step in rising to the challenge.

NOTES

1. This material is partially adapted from Bradford W. Sheafor and Lowell E. Jenkins, "Issues That Affect the Development of a Field Instruction Curriculum," *Journal of Education for Social Work*, Vol. 17 (Winter, 1981), 12–20.
2. Items a–i on Figure 1-1 relate to the roles and responsibilities of several key participants in field instruction. The following descriptions are offered for each:
    a. *Program Director/Dean*—leadership and support; secure resources; public relations
    b. *Field Coordinator/Director*—administrative leadership; develop-implement-evaluate policies; develop field instruction resources; care and maintenance of field program
    c. *Field Liaison*—consultation, monitoring, and evaluation; link to classroom
    d. *Field Instructor*—teach, plan, evaluate, and facilitate learning process
    e. *Field Supervisor*—task management; facilitate integration into agency; not necessarily a social worker
    f. *Agency Administrator*—administrative support; resource allocation; not necessarily a social worker
    g. *Agency Board*—sanction through agency policy
    h. *Student*—active learning; assume role of a staff member; selection-planning-execution of learning/service tasks; engage in knowledge-value-guided practice; professional socialization; evaluation of own performance
    i. *Clientele*—expect quality services, protection of confidentiality, and right to accept or reject student as service provider
3. Council on Social Work Education, "Summary Minutes: Meeting of the House of Delegates, March 4–5, 1976" (New York: Council on Social Work Education, 1976), p. 3.

4. Armando Morales and Bradford W. Sheafor, *Social Work: A Profession of Many Faces*, 2nd edition (Boston: Allyn and Bacon, 1980), pp. 340–344.
5. William E. Gordon and Margaret L. Schutz, *FIRP: Final Report Field Instruction Research Project* (St. Louis: George Warren Brown School of Social Work, Washington University, 1969), pp. 7–14. *See* Chapter 2 for a more elaborate discussion of the Gordon-Gordon paradigm.
6. Jerome S. Bruner, *The Process of Education* (New York: Vintage Books, Alfred A. Knopf, and Random House, 1963), pp. 17–18.
7. Walter L. Kindelsperger, "Modes of Formal Adult Learning in Preparation for the Service Professions" (Paper delivered at the Working Party on Field Learning and Teaching, Tulane University, New Orleans, October 30–November 1, 1967), mimeographed, pp. 4–6.
8. *See* Chapter 10, "The Rights and Responsibilities of Clientele in Field Instruction," for what may be the first serious exploration of this subject.
9. W. Richard Scott, "Professionals in Bureaucracies—Areas of Conflict," *Professionalization*, ed. Howard M. Vollmer and Donald L. Mills (Englewood Cliffs, NJ: Prentice Hall, 1966), pp. 265–275.

2

The Role of Frames of Reference in Field Instruction

William E. Gordon
Margaret Schutz Gordon

All human action that is guided by knowledge is carried out in some frame of reference. This chapter focuses on the nature of a frame of reference and its function in professional practice and concludes with descriptions of a social work practice frame of reference, a learning frame of reference, and the function of both in field learning in social work.

THE NATURE AND UTILITY OF A FRAME OF REFERENCE

The major function of a frame of reference in a profession is to mark out or bound the primary scope of concern of that profession—a special need in social work because of its traditionally broad scope and the difficulty experienced in bounding its own terrain.[1] Professions as well as disciplines need a focusing frame of reference that can mark out broadly not only that part of reality with which they will concern themselves but also how they will view it from their respective frames of reference. The same apparent piece of reality may be viewed differently. Thus, the same rock may be looked at by a crystallographer, a mineralogist, a historic geologist, or a builder; and each will view it in a way limited by his or her respective frame of reference.

The following part of a case description will illustrate how a frame of reference limits or determines what a field teacher and a student will attend to as the student learns to become a social worker. A male student, in his first field setting—a hospital social work department—is assigned the case of a 75-year-old woman who has suffered a mild stroke and for whom discharge planning is necessary. The patient, Mrs. A, has lived alone in her own little house, has a very modest but generally sufficient income from Social Security and her husband's insurance benefits, and has been able to take care of herself. She is now somewhat incapacitated by a definite left-side weakness, though not paralysis, and she will need to get more rest and will be unable to walk as much as she did. Unable to drive and having no nearby public transportation, Mrs. A formerly walked several blocks to the nearby shopping center for her groceries, drugs, and other daily living needs. From the doctors' and the hospital's frames of reference, it is recommended that Mrs. A be sent to a nursing home.

Here the student and field instructor enter the picture. The simplest action (assuming there are nursing home beds available in town) would be to locate a nursing home which could accept Mrs. A and to arrange the necessary papers, and other matters, for her to be moved there. But the student, having learned in class how to know and understand the practice framework presented here, knows he must consider not only the patient's immediate impinging environment—the hospital, including the doctors and nurses—but must extend his assessment to include other aspects of the patient's environment beyond the hospital and to get a full picture of the patient's coping ability both currently and potentially. For example, how will the patient's usual independent functioning (coping behavior) be affected by her limited ability to get around? Accordingly, the student interviews the patient further to learn what her preference for care is, what the strengths and limitations of her situation are, what other environmental impingements are present to contribute or detract from the situation. In other words, the student considers the interface of this patient with her current (hospital) environment and also the other significant interfaces in this woman's current life. He considers the "whole" person in her "whole" environment, using the immediate "problem" interface as the entry point from which to make the overall social work assessment called for by this frame of reference.[2]

Note that to this point the frame of reference has both limited what will be attended to (the color of the woman's hair, her parents' occupations are not relevant) and extended what will be attended to (the previous living arrangements and functioning of the patient).

A frame of reference serves to reduce the complexity of observed reality by organizing it. Since our senses always present us with more than can be readily comprehended—more apparently separate, nonordered pieces than we can handle—there is a basic need to reduce this complexity by both a reduction in separate pieces and replacement of disorder with order to improve comprehension.

The student is then helped by his field instructor to appreciate the needs of the particular setting which calls for the patient to be discharged within a couple of days, so now he must move quickly. He is also helped by his field instructor to get the full picture so as not to move too quickly to a solution that will meet the hospital's needs but will fail to meet the patient's needs. Doing that would deny the values of the profession into which he has moved and within which he is putting to use (practicing) his newly learned knowledge and values. Learning that the patient very much wants to return to her own home and is fearful of a nursing home, the student seeks other environmental supports to see if remaining in her own home is possible. Although there are no children, the patient has three nieces who live in town, and also a great-niece, all of whom are fond of Mrs. A but have not paid much attention to her lately. The social work student rallies them around, calling forth a strength from the environment, and they, together with visiting nurses and meals-on-wheels, both of which the student refers the patient to, can assist Mrs. A enough so that she can remain in her own home. There she will still be able to have her ten-year-old neighbor come after school, which he regularly has done, waiting there until his mother returns from work about 5:00. The boy can help by carrying out papers and trash and doing other little jobs which need doing about the place. Additionally, the boy and Mrs. A provide companionship for each other.

Finally, a frame of reference serves to determine what perceptions of the human scene are consistent or compatible with that of the profession or discipline. The familiar goal of "the greatest good for the greatest number" is incompatible not only with the mathematical perspective which holds that two things can not be maximized simultaneously but also with the social work frame of reference which does not hold to sacrificing even a few individuals for the greater gain of the majority. For example, in the case above, if the student quickly moves to make the nursing home arrangements, neither the client's goals nor the goals of the profession will be met. The student, by attending to the patient's preferences and strengths, permits the patient to remain in her own home, thus helping her maximize her own potential and contribute to others (ameliorate her environment).

Thus, a frame of reference bounds or selects out that part of reality about which the profession or discipline claims some expertise. It further reduces the complexity of reality by organizing it, by reducing and ordering the number of entities that must be attended to; and finally, it serves as a screen for selecting the knowledge and values which will guide practice.

Field instruction in social work, unlike social work practice itself, requires two frames of reference: (1) the professional-practice frame of reference which marks out and begins to structure the part of social reality that constitutes its practice and (2) a learning frame of reference which guides the teaching and learning of the practice frame of reference. We now move to a more explicit and detailed description of these two frames of reference.

A SOCIAL WORK PRACTICE FRAME OF REFERENCE

This is a frame of reference that a student learns to use as a guide for approaching social reality as a professional social worker. In broad terms, it suggests the perspective from which a social worker sees people, how clientele are related to their environment, what goals the social worker may help them achieve, where there may be difficulty, and what changes may be needed in order for them to achieve their goals.

This frame of reference rests upon the fairly well documented position that social work is a nonnormative profession in that it has generally espoused no form of a utopian society and no ideal conduct behaviorally. Its ultimate goal, rather, has been to bring the realities of a person's capabilities and his or her social situation into sufficient balance so that the individual may realize his or her maximum potential, on the one hand, and make a contribution to others seeking the same goal, on the other. Sometimes this is referred to as striking some balance between self-realization and social contribution without specifying for any person where the balance will be struck. As social work has become tinged with the scientific perspective, it has been forced to translate this philosophical stance into a conceptual form which is compatible with the findings of the social-behavioral sciences and thus, hopefully, illuminates the professional practice of social work. For example, realization of potential can occur only as a result of the individual's growth and development, and contribution to society can occur only if the individual somehow brings about an ameliorated change in the environment (social milieu) conducive to the growth and development of others.

It is also fairly well documented that the underlying mechanism for growth and development of individuals and amelioration of the environment is *exchange* between person and environment. Put more technically, people, like all organisms, are open systems into which there is input and from which there is output. Further, this exchange must occur in the context of an *action* field which can sustain it. To sustain or permit exchange, this action field must have certain qualities—just any action field will not suffice. At the moment, these qualities are unnamed and unknown but are thought to be dependent on the extent to which the individual can match his or her environment-directed behavior with the impinging environment in such a way as to render the activity mix (transaction field) permeable to controlled exchange between person and environment.

The two sources of this activity mix are the environment-directed behavior of the person(s) and the impinging environment. We regard coping behavior as that behavior of the individual consciously directed to management of this transaction field. Impinging environment is the part of the person's environment that reaches the interface between

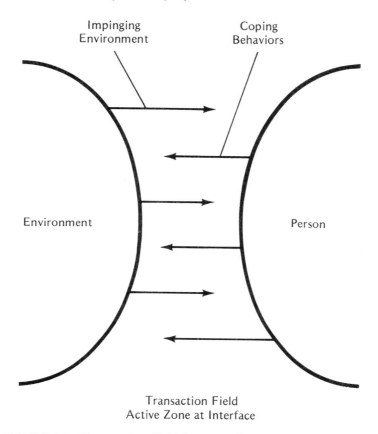

Transaction Field
Active Zone at Interface

FIGURE 2.1   Transaction Field Between Person and Environment.

person and environment. This frame of reference is schematically shown in Figure 2-1.

The interface and its attendant phenomena is the focal point of social work concern. From this focal point, social work moves back from the interface further into the environment, on one hand, and toward what lies behind the coping behavior of the person(s), on the other: (1) to identify "causes" of coping behavior and "causes" of impinging environment that may be responsible for the dysfunctional mismatch and in search of points of intervention and (2) to anticipate consequences to the environment and to the individual(s) of the proposed intervention.

The reader will note that this frame of reference is quite independent of the traditional "methods" of social work: casework, group work, and community organization. It is a person-environment—centered perspective which remains the same whatever the method that is used. In a group, each member's impinging environment consists of the output of all other members with which a given member may or may not be able to cope, with resulting deleterious effect on that person and on the group. Thus, a group may become a highly controlled environment specifically designed to modify the coping ability of its members, as is well demonstrated in therapy groups. That the transactions among members may set in motion certain predictable regularities gives rise to group theory that may be utilized by social work practitioners within the context of the social work frame of reference. Similarly, other techniques of group or family behavior may be used in the social work frame of reference so long as they are consistent with the concern for *every* member's transactions that will produce growth and development and be constructive to the environment.

Adherence to this frame of reference would not condone the use of procedures to select the most productive members of a task force without concern for the consequences to those who are not selected. Any of the technologies of Gestalt, family therapy, or behavior modification, and so on, may be used as long as the overall perspective of the social work frame of reference is maintained so the practitioner is always focused upon both *person and environment* with respect to the causes and consequences of the match or mismatch between them.

Since the central focus of social work practice is the interface between person and environment, with particular attention to how the match of coping behavior and impinging environment affects the transaction and hence the outcome for both, it follows that as one moves "deeper" into the person or the environment in search of causal conditions behind that interface, the closer one comes to the outer boundaries of social work expertise. Exclusive concern with the intrapersonal factors controlling human behavior is the basis of several behavioral sciences; and beyond them lie fields such as physiology, neurology, and genetics on the person side, and on the environment side, all those disciplines that attempt to explain the development of the current environment and its impingement on the human condition. While social work may well utilize some of the insights from these disciplines, it only becomes social work practice when one focuses *simultaneously* on person and environment, and most clearly when that focus centers on the actual interface.

THE LEARNING FRAME OF REFERENCE

The primary objective for the field students is learning in both classroom and field, and while they may and do engage in some practice, learning should be the paramount concern. Where practice is regarded solely as an art, there is no way but to "learn by doing." However, where practice purports to be in some degree consciously knowledge-value-technique guided, there are at least three kinds of learning to be accomplished: (1) learning to "know"; (2) learning to "understand"; and (3) learning to "do."[3]

We assume that the conditioning of the human organism to perceive and act in reality situations through the mediation of knowledge (cognitive maps) is a complex process involving at least three different kinds of objectives in our testing and our teaching.

Knowing refers entirely to the cognitive realm and specifically to conceptual mastery of knowledge—to the acquisition by the student of constructs, generalizations, and concepts—the building blocks of knowledge. Knowledge, the stuff to be mastered by the students, and which results in their knowing, is used in two senses. First, there is the symbolized form, usually verbal descriptions and definitions referred to as S-state knowledge; and second, there is the in-the-mind form, related to whatever changes are induced in neurological paths and patterns by exposure to the symbolized form of knowledge in various learning contexts, called N-state knowledge.[4] Knowing, in our view, is achieved when exposure to symbolized knowledge in the context of various learning situations results in neurological pattern changes. Thus, knowing is influenced not only by the learning experiences in the traditional sense but also by the nature and progression in the S-state knowledge itself. These changes in N-state knowledge, of course, can be judged at present only through a response to test stimuli or by introspective judgments reported by the student.

Understanding, as used here, refers to that part of human behavior occurring when perceptual inputs or reports thereof are brought into juxtaposition with the cognitive mapping system of the student and are organized by those maps to yield explanations and predictions with respect to the perceptual inputs. Conceptually, the significant element here is the student's confronting directly or vicariously the reality instances wherein his or her cognitive maps come into play, not only to explain the inputs but to suggest what to further look for, how to interpret what has come in, and what to expect. In general, the approach to understanding is similar to, but not identical with, Kelly's idea of the function of his constructs when he says, "Man looks at his world through transparent patterns or templets which he creates and then attempts to fit over the realities of which the world is composed."[5] The idea of understanding is roughly similar to Sarbin's, et. al., approach to conceiving of clinical inference in that an objective input to the human senses is assumed (though not particularly realized); the organism then has the task of organizing these inputs or "structuring" that part of the environment from whence these inputs came before it can take rational and knowledge-based action with respect to that environment.

Doing objectives include the field performances conceived to be directed toward professional intervention. No matter what levels of knowing and understanding are attained, there is no professional intervention until the practitioner has acted on his or her surroundings; that is, until something has crossed over the practitioner's boundary that has impact on those surroundings. No matter how much activity goes on within the practitioner, there is no interventive effect unless some of the action emerges to reach her or his surroundings. At a less fundamental, more common-sense level, we do recognize that a critical part of practice is what reaches those toward whom the practice is directed. It involves a range of human activity which can be sensed by others—talking and other communication by tone of voice, facial expression, bodily movements, and so on. A part of becoming a good practitioner is the coordination of all modes of communication to others so that the same message comes through on all channels or, more generally, the organization of motor behavior in such a way that one part supports or reinforces another toward a goal that has been determined from understanding a situation.

The conceptual separation of knowing, understanding, and doing is an attempt to recognize that the respective neurological systems (cognitive, perceptual, and motor) are different and, therefore, probably call for different kinds of learning experiences and different kinds of testing. It also attempts to recognize that students may acquire a concept without being able to use it with incoming data or information, or they may be able to apply the concept, in the sense of explaining or making predictions about a given situation, without it following that their motor system will then act in accordance with their understanding of the situation. The person who acts without being able to give the knowledge basis for this action (one form of intuitive practice) is presumably being guided by some kind of programming of his or her neurological system. The fact that he or she cannot report the knowledge basis does not mean that some kind of knowledge is not being used preconsciously (learned intuition). Learning, which progresses from knowing to understanding to doing, however, becomes a more clearly time-related process requiring subprocesses involving not only three different neurological systems but their final interlocking—the penetration of the knowledge to the point where the student's behavior is finally predictably affected by that knowledge.

In summary, we assume that in approaching a real situation one is working with a personally constructed form of that situation. We also assume that the nature of that constructed reality is strongly influenced by the constructs or cognitive maps available (known) to the individual. It follows, therefore, that the acquisition of this mapping system and its progress toward a behavior-influencing state becomes of central concern to the evaluation of learning. Modification of human behavior, to whatever extent it is controlled by rational procedures, is a slow and gradual process which presumably can stop at various stages in the process. This would seem to require that we tap in with our measurements at the various stages, specifically "knowing," "under-standing," and "doing."

IMPLICATIONS FOR FIELD INSTRUCTION: PRACTICE AND LEARNING

Mutual Reinforcement of Class and Field

When a practice frame of reference, such as the one described, is adopted by the profession (or at least by a school), then both class and field teachers will be teaching it and students will get continued re-inforcement of their learning, that is, an articulated approach. This obviates the need for an entirely separate field curriculum. Rather, field teaching can become a true facilitation of the knowledge and understanding that students gain in the classroom or bring in from other sources and the enrichment and deepening of that learning as they are helped to apply it in the great variety of real-life situations presented as assignments in the field. In the case described earlier, the field instructor needs to help the student consider how to approach a 75-year-old hospitalized woman since the student has not talked with many older people—much less hospitalized older people—except his own grandparents. The field teacher capitalizes on that experience and helps the student see how to use it in the new situation. The field teacher also helps the student to consider what the patient's impinging environment outside the hospital looks like and what it can yield; what specific community resources may become part of the patient's imping-ing environmental supports; what the personal strengths of the patient are—her general sense of independence, her positive attitude toward her exercises, which are expected to strengthen her ability to walk around and to do more for herself, and her need and wish to feel of value to others.

Students need not spend time figuring out the differences between the practice frameworks of their classroom teachers and field teachers. Rather, they can gain the sense of strong professional identity that comes from seeing the same fundamentals of professional practice taught in both class and field and the different ways in which they can be applied and amplified. With this approach, the field teacher helps the student gain first-hand knowledge of the specialized population being worked with in the field and also gain an understanding of a particular social-service delivery system and of the specialized tech-niques used in that field. "Learning the setting" in this sense is a particu-lar case of the application of generalized knowledge of organizations, agencies, policies, work with people, and so forth, learned in the class-room. Thus, the student in the example is able to take the social work frame of reference which he already "knows" from class, and with careful guidance from the field teacher, apply it with confidence in this new and, for him, untried situation, thus strengthening his command of the frame of reference and seeing how additional knowledge of the particular interface is essential for developing the kind of plan that will potentially lead to desired outcomes for the patient and her environment.[6]

Unless and until class and field operate from the same practice frame of reference, we will continue to find essentially two different curricula presented to students—one in class and another in field, with the field curriculum often not providing any opportunity for the students to put to use their new-found classroom knowledge and sometimes even requiring them to do the reverse of what they are being taught to know and understand. There is usually no intent by field teachers to confuse or frustrate students; rather, there is simply lack of agreement on the fundamentals of our practice. Surely it is less than an optimum learning situation when a student reports to the field teacher that the practice teacher, commenting on a field learning ex-perience of the student, said the assignment was not "social work" and never should have been given to the student! Instead, the student can return to the classroom with a clear-cut example of having put his or her knowledge to use and is ready to add more knowledge to his or her developing professional repertoire.

Mutual Field-Class Curriculum Planning

Another important implication arising from this line of reasoning is that classroom and field faculty together must plan the curriculum which is to be adopted so that the common frame of reference has the benefit of both inputs. This allows for the reality testing necessary by practitioners so that the framework has teeth and is not offered as some abstract nicety that seems to have no relevance for, nor ready applicability to, the practice students will be exposed to in their field settings. The education of our upcoming social work practitioners is too important to be left to educators alone! Such collaboration should help both class and field to make the essential separation between a so-cial work practice frame of reference and the many and varied metho-dological modalities that may be utilized interventively to carry out the goals established by the basic frame. No longer would we hear ques-tions such as, "Can behavior modification be considered an appropri-ate *social work* treatment method?" Of course it is not a social work method. It is a plan for intervention which may be used by social workers, including social work students, *if* careful assessment of the person-environment interface suggests that behavior modification is the method of choice likely to attain the desired goal of maximizing indi-vidual potential and ameliorating the surrounding environment. Be-havior modification becomes a means to the social work end, never the treatment method preferred regardless of the presenting situation or the likely consequences of its application.

Reduced Premature Use of Inappropriate Methods

Use of the practice frame of reference should reduce a common problem in the field—students moving too quickly to apply a more narrow treatment method, probably from their urgently felt need to intervene immediately (perhaps not knowing what else to do). Application of this frame of reference will help students achieve a balance between an individual's capacities and limitations and the impinging environmental conditions which may not only be playing a part in the client's problem but which have to be contended with in solving the problem. Students who too quickly apply transactional analysis (TA), family therapy, or other methods to situations that have not yet been adequately assessed from a social work practice frame of reference may cause dysfunctional outcomes for clients who may suffer the consequences of excellent technical skills applied inappropriately. For example, if a student approaches a parent and child having difficulty with their relationship from the viewpoint of TA, without first applying the social work practice "screen" (frame of reference), he or she may fail to see that a big part of the difficulty lies in the mother's dissatisfaction with her boring and underpaid job which is having spillover effects on her relationship to her son. Even very skilled application of TA, while possibly helpful, will not be dealing with one of the major concerns and will be failing to utilize social work's greatest strength—its concern for the whole person and that person's interfacing with his or her whole environment. Too quickly moving to a narrow treatment method before applying the unique, broader social work frame of reference neither fits the perspective of our profession nor provides the best service for clients.

Reduced Student Dependence on Field Instructor

Another advantage of the students having a clear understanding of the social work practice frame of reference is that they are not so dependent on the field teacher or the practice setting to provide the learning structure necessary. That is, students are clearly not "apprentices" in a given agency, unable to move unless given the specific steps prescribed by the setting or field instructor because they will come to each situation well armed with the basic frame of reference, and how to go about applying it initially. Field teachers will need to help them sharpen up the application in a particular setting and certainly with interventive techniques to carry out the plans made. However, students can move into new, untried situations with some sense of knowing how to start out since the practice frame of reference provides them a basis for so doing.

Broader Social Work Role Revealed

This frame of reference also allows students to discover limitations in agency and community services and permits field teachers to help them see their larger professional role. If the student in our example, upon assessing the situation in accord with the practice frame of reference, finds an aged client able and desirous of remaining in her own home rather than moving to an institution but finds neither the field setting nor the community ready to provide the homemaking and transportation services necessary, the student won't stop there. He will take at least beginning steps to focus the community's attention on the client's needs instead of merely saying "our agency is unable to help you" or merely being content to place the client in a nursing home.

Strengthened Sense of Being Professional

A firm professional perspective provides students the knowledge and value base for them to move into any agency and use themselves as professionals, abiding by the policies of the agency, of course, but not being cowed by the rules or having a sense of prostituting their professional knowledge and values to a delivery system. If we may be pardoned this analogy to medicine, doctors—even when salaried as in government hospitals—do not give up their professional stance or fail to be guided by their knowledge just because they are in a certain hospital. Should a hospital's rules seem to require them to give up their professional standards, the doctors would most assuredly get those rules changed! Social work students, perhaps too willingly, report things like (if serving as a probation officer), "I'm not allowed to work with the family. There's only time to work with the youngster"—even though a careful social work assessment has clearly indicated that the family must be involved for there to be any likelihood of preventing a repeat offense! Consistent and skilled teaching of the social work practice frame of reference would push students to say that they could not practice "social work" in that setting.

Presently, we tend to let the setting outline what our practice will be, instead of having our practice frame of reference determine what we will practice, no matter what the setting. We should be professionals, bringing our practice into a variety of settings, not merely employees bending our knowledge and values to the peculiarities of various agencies. We can do this only if we teach students to learn well this unique and powerful frame of reference which they will carry with them to the field setting, where they will apply it fully, with their field teacher's help, even though it means they may find limitations within the agency, within the community, within themselves, within social work knowledge. Then, and only then, will social work move ahead on its own, rather than be tossed to and fro by whatever new "treatment method" or new theoretical perspective from sociology, business, psychology, or other field comes along. We will help students find gaps in social work knowledge, and they will push us or themselves— or if that's not their "bag," their fellow social workers who are knowledge builders—to work to fill those gaps.

Implications for field instruction of adopting the learning frame of reference described—moving from knowing to understanding to doing—have been hinted at previously. They are amplified below.

Delayed Entry Into Field

The first is that if we take seriously the notion of knowing well, before doing—that is, to apply what we know rather than, through trial-and-error learning, stumble through what we do—we would clearly not place students in the field immediately upon entering a professional social work program. We would indeed arm them with some social work knowledge and a social work value stance before sending them out to behave as professionals, supposedly guided by professional knowledge and values. We are not talking about concurrent vs. block field arrangements. We are saying that under either system, we would have students know and understand the social work practice frame of reference and its initial application before expecting them to use it in a real-life situation in the field. We get frequent criticisms about what students in the field "don't know" and what field teachers must therefore teach on what might be called an instant-knowledge basis in order for them to handle even passably the tough situations confronting them in field assignments. It is probably surprising that ill-prepared students don't cause more disasters in their first weeks and months in the field. We'll probably never know how many lives *may* have been harmed or how many folks have failed to be helped because of this—and we probably won't try to find out. Students who know well the practice frame of reference should reduce the likelihood of this happening.

Broader Scope of Learning in Field

Further, this learning framework has the potential for permitting the field instructor to help students apply conceptual formulations brought from the classroom but which the field instructor does not know. We are aware that new formulations are put before students in classes that field teachers, who have been out of school for two to twenty years, may only have heard of and clearly do not command. Yet, the new ideas seem plausible, the students are eager to try them out, and the field instructor thinks they will work but does not really know that material well enough to ensure that the students are properly applying it. However, with the assurance that a student knows and understands a particular theory or construct system, for example, behavior modification, the field instructor, even though not really knowledgeable about "behavior mod" as a system of intervention, should be able to test out with the student whether or not it is appropriate and safe for the student to try in a given situation. If students know and understand a conceptualization so that they can satisfactorily explain its use to the field teacher and indicate probable consequences of the success or failure of its use, and if the teacher finds affirmative responses to the following questions, there should be no danger to clients, agency, or students in permitting them to put the new formulation to actual use.

These questions must be answered affirmatively in order for the field instructor to monitor satisfactorily a student's use of a new conceptual construction.

1. *Can the student construct reality-confronting situations with this formulation?* As with behavior modification, can the student define an assigned situation so as to determine clearly what is the behavior to be modified, whose behavior is to be modified, and who are the essential "actors" in the situation? Does the student understand how to establish baseline behavioral data and what constitutes positive and negative reinforcement? In other words, can the student satisfactorily explain the major constructs of the formulation, their relationship to each other, how they become a "treatment scheme," and so on?

2. *Can the student intervene in accord with the construction being considered?* Do students know clearly what is acceptable and unacceptable behavior on their own part if they are to be consistent with the formulation? Can they establish the ground rules necessary for the clients and students to operate within? Can they, through role play, actually engage in the professional interventive behavior called for, even if it means some confronting, some nonsupportive kinds of statements?

3. *Does the formulation suggest feasible interventions with reasonably predictable outcomes?* In other words, using behavior modification as an example, is the behavior to be changed such that what seems possible and feasible for the client to do to change it and what seems possible and feasible for the student to do in helping the client make those changes seem reasonably likely to lead to success? If the answer can't be yes, it would seem better to consider other modes of intervention in which predictable outcomes seem more likely to be positive.

4. *Can the formulation (theory or subset of constructs) be subsumed*

under the professional practice frame of reference? If not, the field instructor would not appropriately help students to know, understand, or intervene in accordance with it. For example, if the use of behavior modification as the student plans seems to omit consideration of some significant aspect of the environment, questions will need to be raised. If the behavioral change in a woman is all being directed toward her husband, ignoring her dominating mother, then one significant part of the impinging environment is being omitted. Thus, one essential piece for maximizing the client's potential and ameliorating the client's environment is being ignored, and the fullness and breadth of the social work practice frame of reference is not being considered, so the field teacher would need to be sure the student did draw this into the interventive plan. In this example, behavior modification itself is not ruled out. Rather, its use must be extended to include at least one other element in the environment, the definition of the interventive unit cannot be so narrow. If, however, the proposed behavioral change by the client, as conceived by the student, was to harm other individuals in that client's situation in some way, that would be totally out of line with the social work practice frame of reference, and the field teacher would prevent a student's applying that particular mode of intervention in that instance.

Thus, even without knowing much about behavior mod, a field teacher could help a student learn to apply it within a social work frame. The student's strength of knowing and understanding as demonstrated to the teacher before application to a client can help guide them both to proper and effective use of that knowledge on behalf of a client and give them a basis for evaluating the student's work.

SUMMARY

In summary, the social work practice frame of reference is learned as the characteristic professional way of viewing practice reality in the cause of professional intervention and the conceptual structure within which the great detail of more specific practice knowledge and values is given some ordering and focus for use. It thus serves as a bridge between classroom and field, and like any bridge, if it is not well anchored on both sides, it will not connect the two parts nor bear the essential traffic between. The learning frame of reference is a blueprint for how the educational bridge will be anchored and built between the classroom and the field; that is, how the practice frame of reference and all other classroom knowledge will come to guide the student social workers' professional behavior as they confront practice reality.

NOTES

1. In the natural sciences, a frame of reference is frequently a set of lines or points that bound an area of interest. For the astronauts, the orbit of the moon around the earth marked out a special territory in which they must operate on the moon and return again. In the social sciences, "a frame of reference is used . . . to denote a set of basic assumptions necessary to delimit and determine a subject matter of a science or a theory." Accordingly, "the frame of reference of the theory of action (Parsons and Schills) involves actors, a situation of action, and the orientation of the actor to that situation." Thus, the fixed points, lines, or planes of the more physically oriented frames of reference become the fixed "constructs of the social sciences which it is necessary to assume . . . to make meaningful observations . . . and determine upon which aspects of reality the scientist is directing his attention. . . ." (Julius Gould and William Kolb, eds., *Dictionary of Social Sciences* [New York: Free Press of Glenco, 1964], p.275).

2. See Margaret Schutz, "Assessing, a Bridging Skill in Social Work" (Paper presented at the 1975 National Association of Social Workers Symposium, Hollywood-by-the-Sea, Florida), mimeographed.

3. William E. Gordon and Margaret Schutz, *FIRP: Final Report Field Instruction Research Project* (St. Louis: George Warren Brown School of Social Work, Washington University, 1969), pp. 7–14; George A. Kelly, *The Psychology of Personal Constructs, A Theory of Personality*, Vol. 1 (New York: W.W. Norton & Company, 1955), p. 9; Theodore R. Sarbin, Ronald Taft, and Daniel E. Bailey, *Clinical Inference and Cognitive Theory* (New York: Holt, Rinehart, and Winston, 1960), p. 29.

4. S-state or symbolized knowledge is recognized as containing constructs, generalizations, and concepts; their counterparts in N-state knowledge have, as far as we know, not been named (William E. Gordon, "Notes on the Nature of Knowledge," *Building Social Work Knowledge: Report on a Conference* [New York: National Association of Social Workers, 1964], pp. 60–75). Because of this distinction maintained between N-state and S-state knowledge, it is probably only the N-state that is comparable to what Kelly refers to as "constructs" (Kelly, *op. cit.* p. 9), or to what Sarbin, Taft, and Bailey refer to as "modules" (Sarbin, Taft, Bailey, *op. cit.*, p. 29). The latter refer to other terms such as Vernon's "schemata," the "mental maps" of Hayek, and the "coding systems" of Bruner, etc. One would infer, therefore, that these terms allude to the in-the-mind knowledge corresponding more closely to our N-state than S-state knowledge.

5. Kelly, *op. cit.*, pp. 8–9.

6. It should be noted that no special mention is made herein of the important and considerable task of the field teacher in helping the students gain an understanding of their own feelings and those of clients and others in their work. It is thought that this task would not be altered particularly by these frames except perhaps the aspects given attention and the order of the learning as indicated.

3

A History of Social Work Field Instruction

Apprenticeship to Instruction

Aase George

This chapter provides a perspective on field instruction through tracing briefly its development as an integral part of social work education. It seeks to provide answers to the following questions: How and when did field instruction begin? What approaches to instruction have been used? What major changes in content and method have taken place? What have been the different patterns of field instruction in graduate and undergraduate education for social work? Data was secured through review of professional literature and interviewing of some educators in other professions and of social work educators, who, like the writer, had experienced change in field instruction patterns over the years.

THE BEGINNINGS OF FIELD INSTRUCTION: THE APPRENTICESHIP APPROACH

As in other professions, education for social work began with apprenticeship training. In fact, it was through doing in the field under the direction of others who had learned in the same way that both the "paid agents" and "friendly visitors" in Charity Organization Societies and Associated Charities were taught social work skills before the founding of the New York School of Philanthropy in 1898.[1] It was the actual provision of service that was the means of training, with group meetings and individual conferences used to discuss the cases, determine what could and should be done to improve the conditions of the needy, and influence behavior in socially desirable directions. Later, informal evening reading groups were started in some agencies to meet the need for more knowledge.

In 1898, the New York Charity Organization Society started a six-week summer training program for volunteers, essentially an apprenticeship system with some lectures and field visits.[2] This program was extended to a full year in 1903–04 under the New York School of Philanthropy and in 1910 became a two-year program, known later as the New York School of Social Work and today as the Columbia University School of Social Work. Similar training programs in the family casework agencies of that period eventually led to the founding of other schools—Boston, Philadelphia, Cleveland, and Saint Louis, for example, had independent training centers in family casework agencies that grew into schools of social work.

One of the early trainees of the Associated Charities program that became what is now Case Western Reserve School of Social Work describes the seven-month training program in which the class of four or five young women performed an appreciable amount of work in return for scholarships of $30.00 per month.

> It consisted of a weekly lecture given by a member of the A.C. staff (most often Mr. Jackson [the executive] or representatives of agencies whose work touched closely that of the A.C.; occasional trips to other agencies and institutions; assigned readings; and, most important of all in the minds of the scholarship holders, what amounted to practically a full-time job. There was not much tempering of the wind to the training class lambs. It was a stimulating dose of responsibility that was handed to them. Very early in her career the trainee was told that to some people she would be their only contact with the agency and by her conduct the 'whole Associated Charities' would be judged. A sobering thought, but a little intoxicating, too![3]

Another of the early training programs, which developed into the School of Social Service Administration at the University of Chicago, grew out of a settlement house undertaking and an early effort to offer extension courses in what was then (1907) the Chicago School of Civics and Philanthropy.[4] Still other schools developed out of training courses offered in colleges and universities, usually through departments of sociology, and these courses were also often related to practice through use of Charity Organization Societies for laboratory work for the students.[5]

When one reads the papers written by early leaders in the field of social work on the need for training schools, it is clear that learning through doing was always seen as an important part of education for social work. Mary Richmond, for example, in 1897 called for a permanent group of instructors to direct the work of students, giving them theory and practice together.[6] She pointed out that while many learned from doing, learning by doing alone is not efficient and must be supplemented by theory. As in medicine, a long apprenticeship must still be served for skill, and training schools would allow volunteers and staff to profit from the experience of the more skilled.

FIELD INSTRUCTION IN THE PERIOD BEFORE 1940

The Academic Approach

The period before 1940 was marked by the establishment of an increasing number of schools of social work. With the 1918 organization of the Association of Training Schools for Professional Social Work, which in 1927 became the American Association of Schools of Social Work (AASSW), opportunity to discuss common interests and problems was provided. Some important results were the setting of the first curriculum standards in 1932, the decision in 1935 that approved programs must be within institutions of higher learning accredited by the Association of American Universities, and the requirement in 1939 that members must offer a two-year, graduate-level program leading to a master's degree.[7] Field instruction, most commonly referred to as field work in this early period, was recognized as an essential part of education in the programs established and in the 1932 curriculum standards. Only in one study, that published by James Hagerty in 1931, was field work designated as unsuitable for graduate work and relegated to vacation periods; it was to be done on a noncredit basis—but carefully organized and supervised nevertheless.[8] Werner Boehm found Hagerty reflecting the view of public-supported universities in the West and Middle West rather than the view of private institutions and voluntary agencies of the eastern establishment which prevailed in social work education at that period.[9] That educators from the social science field rather than from practice did not always find it acceptable to give graduate credit for field work is evident from the fact that after a two-year course in family casework was established at Western Reserve University in 1920, it took three years and some intercession by the family-agency staff to get the credit for field work granted which enabled students to earn master's degrees. Learning that the dean, a social scientist, and others on the faculty had had some doubt that supervisors were sufficiently attentive to relating casework principles to the cases the students carried, the supervisors responsible for field instruction were spurred on to work all the harder on improving standards for field teaching and updating their own knowledge.[10]

Although group workers were beginning to organize to study their area of practice and a one-year program in group service was offered at Western Reserve University beginning in 1925, it was the more fully developed casework method on which field instruction centered. This might be expected when many of the schools developed and drew faculty from family training programs. Also, it was in the agencies where the first training programs had operated that field placements could be found for the majority of students. There was even thinking that field work in family agencies was so basic that it should be used for all first-year students, no matter what specialty they elected.[11] Even group work students were sometimes given a period of field work in a family agency, though the reverse was rarely possible.[12] One family agency reported that 408 students had field-work placements in the agency throughout the period between 1920 and 1940;[13] the peak student group in 1931 was 99 first- and second-year family casework students, 7 medical social work students, and several public health nurses.[14] Students were undoubtedly a big help in carrying the load since each first-year student was expected to carry twenty-five cases, and second-year students carried a caseload of thirty-eight in 1926.[15] Expectations were lowered later, but until the fall of 1934 students were expected to be at work in the agency except when they had time off to attend classes, and at least through 1940 they usually remained for both years, working in the field during the intervening summer except for a three- or four-week vacation.[16] Field work was central, and any class preparation had to fall into evening or weekend free time unless courses were scheduled so that a period in between was too brief to permit return to the agency.

Other settings in which casework was the principal method were also in use, for this was a period in which practice was seen as occurring in many areas of specialization. Medical social work had developed in Massachusetts General Hospital in Boston and Bellevue Hospital in New York as early as 1905;[17] and one of the early schools, Simmons, was especially noted for education appropriate for that area of practice. Psychiatric social work had also developed out of the introduction of the psychoanalytic theory of personality, the efforts to rehabilitate shell-shock victims of World War I, and the mental hygiene movement which led to the establishment of mental guidance clinics in the twenties. Smith College School for Social Work, which has always been especially known for its education of psychiatric social workers, grew directly out of the efforts of Mary Jarrett, chief social worker at Boston Psychopathic Hospital, who wished to establish training to meet the needs of the hospital program.[18] Child welfare, school social work, and Red Cross work were among early specializations. Public administration was also recognized early as a special field, and later in the depression years of the 1930s, when the Federal Emergency Relief Administration was sending students to schools of social work to be educated for public welfare positions, field work in this area also became important. Apparently it was more often regarded as a form of family casework than a specialty, however. Fortunately, the Milford Conference Report in 1929 led to recognition that problems and methods were basically the same in all areas of casework practice, reducing to some degree the trend toward separate educational programs in class and field for each specialty.

The work of Mary Richmond, and especially the publication in 1917 of her book *Social Diagnosis,* was seen as giving a scientific base for casework practice; and the introduction of the psychoanalytic theory as an explanation of personality development led naturally to the focus on helping individuals resolve problems and adapt to stress constructively. Both Freudian and Rankian psychology strongly influenced field teaching, and each had its own proponents. Although Freudian concepts were more widely followed in field teaching, the Pennsylvania School faculty, who were advocates of Rankian psychology, were especially active in producing professional literature through which their views were spread. The 1936 publication of Virginia Robinson's *Supervision in Social Casework,* which describes field instruction of students at the Pennsylvania School, is especially noteworthy.[19] Athough papers were being given at conferences, articles were being published in journals, and seminars were being given for supervisors of students and staff through schools of social work and professional organizations, this was the only book on supervision that was circulated at that period. Its influence can be seen in the practice and field teaching even of those most strongly advocating Freudian concepts.

In a paper published by the Council on Social Work Education based on her unpublished doctoral dissertation, "The Objectives of Field Work in Social Casework, 1898–1955," Mildred Sikkema presents a particularly clear analysis of the changes taking place in field instruction.[20] She saw the early focus as being on professional development in terms of "gaining knowledge, developing attitudes, and understanding values in the context of social and economic conditions" with concern both for the poor as individuals and for social institutions and social justice. The emphasis was then shifted to understanding the individual being helped, through the psychoanalytic and psychiatric knowledge current during the 1920s and 1930s. As earlier, students were taught "orderly methods and organized procedures for helping," but these were associated primarily with the casework method. In the first year of field work, the student was expected to learn to apply "generic" principles; in the second, to acquire skill in a given field of practice. There was some difference of opinion about whether it was the development of a professional use of self or the personal growth and development of the student that was the goal; in either case, the relationship with the supervisor was regarded as the chief means of facilitating professional development, and the student's productive use of supervision became an important objective.

The Therapeutic Approach

Whether the purpose of the student-supervisor relationship was educational or therapeutic was not always clear. This was the period in which Grace Marcus was hailed for presenting a paper at the National Conference on Social Welfare describing the supervisor as a caseworker who must see her casework embracing not only the student's cases but the student herself since symptoms evident in the work situation would persist unless personal problems of the student were worked out.[21] Her use of the feminine pronoun attests to the fact that social work was seen largely as a woman's profession at that period, although male students were sought and highly valued by field agencies as future administrators.[22] The educational goal was always clear to some and became generally accepted with personal growth seen as a by-product of professional development because of the close relationship between the two. Virginia Robinson viewed the process of learning to use oneself in a helping relationship as involving a change and reorganization of thinking and feeling which in the end must be integrated until it becomes one's own and as a stimulated growth experience which must affect the whole self.[23] Field instructors and students influenced by the Freudian personality theory found personal growth occurring through the carry-over to self of what the student learned in helping others in the field and the maturing experience of close relationships in which they received acceptance and learned to assume responsibility.

The articles on supervision of students in the field, published by the Family Service Association of America, are described by the editor as demonstrating preoccupation with the student's emotional problems and the nature of the relationship between supervisor and student.[24] Certainly the sections on field work in the anonymous autobiographical article, "Supervision," shows both constructive and destructive use of the student-supervisor relationship as a means of student learning about his or her own attitudes in the work situation.[25] Similarly, in an article on "learning by doing" in which Doris Byars gives an account of a first-year student's learning from a case assignment and Marjorie Boggs does the same for a second-year student,[26] it was shown that field instructors, in addition to attempting to understand the individual differences and needs of their students, also sought to give them information and guidance in helping their clients, tried to foster awareness of the application of classroom knowledge, and encouraged independent thinking and decision making as the students became capable of this. In a different psychological framework, the same is true of the examples of student field work in Virginia Robinson's *Super-*

vision in Social Casework and other publications of the Pennsylvania School of Social Work at this period.

Other Developments in Field Instruction

Both Bertha Reynolds and Edith Abbott called attention to the apprenticeship quality of much of the agency field instruction of this period and considered, with different conclusions, the use of faculty field teachers rather than agency field supervisors. Bertha Reynolds held that the supervisor's belonging to an agency and having real responsibility to it was important for student assimilation of knowledge under real conditions of practice and that the resolution of the related problems lay in the school's structuring of field experience so that students gained from them not just the skills needed to do the agency job, but a broad base of social work equipment to use in a wide variety of practice situations.[27] This called for adequate education of supervisors for field teaching, something Bertha Reynolds attempted to supply in a special course for field supervisors and teachers. Edith Abbott, on the other hand, believed students should have access to full-time faculty field instructors and should work in as many as five different practice fields, just as medical students are rotated to different services no matter what their specialization.[28] She took pride in the fact that her school, the University of Chicago, did employ field teachers. At least one other school, the University of Minnesota, also did so at the time.

While most schools used concurrent field placements in the 1930s, block placement had been developed at Smith College, where the isolated location made necessary the use of field agencies at some distance from the campus. The delay in field placement until after a summer of classroom work was seen as of some advantage in permitting the student to go to the field equipped with beginning knowledge to apply in practice.

Community organization was recognized as a field of practice but not clearly differentiated from group work for purposes of field work until the 1940s, following the publication and acceptance of the 1939 Lane Commission Report which identified the commonality of this practice activity with other methods.[29] The 1939 decision that professional social work education needed to be at the graduate level relegated undergraduate programs to preprofessional status. Half the programs in social work education were at the undergraduate level in 1931,[30] and undergraduate schools with programs of social work education continued to offer classes and to use laboratory experiences in social agencies when found desirable and possible throughout this period. However, the professional literature examined gave no special attention to the characteristics of field experience in these undergraduate programs.

FIELD INSTRUCTION FROM 1940 TO 1960

Throughout the 1940s and 1950s there was considerable focus on field instruction with efforts to improve standards and find ways of organizing content to provide educationally sound field teaching. Professional publications relating to field instruction were numerous; two important studies of social work education considered and made recommendations regarding field instruction as one aspect of the curriculum. Classes or seminars for field instructors were developed in a number of schools, and the expansion of opportunities for social work that came with World War II and its aftermath was reflected in the increased development of field practice for areas other than casework. The apprenticeship quality of much of field teaching had been recognized before, and still was evident, but there was a strong effort from many directions to achieve educational quality for this component of the curriculum befitting graduate-level, professional education. There were also indications of beginning attention to undergraduate social work education including field instruction.

Developments in Undergraduate Programs

While the decision that a two-year graduate program of class and field work was required for social work education had been made by the American Association of Schools of Social Work, undergraduate-level education was still being offered largely in the land-grant universities and colleges of the Middle West and Southeast accustomed to trying to meet the needs of their geographical area. These schools saw a two-year graduate program as impractical in meeting the urgent demand for staff in public institutions and social welfare agencies and opted for undergraduate majors or combinations of undergraduate and graduate work leading to a one-year master's degree. In 1942, the National Association of Schools of Social Administration (NASSA) was established to meet the needs for joint planning and accreditation for those programs. Their recognition of undergraduate preparation for social work probably was the first attention given to this area of professional education, although it was not sustained! The problems of two accrediting organizations in social work education was soon recognized, joint planning undertaken, and in 1952 NASSA and AASSW merged into the present Council on Social Work Education. Teachers in undergraduate programs continued to feel like stepchildren even though there were committees and meetings to consider undergraduate education which gave opportunity to share thinking and experiences and develop group supports.

    There is evidence that use of field instruction was going on in schools that offered undergraduate social work education. The University of California in Berkeley reported in 1966 that it had used agency visits since 1942 to give students field experience but had to substitute movies, videotapes, and demonstrations when classes became too big to offer field observation in social agencies.[31] That school never used supervised field experience for undergraduates. Others did, but the pattern was very mixed. Ohio State University had a sizable program in the mid-forties, offering undergraduate field experience in such diverse settings as public welfare agencies, children's institutions, correctional facilities, public recreation, and rehabilitation programs. Placements were normally made during the senior year and usually on a block basis. Although the agencies tended to be public ones similar to those in which students might find employment readily upon graduation and the training given was of the apprenticeship type, students had the opportunity to give direct service, and in some instances they participated in innovative extensions of programs to the community. Other schools arranged field experience for students taking undergraduate social work classes in agencies where they might be limited to observation and the activities considered suitable for volunteers. More in line with current practice is Lucille Barber's description in 1956 of a wide range of field learning experiences provided for undergraduate students at Michigan State University with a two-hour weekly field-experience class which allowed additional learning from faculty and other students.[32]

The CSWE curriculum study of 1959 reported that 92 percent of the students in social work departments or social science divisions of member schools offering a social work major were given field-experience programs, while in member schools with social work courses located in a sociology department more than 60 percent were offered field experience.[33] The 1951 Hollis-Taylor report points out that undergraduate education should be considered part of professional education, as it is in medicine, dentistry, and education, rather than being labeled preprofessional and neglected in curriculum planning.[34] The further point is made that field learning is the only rule of thumb on which the student can depend before he or she has "elementary working knowledge of the content, methods, and techniques of the scholarly disciplines that underlie or apply (to social work practice), along with technical social work skills."[35] Seen as unsound were both the teaching of professional skills and the field practice of casework or other methods "prior to undergoing a series of learning experiences that include both a knowledge and a feeling component" and the teaching of technical and vocational skills more efficiently taught through on-the-job training or specially designed semiprofessional programs of a terminal character.[36]

The 1959 curriculum study pointed out the many areas of confusion and illogical thinking concerning undergraduate field experience.

For example, field experience and agency experience are sometimes regarded as synonymous, and schools that did not permit regular undergraduate field experience in some instances were found to encourage
participation in the summer institutional program of the American
Friends Service Committee, work as dormitory counselors, or volunteer work requiring considerable skill in interpersonal relations.[37]
Again, lack of maturity was used as a basis for not involving undergraduate students in a carefully supervised field experience, but the
same students might be recommended for employment in public welfare three months later. Bisno found that undergraduate field-
experience programs suffered from the attitude held by some social
work practitioners and graduate-school faculty that field participation
belonged on the graduate level and, therefore, was inappropriate for
serious analysis in the undergraduate curriculum. Partly for this reason,
planning and funding seemed to be inadequate. Werner Boehm, in his
proposals, placed field observation in the junior year with basic social
work knowledge, and field experience in the senior year on the level of
intermediate responsibility along with content in human growth and
behavior, social work values and ethics, and social welfare policy and
services.[38]

Although neither the Hollis-Taylor nor the Boehm recommendations were accepted and tested in operation, serious consideration of
an undergraduate continuum, including field instruction, seems to
have begun.

Developments at the Graduate Level

In graduate social work education there was an effort to strengthen the
educational quality of field instruction. The 1940–41 report of the
CSWE Subcommittee on Field Work stressed the importance of regarding field work as a portion of the educational program as valuable as
class teaching, demanding equally qualified teachers, use of definite
criteria in the selection of field agencies, and attention to the school-to-
school variations in amount of credit given for field work, the time
devoted to it, and the budget available for it.[39] The 1932 curriculum standards called for "not more than ten semester or fifteen quarter credits
of field work" in the first year and had not yet been changed. For the
second year no standards had been developed.

Both the 1944 and 1952 CSWE curriculum statements continued to
stress educational standards for field instruction, and there were many
efforts to find ways of assuring more educationally adequate and uni-
form learning experiences in the field for students. Some attempts
were related to identifying the content for field teaching in relation to
the method taught. Outlines were worked out, specifying such items
as the structure, function, and program of the field agency; the case-

work or group-work method and process to be taught; the psycho-analytic and psychiatric concepts; and the professional attitudes and work habits, responsibilities, and skills.[40] Other attempts focused on devices for integrating class and field as a way of assuring educational focus. For example, course outlines were shared with field instructors and seminars on new class content were provided for them. Student integration of class and field was also one approach. Class assignments calling for analysis of field experience in terms of class content and periodic written reports on field experience, relating it to reading and class content, were among the devices used. Still other efforts to achieve educational focus were made through developing "criteria for student progress." These tended to be individualized in terms of the growth and progress of each student rather than generalized in terms of similar standards of achievement for all students, though eventually there was some effort to set minimum standards for all.

Designing field work as a course with identified objectives, selected content, and planned learning opportunities was discussed; but opposition to the idea came from those who saw it as too intellectual and incompatible with the day-to-day practice within an agency. In the 1950s there was work on the educational objectives of field work in terms of knowledge, attitude, and skill, based on newly developed principles of curriculum construction that related field work to classroom curriculum. Efforts to make these objectives meaningful to field instructors and field-planning faculty were not too effective in spite of consultation visits from the CSWE staff.

Mildred Sikkema, whose work as a consultant on field instruction for CSWE during this period gave her considerable perspective on the developments in this aspect of social work education, saw renewed interest in the significance of social needs and social conditions and a beginning appreciation of the importance of values and developing individual social responsibility. However, she found no general acceptance of social responsibility as an objective of field instruction. There were still many who thought learning the practice of a social work method was as much as could be accomplished in the field and that professional development, or the development of a professional self, was the means through which students achieved responsible use of themselves in practice.[41] With reliance on the student-supervisor relationship for teaching and learning, there was fear that a damaging dependency was being created in the student. Dr. Sikkema found both implicit and explicit apprenticeship approaches and goals in use at this period. Similar findings were made in the Hollis-Taylor study of social work education and the 1959 curriculum study.[42]

Some of the professional literature in this period show a clarity of thinking and depth of understanding of the educational aspects of field instruction that give them as much value today as when they were written.[43] Although much of the literature illustrated field instruction in which casework was the major method used, they were written in a period when field instruction in group work, which had started in 1925, developed rapidly with the extension of field settings from the neighborhood and settlement houses used earlier to institutions for children and youth, hospitals, clinics, day nurseries, and housing developments. There was also the beginning of effort to teach practice generically, with students specializing in casework being taught the use of group experiences and group work students being taught individual treatment. All students were also to be aware of elements of administration, community organization, and research in their practice, but Hilda Arndt correctly assessed that the generic nature of field instruction was not something that became actuality just from the considerable lip service given to its concept.[44] As for casework, content for field teaching of the group-work method had been analyzed in an effort to assure educational focus and standards.

Field teaching of community organization also developed in the 1940s, although education for this area of practice was described as still "in the infancy of its development" in the 1947 *Social Work Yearbook*.[45] One school, Ohio State University, served at this period as the training center for what became the United Community Funds and Councils of America, maintaining a special relationship with the national agency and trying to meet its needs for staff.

There were some field placements in administration and research and experimentation in offering field instruction in supervision. Advanced-practice field instruction was also available through some of the schools offering a third-year or doctoral program. Except for efforts to select agencies and field instructors of high quality, however, this advanced instruction was similar to that at the master's level.

Both the 1951 and 1959 studies of social work education had recommendations to make about field instruction. The Hollis-Taylor report suggested the use of panels of school and agency teachers in the field for first-year professional students rather than the tutorial system. With objectives and content identical to those used in class, methods could be suited to the content with the result that students might have more than one field teacher and experience in more than one social agency during the year. Responsibility could be placed with the field teacher and student or the group of students and field teachers learning through a sequence of observation and group participation, and finally, full, direct responsibility for service could be given to the student alone by the end of the year.[46] In the second year, field instruction in the area of specialization was suggested, but what this would consist of was not worked out, although it was thought a two-year or longer program leading to the doctor's degree might be necessary.[47]

In the 1959 study, Boehm visualized a continuum with the social agency complementing all stages of class learning and increasingly involving the student. What he termed the "selection stage" called for observation and would be followed by a "focusing stage" in which there would be highly circumscribed responsibilities with recipients of service. The "application stage" in which students would learn the method component of the curriculum had three parts with field instruction in only the first two. In Boehm's proposal, a year of field learning identical to the concurrent plan at the master's level would be followed by nine to eleven months of practicum experience, with remuneration in selected teaching agencies, under intensive supervision with no class work. The final stage involved a summer period of integrative seminars.[48] Response to both the Hollis-Taylor and Boehm recommendations was generally negative, but with time some of the ideas presented gained more favorable consideration.

FIELD INSTRUCTION
FROM 1960 TO THE PRESENT

The 1960s were years marked by experimentation and a concentrated effort to achieve educational quality in field instruction. This effort continued in the 1970s but without the funding through government grants and the strong leadership from CSWE staff it had received in the previous decade. On the undergraduate level, there was rapid progress in building educational programs recognized as educating students for the first level of professional practice and replacing the first year of graduate study for some students.

The Development of Professional Undergraduate Programs

Partly as an outgrowth of the 1959 curriculum study, in 1961 the Board of Directors of CSWE adopted a guiding statement on undergraduate education and, through funding by a federal grant, brought to its staff an educational consultant to work with undergraduate programs. Hundreds of colleges and universities were reached by the consultant, group meetings were held with faculty and practitioners, special sessions were planned for the Annual Program Meetings of CSWE, publication of materials helpful to undergraduate social work educators was stimulated, and institutes were held for faculty.[49]

A 1966 survey of schools offering undergraduate programs in social welfare brought responses from 190 schools, both members and nonmembers of CSWE. Of these, 159 offered field experience and most (72.2 percent) limited the placement to one agency with direct responsibility for service activities.[50] A small proportion (7.9 percent) only had opportunity for visits to social agencies; others could observe the work of the agency.

At the 1956 Annual Program Meeting of CSWE, Ernest Witte called for the imaginative use of field experience under well-planned educational direction, whether undergraduate students were preparing for immediate employment or graduate-level professional education for social work, because of its potential for stimulating learning as well as teaching useful content regarding the organization and functioning of social agencies.[51] He reported that a Western Interstate Commission for Higher Education (WICHE) survey had shown there was insufficient use of rich, live field experiences in educating undergraduate students and suggested collaboration between WICHE and CSWE in developing educational models through which ideas could be tested.

In 1956 a workshop on field experience defined objectives for this curriculum area and identified ways to increase the use of a variety of agency settings and assure quality in field teaching. It was recognized that the use of nonprofessionally educated agency supervisors might be necessary and could be educationally sound provided the field experience was carefully defined in relation to a college course.[52] From this workshop a guide to objectives, content, field experience, and organization was published[53] as well as a special monograph by Margaret Matson on field experience in undergraduate programs.[54] The latter was a useful guide to the why and how of field experience in undergraduate programs in social welfare, complete with suggested forms and bibliography.[55] Matson illustrated the application in field experience of the Tyler framework of building curriculum (see Chapter 4) from objectives, and she discussed the use of learning principles in field teaching, activities through which field learning takes place, and integration of classroom and field learning through the student bringing to the field prior foundation knowledge and social welfare content which the instructor can consciously plan to reemphasize, illustrate, and integrate. The use of a field seminar conducted by a faculty member as a tool in integration was emphasized, although in block placements it often is impractical. Certainly what Matson presented is an educational focus rather than apprenticeship learning. Differentiation between field observation and experience had already been made and some consensus reached that the former belonged in the junior year or earlier, the latter in the senior year, as suggested in the 1959 curriculum study.[56]

A 1969 CSWE publication, *Continuities in Undergraduate Social Welfare Education*, shows some of the struggle at this period to develop educationally sound plans for field experience for undergraduate students. In one of the papers, Zelda Samoff called for using every opportunity to get undergraduate students into the community and advocated flexible planning to permit student use of field experience at points before the junior year when they have need for an elective through which they may find identity, meaning, and relevance in life and education.[57] She considered this experience so illuminating of the foundation courses that she thought it unwise to postpone field placement until the student can bring foundation knowledge and social welfare content to it. Ernest Witte, in another paper, described the curriculum at San Diego State College which called for a one-semester field experience in both the junior and senior years with weekly group meetings with the faculty member responsible for the field experience in addition to two four-hour periods in the field agency each week.[58] An elective, one-semester field experience in the junior year was also offered by special permission when circumstances warranted. Emphasis was clearly on assuring educational focus and careful planning between school and agency to avoid exploitation of the student through routine and repetitive assignments of little educational value.

Two events in 1970 put new emphasis on use of field experience to educate undergraduate social work students for beginning entry into the profession: the decision of NASW to admit BSW graduates of CSWE-accredited programs to full membership, and the establishment by the board of directors of CSWE of new standards for constituent membership in the Council by colleges and universities offering undergraduate programs in social work. These standards included requirement of "an appropriate directed field experience with direct engagement in service activities as an integral part of that program."[59]

An analysis of undergraduate social work programs approved by CSWE in 1971 showed that there was still a wide range in arrangements for field experience among member schools, although educational standards and clock hours in the field now had a new importance.[60] Clock hours in the field ranged from 56 in the first quartile to 540 in the fourth, with 190 the average and 168 the median.[61] Most schools used only concurrent placements, but eleven used only block and twenty-three both block and concurrent placements. The field seminar was in quite general use, with only twenty-eight schools, or 19 percent, not offering it. Traditional agencies were the major resources for field placements, but some innovative plans allowed students to work with grass roots social-action movements or in setting up services such as day care and, in a few instances, placed students in offices of political leaders.[62] Although only 30 percent of the schools held strictly to the requirement of MSW field instructors, because of the difficulty in finding them available especially in rural areas, most of the schools offering a field seminar to integrate theory and practice did require that the instructor be an MSW.[63] Alfred Stamm reported that field instruction was the component in the educational programs examined that required the most remedial attention, since not all schools had successfully shifted from observation to direct involvement of the student in service delivery.[64] One can speculate that this was probably even more true of schools not members of CSWE.

Cordelia Cox, CSWE consultant to undergraduate programs, gave a somewhat more positive picture in a paper published the same year.[65] She saw as trends the progression from field observation to field experience to field instruction with faculty field teachers, the use of field centers that offer multifaceted learning, and the granting of faculty status to agency field instructors. She reported some use of MSW students as field instructors for undergraduates, usually second-year students with experience who would be going back to supervisory positions. The value of two placements, one traditional, the other innovative, was under consideration. The reported trend to teach practice as an entity was also noted.

A number of other papers published after 1970 consistently focused on building field instruction programs educating students for beginning-level entry into the profession and efforts to find objective means of testing for competency.[66] Certainly the CSWE curriculum standards for field experience, adopted in October 1974, show expectation of educational planning far beyond the apprenticeship model with which field work began. These standards called for a "sound, educationally directed field experience sufficient to prepare for social work practice"; stated that the educational institution needs to assume "primary responsibility for philosophy, content, organization, and implementation of the field curriculum"; and called for the opportunity to apply and integrate classroom content with field experience and develop skills requisite for beginning-level professional practice through engagement in service activities for a minimum of 300 clock hours. To this end it is stated that the activities must be "sufficiently broad to familiarize students with a variety of social work interventive modes."[67]

Developments at the Graduate Level: Moving toward an Articulated Approach

Social work educators in the 1960s were involved in efforts to conceptualize knowledge for teaching in both class and field and drew on Ralph Tyler and Jerome Bruner for learning principles to use in organizing content and selecting methods of instruction. Articulation of learning activities between class and field became a sought-after goal. Federal grants were available to help fund a number of exploratory studies on field instruction, stimulated in part by the CSWE project on that subject. Active interest in that area of the curriculum was evident in the number of papers read at professional meetings, the special meetings held, and the many monographs and articles published.

For agency field instructors and executives comfortable with traditional patterns of field teaching, it was not an easy period—nor was it so for some faculty. There was new language to learn, and demands made on agency staff were much heavier than in the old days of apprenticeship training. In schools where practice was taught generically in the first year, the expectation that students be provided with learning experiences in direct work with individuals, groups, and community sometimes required that instruction of the student and the student's time be shared with one or more staff members serving as adjunctive field instructors or even that the student's time be divided between two agencies. It also called for more preparation by field instructors. Often agencies found less immediate return in service from students because of their educational needs and lack of specific preparation in method or perhaps psychiatric content viewed as essential in the practice setting. That enthusiasm and interest continued among agency field instructors and that social agencies, hard pressed to meet service needs, still offered field facilities gave evidence of commitment to participation in the professional education of future social workers even though it was costly. Without the agency field faculty, schools would have been hard pressed to place students since most field instructors were still agency paid.

However, out of the conviction that schools had to carry primary responsibility for all teaching including field instruction, there was increased interest in developing teaching and service centers and in use of faculty field instructors. Tulane University's experimental design for first-year field instruction led the way but was only one of a number of efforts to assure educational focus fitting the curriculum of the particular school involved. That design called for establishing community-based teaching centers in areas where a sizable group of students with faculty field instructors could learn neighborhood needs and participate in varied types of service delivery, learning through both individual and group teaching, but largely the latter, with care observed in applying educational principles. Class content was also taught in the field and tests administered as in other classes to evaluate field learning.[68] The University of Chicago sought a similar educational goal by establishing a center to meet the needs of a city neighborhood through clinical research and demonstration in collaboration with agencies serving the area. Staff at various educational levels delivered a variety of services, and students assigned to the center had a carefully planned progression of field learning experiences integrated with practice classes under faculty instructors.[69] Still other schools set up field units with a focus on problem rather than method, planning learning experiences that gave opportunities to know the needs of a client group such as the aged or handicapped and the service delivery systems working in that problem area.[70]

Efforts were also made to work with agency field instructors to share with them the knowledge needed to collaborate with schools in innovative field programs or to encourage their planned teaching of content not usually given special attention.[71] Research efforts to develop instruments for evaluating field learning were further evidence of the active interest in developing educational resources to use in field instruction.[72] Even the collection of articles from *Social Casework* published in 1966 as *Trends in Field Work Instruction* reveals experimentation by agency field instructors in traditional settings, although not on so large a scale as in some of the schools.[73]

While interest in maintaining and improving the educational quality of field instruction continued in the 1970s, there was not the level of activity in sharing exploratory studies and research at professional meetings and through publications that marked the 1960s. This was probably related to the decrease in availability of funding through government grants and the termination of the CSWE project on field instruction which provided much of the stimulus to study field teaching and learning in the 1960s. Faculty responsible for field instruction programs have expressed a need for more consultive help and planned meetings to consider common problems and their solution. Meanwhile the accreditation standards adopted in April 1971 allowed individual schools considerable latitude in developing their own criteria for learning experiences to be provided through the practicum so long as all arrangements derive "from clearly stated educational purposes, articulated with other components of the curriculum" and there is provision for direct involvement of students in service activities in agencies that meet specified professional standards.[74] The educational focus is clear, but there is also considerable diversity in current field instruction programs.

It should also be noted that during the 1960s and 1970s efforts to develop articulated approaches between class and field instruction emerged. Field settings were viewed as laboratories where students could test and reify what they were learning in the classroom. This approach was consistent with the knowing-understanding-doing paradigm presented by Gordon and Gordon during this period and reported in Chapter 2. A field instruction structure was used which allowed for ready linkage between class and field content and could be tailored to the learning style and practice background of the individual student. The articulated approach to field instruction is described in depth by Sheafor and Jenkins in Chapter 1.

CONCLUSION

What stands out in the development of field learning and teaching in education for social work is the important place clinical experience has had from the early days of apprenticeship training to the most educationally and clearly articulated, focused program of present-day field instruction. Not only has field learning provided the live experience important to students in arousing their interest, giving meaning to classroom theory and allowing them to test their career commitment, but it has also been an indispensable method of teaching, when knowing, understanding, and doing are seen as steps in the learning process. The early, narrow focus on casework, often for use only in a particular agency, has broadened with the effort to relate field experience to the total curriculum and to teach multimethod skills; and there has been a concerted effort to help field instructors understand and use sound educational principles. Faculty field instructors in teaching or service centers operated by schools or based in social agencies have led the way in testing methods of strengthening the educational values of field teaching, but the collaboration of agency field instructors and the investment of social agencies in this aspect of the curriculum has been considerable through the years. The use of group methods in field teaching, the sharing of teaching responsibility by more than one instructor, the moving from generic practice experience to more specialized and advanced placements, and the continuum from undergraduate to graduate field instruction are among current trends. While there is still much unevenness and many lags in achieving what leaders in social work education envision, progress is clear.

NOTES

1. Alfred Kadushin, *Supervision in Social Work* (New York and London: Columbia University Press, 1976), pp. 6–8.
2. Ernest Hollis and Alice L. Taylor, *Social Work Education in the United States* (New York: Columbia University Press, 1951), p. 9.
3. Florence T. Waite, *A Warm Friend for the Spirit: A History of the Family Service Association of Cleveland and Its Forbears 1930–1952* (Cleveland: Family Service Association of Cleveland, 1960), p. 84.
4. Kadushin, *op. cit.*, p. 12.
5. *Ibid.*, p. 11.
6. Mary Richmond, "The Training of Charity Workers," *The Charities Review*, Vol. 6 (June, 1897), 308–321.
7. Diane Bernard, "Education for Social Work," *Social Work Encyclopedia*, Vol. 1 (1977), 290–300.
8. Werner Boehm, "Education for Social Work Studies," *Social Work Encyclopedia*, Vol. 1 (1977), 309.
9. *Ibid.*
10. Waite, *op. cit.*, pp. 210–212.
11. Bertha Reynolds, *Learning and Teaching in the Practice of Social Work* (New York: Farrar and Rinehart, 1942), p. 6.
12. Waite, *op. cit.*, p. 216.
13. *Ibid.*, p. 326.
14. *Ibid.*, p. 233.
15. *Ibid.*, p. 212.
16. Florence Hollis, "A Study of the Case Work Performance of Graduates as a

Measure of the Effectiveness of Professional Training," in *The Skills of the Beginning Case Worker as Evaluated by the School, the Agency, and the Worker* (New York: Family Welfare Association of America, 1941), p. 2.

17. Ernest Hollis and Taylor, *op. cit.*, p. 13.

18. Victoria Roemele, "1918–1968: Challenge, Innovation, and the Smith Tradition," *Smith College Studies in Social Work*, Vol. 39 (June, 1969), 178.

19. Virginia P. Robinson, *Supervision in Social Case Work: A Problem in Professional Education* (Chapel Hill: The University of North Carolina Press, 1936).

20. Mildred Sikkema, "A Proposal for an Innovation in Field Learning and Teaching," in *Field Instruction in Graduate Social Work Education: Old Problems and New Proposals* (New York: Council on Social Work Education, 1966), pp. 2–5.

21. Grace Marcus, "How Casework Training May Be Adapted to Meet Workers' Personal Problems," in *Proceedings of the National Conference of Social Work, 1927* (Chicago: University of Chicago Press, 1927), pp. 385–392.

22. Waite, *op. cit.*, pp. 151, 327.

23. Robinson, *op. cit.*, pp. 3–7, 43.

24. *Supervision Philosophy and Method*, a reprint of fourteen articles from *The Family* (New York: Family Service Association of America, 1929–30).

25. Anonymous, "Supervision: An Autobiography," *Ibid.*, pp. 12–17.

26. Doris Byars and Marjorie Boggs, "Learning by Doing," *Ibid.*, pp. 44–55.

27. Bertha Reynolds, *op. cit.*, pp. 141–144.

28. Edith Abbott, *Social Welfare and Professional Education*, revised and enlarged edition (Chicago: University of Chicago Press, 1942), pp. 57–61.

29. Robert P. Lane, "Report of Groups Studying the Community Organization Process," in *Proceedings of the National Conference of Social Work, 1940* (New York: Columbia University Press, 1940), pp. 455–473.

30. Herbert Bisno, *The Place of the Undergraduate Curriculum in Social Work Education*, A Project Report of the Curriculum Study, Vol. 2 (New York: Council on Social Work Education, 1959), 5.

31. Milton Chernin, "Principles of Organization of Undergraduate Social Service Education Programs: Content and Supporting Courses," in *Observations on Undergraduate Social Welfare Education* (New York: Council on Social Welfare Education, 1966), p. 25.

32. Lucille K. Barber, "Objectives of Community Field Experience in Undergraduate Education for Social Work," in *Education for Social Work: Proceedings of the Fourth Annual Program Meeting* (New York: Council on Social Work Education, 1956), pp. 123–130.

33. Bisno, *op. cit.*, pp. 55–56.

34. Ernest Hollis and Taylor, *op. cit.*, p. 174.

35. *Ibid.*, p. 177.

36. *Ibid.*, pp. 182–183.

37. Bisno, *op. cit.*, pp. 50–53.

38. Werner W. Boehm, *Objectives of the Social Work Curriculum of the Future*, The Comprehensive Report of the Curriculum Study, Vol. 1 (New York: Council on Social Work Education, 1959), 175–178.

39. Bertha Reynolds, *op. cit.*, pp. 137–138.

40. Sikkema, *op. cit.*, p. 6.

41. *Ibid.*, p. 7.

42. Ernest Hollis and Taylor, *op. cit.*, pp. 230–234; Werner W. Boehm, *The Social Casework Method in Social Work Education*, A Project Report of the Curriculum Study, Vol. 10 (New York: Council on Social Work Education, 1959), pp. 74–75.

43. Of particular importance were Bertha Reynolds's *Learning and Teaching in the Practice of Social Work* and Charlotte Towle's *The Learner in Education for the Professions as Seen in Education for Social Work* (Chicago: University of Chicago Press, 1954). Of interest also is Annette Garrett's monograph, "Learning through Supervision," published in *Smith College Studies in Social Work*, February, 1954. The University of Pennsylvania faculty continued to contribute professional field-related literature with Virginia P. Robinson, ed., *Training for Skill in Social Casework: Social Work Process Series* (Philadelphia: University of Pennsylvania Press, 1942) and Rosa Wessel and Goldie Basch Faith, *Professional Education Based in Practice: Two Studies in Education for Social Work* (Philadelphia: University of Pennsylvania School of Social Work, 1953). In addition, there were many papers dealing with field instruction given at professional meetings and later published. These include an interesting series of articles from *The Family* in 1941 and 1942, reprinted in pamphlet form under the title *Field Supervision of Casework Students* (New York: Family Welfare Association of America, 1941–42) and illustrating field-work content and teaching in a range of settings from public welfare to child-guidance clinics. Hilda Arndt's paper, "The Learner in Field Work," in *Education for Social Work: Proceedings of Fourth Annual Program Meeting* presents in some detail the educational objectives, content, methods, and arrangements through which it was hoped that field instruction was moving away from the apprenticeship approach. Other papers that dealt with evaluation of field work and skills learned were: Rosemary Reynolds, *Evaluating the Field Work of Students* (New York: Family Service Association of America, 1946); Florence Hollis, *op. cit.*; Margaret Schubert, "Field Work Performance: Achievement Levels of First-Year Students in Selected Aspects of Casework Service," *Social Service Review*, Vol. 32 (June, 1958), 120–137.

44. Arndt, *op. cit.*, p. 41.

45. Wayne McMillen, "Community Organization for Social Welfare," in *Social Work Yearbook, 1947* (New York: Russell Sage Foundation, 1947), p. 115.

46. Ernest Hollis and Taylor, *op. cit.*, pp. 241–244.

47. *Ibid.*, pp. 247–262.

48. Boehm, *Objectives of Social Work Curriculum*, pp. 86–88.

49. Sherman Merle, *Survey of Undergraduate Programs in Social Welfare: Programs, Faculty, Students* (New York: Council on Social Work Education, 1967), pp. iv–v.

50. *Ibid.*, pp. 16–20.

51. Ernest F. Witte, "Articulation between Graduate and Undergraduate Education for the Social Services," in *Observation on Undergraduate Social Welfare Education*, p. 33.

52. Cordelia Cox, "Planning for the Undergraduate Social Welfare Sequence: The Role of the 1965 Faculty Workshops and Institute," in *Observations on Undergraduate Social Welfare Education*, pp. 1–2.

53. *Undergraduate Programs in Social Welfare: A Guide to Objectives, Content, Field*

Experience, and Organization (New York: Council on Social Work Education, 1967).

54. Margaret B. Matson, *Field Experience in Undergraduate Programs in Social Welfare* (New York: Council on Social Work Education, 1967).

55. *Ibid.*

56. *Undergraduate Programs in Social Welfare*, pp. 14–16 and Boehm, *Objectives of Social Work Curriculum*, pp. 175–178.

57. Zelda Samoff, "The Continuum Revisited—The Undergraduate Underpinnings," in *Continuities in Undergraduate Social Welfare Education* (New York: Council on Social Work Education, 1969), pp. 23–39.

58. Ernest F. Witte, "Implications and Next Steps for Undergraduate Education," in *Continuities in Undergraduate Social Welfare Education*, pp. 69–71.

59. Dorothy Bird Daly, "The Future Baccalaureate Degree Social Worker—Implications for Social Work Education," in *Continuities in Undergraduate Social Welfare Education*, p. 98.

60. Alfred Stamm, *An Analysis of Undergraduate Social Work Programs Approved by CSWE, 1971* (New York: Council on Social Work Education, 1972), pp. 6–11.

61. *Ibid.*, p. 9.

62. *Ibid.*, pp. 7–8.

63. *Ibid.*, p. 10.

64. *Ibid.*, p. 7.

65. Cordelia Cox, "Characteristics of Undergraduate Programs in Social Work Education," in *Undergraduate Social Work Education for Practice: Report of the Curriculum Building Project Conducted by Syracuse University School of Social Work Under Contract with the U.S. Veterans Administration*, Vol. 1 (Washington, D.C.: Education Service, Department of Medicine and Surgery, V.A. Administration, 1971), pp. 7–21.

66. See Harold L. McPheeters and Robert M. Ryan, *A Core of Competence for Baccalaureate Social Welfare and Curriculum Implication* (Atlanta: The Undergraduate Social Welfare Manpower Project, Southern Regional Education Board, December, 1971), pp. 121–127; Morton Arkava and E. Clifford Brennen, eds., *Competency-Based Education for Social Work: Evaluation and Curriculum Issues* (New York: Council on Social Work Education, 1976); and Robert T. Constable, "Preparing for Practice: Field Experience and Course Work in the Undergraduate Social Work Program," in Lowell, *Teaching for Competency in the Delivery of Direct Services* (New York: Council on Social Work Education, 1976), pp. 9–17.

67. *Baccalaureate Social Welfare Programs* (New York: Council on Social Work Education, October, 1974), pp. 5–6.

68. Helen Cassidy, "Role and Function of the Coordinator or Director of Field Instruction," in *Current Patterns in Field Instruction in Graduate Social Work Education*, ed. Betty Lacy Jones (New York: Council on Social Work Education, 1969), pp. 148–155.

69. Donald Brieland, "A Social Services Center for a Multi-Problem Community," in *Current Patterns in Field Instruction*, pp. 61–67.

70. Howard W. Borsuk, "Agency – School Communication: The Influence of Changing Patterns of Education," in *Current Patterns in Field Instruction*, pp. 55–57.

71. Josephine DiPaola, "Helping Field Instructors Retool When a School Changes Its Approach to the Teaching of Methods," in *Current Patterns in Field Instruction*, pp. 165–175.

72. Mildred Sikkema, "Analysis of Explorations Reported by Schools in the Working Party," in *Field Learning and Teaching: Explorations in Graduate Social Work Education* (New York: Council on Social Work Education, 1968), pp. 22–24.

73. See Minna Green Duncan, "An Experiment in Applying New Methods in Field Work"; Esther E. Urdang, "An Educational Project for First-Year Students in a Field Placement"; and Francis J. Ryan and Donald R. Bardill, "Joint Interviewing by Field Instructor and Student," in *Trends in Field Work Instruction* (New York: Family Service Association of America, 1966), pp. 36–42, 43–48, 61–64.

74. *Manual of Accreditation Standards* (New York: Council on Social Work Education, revised April, 1971).

Part II

FIELD INSTRUCTION AS A CURRICULUM UNIT

In this section two chapters examine field instruction as a part of the curriculum of the social work program. Based on the objectives of the program and the materials encompassed in classroom instruction, it is essential that objectives for field instruction clearly be specified and the ability of students to meet those objectives be fairly evaluated.

The explication of teaching and learning objectives for field instruction is addressed by Ann Pilcher in Chapter 4, "The Development of Field Instruction Objectives." She stresses that these objectives must be carefully planned and clearly related to the objectives of classroom instruction and shows that, otherwise, a school may in effect be operating two curricula. Pilcher argues that field objectives must relate to professional competence in all areas of the curriculum.

To establish appropriate goals, the school must first clearly identify the practice behaviors expected at different levels of a student's education. With the practice objectives specified, the educational objectives can be delineated and a teacher can identify the behavioral changes required of the student.

Pilcher explores alternatives for developing these behavioral objectives. She provides helpful explanation and illustrations of the manner in which a school can develop these objectives. Specification of objectives by a school is prerequisite to the development of appropriate forms of evaluation. In Chapter 5, "Evaluation of Field Teaching and Learning," E. Clifford Brennen discusses means of evaluating field education.

Brennen helpfully examines the double function carried by the field instructor—teaching and grading. Although there is often strong resistance to evaluation in field education by both teacher and student, Brennen argues that it is an essential task that can be accomplished successfully through clearly stated learning objectives and a series of evaluative efforts that sample the work of the student throughout the field placement.

A theme of Brennen's chapter is the importance of an appropriate structure to the field evaluation activity. He contends that students should produce a series of examples of their work which contain clear statements of the rationale for their actions. With this material, the field instructor must be prepared to assess the student's work and identify procedures that might be used to strengthen this performance.

Finally, Brennen discusses the strengths and limitations of efforts to design rating instruments for field instruction. Such instruments must be specifically related to objectives developed by the individual school. They must be used somewhat flexibly but can serve to clarify expectations for student performance and methods of evaluation.

4

The Development of Field
Instruction Objectives

Ann Jackson Pilcher

Competence in practice is the overall goal of social work education, and the level of competence expected in the graduate is one that is sufficient for responsible professional practice. Professional competence in social work derives from the acquisition of knowledge, values, and skills learned in the basic curriculum; it is fostered through successful experience in practice and continuing professional development.[1] In the training of social workers, educators continue to rely heavily on field instruction to develop professional practice competence.

This chapter focuses on quality field instruction as a unique but integral part of the total curriculum and the development of clear behavioral objectives in the field.*

TWO PERSPECTIVES ON FIELD INSTRUCTION

There appear to be two major and opposing perspectives about professional field instruction, each referred to frequently in the literature. One is that field instruction is a separate sequence or component of

---

* Although I take complete responsibility for the material presented in this chapter, sincere appreciation is expressed for the invaluable opportunity of discussing some of these ideas with my colleagues, Don Pilcher and Herb Bisno.

the school curriculum as is social policy, human behavior, methods, or research. As such, the implication is that it should have its own clearly delineated objectives, curriculum content, and evaluation procedures. The other view is that field instruction is a learning opportunity or special field laboratory for the total school curriculum along with the classroom, the skills laboratory, and the integrating seminar (i.e., the articulated approach).

Frequently both viewpoints seem to be held by the same faculty. The confusion about these two perspectives has clouded the central issue of designing a curriculum that assures professional competence through quality field instruction.

The classroom has traditionally been seen as the place where students "learn about" practice, and the field where they practice what they have "learned about." The field was recognized as a place for applying knowledge under supervision, but one has to ask, What knowledge? People teach what they know, and since field instructors are often unaware of classroom content, they may very well teach what they learned three to fifteen years ago. Without one set of clear behavioral objectives, we may have two curricula—one for the classroom and one for the field. And with the students' delight in experiential learning, the dichotomy between class and field grows apace. Unfortunately, this separation between academic knowledge and field practice during professional education may hinder the goal of professional competence. This schism, too, may be responsible for the general disinclination of many social work practitioners to keep up with the expanding knowledge base and for the meager contributions of practitioners to the development of new knowledge.

With the growing emphasis on more rigorous professional training, classroom teaching and academic content have received a greater impetus than the field. This is also reflected in the development of more doctoral programs in the 1960s. It's as if the university became preoccupied with the development of classroom curriculum and left the field to carry on as best it could.

At the same time concern was increasingly expressed from academic quarters in the form of exhortations to upgrade the field and make it an academic experience. This demand has generally been taken to mean the development of field objectives but with a separate curriculum; this in turn was an attempt to make the field more like the other sequences and, therefore, separate. Thus, field experience has come to be regarded as both a separate sequence with its own objectives, as well as a vehicle for the application of classroom learning, taking its objectives from the school objectives. Since the perspective one takes has a tremendous impact on curriculum design, the need for clarification is paramount.

It is my contention that field instruction as a vehicle for learning cannot reflect the total curriculum and at the same time have a curriculum of its own (in the academic sense of the word). The two stances are incompatible, just as having separate objectives for the field, apart from the overall objectives of the educational program, is inconsistent.

There must be field objectives, but they must be clearly delineated behavioral objectives that relate to professional competence in all areas of the school curriculum. Curriculum includes objectives and academic content; the objectives of the field derive from the objectives of the total program, and the content of the field refers primarily to the rich and varied learning experiences available only in the pragmatic world of professional practice. However, the field can certainly be used to teach theoretical content, such as the theory of practice, as well as research, social policy, and substantive knowledge on the social problem area with which the agency is involved. Nevertheless, such content is not restricted to the field and does not constitute a complete curriculum for the field. Decisions about *what* will be included in the total curriculum come first, and then it must be decided *where* and *how* it will be taught and reinforced. The uniqueness of the field lies in the availability of practice activities, and the opportunity for integration of knowledge, values, and skills by the student through actual practice.

Clarity and conviction about the field as a mode of learning and not as a separate sequence of the curriculum with separate objectives may well provide the necessary base for the development of quality field instruction. As one social work educator put it, "The purpose and objectives of field instruction should be derived from the purposes and objectives of the social work curriculum, and these should dictate the content and methods of teaching in the field."[2]

The clarification of this issue and the decisive intent to assume the perspective of a unified curriculum offered in different arenas should enable us to avoid some of the present confusion about goals. It should also provide us with a firm base to develop crisp and seminal objectives.

THE CONTINUUM AND EDUCATIONAL OBJECTIVES

In setting outcome goals many schools are faced with the need for a clear explication of practice behaviors at different levels of education. What do we expect of the BSW and MSW graduates? Unfortunately, clear guidelines do not yet exist. In fact, as the *Report to the Task Force on Structure and Quality in Social Work Education* made clear, the articulation of educational content between undergraduate and graduate programs was the most crucial issue facing social work education in the seventies,[3] and it remains controversial.

Increasingly, it seems apparent that the BSW will be a "generalist" graduating from a "core" curriculum with the first professional practice degree.[4] Although the core curriculum has not yet been developed officially, the CSWE statement on accreditation standards does provide curriculum guidelines. In addition, developments in various programs have been documented and are available.[5] Generally speaking, there appear to be developments with more consistency and uniformity at the BSW level than at the MSW level. Unfortunately, graduate faculties have not yet seen fit to build on this development in a consistent manner.[6]

Paradoxically, inputs for program development are specified and monitored for accreditation, but outcomes are not; and universities are morally, if not officially and legally, accountable for the practice competency of their own graduates. Thus, behavioral objectives and outcome goals for different levels of education need to be clearly differentiated by each school or program.

Differentiation of objectives and content may be conceptualized by task and/or level of performance. Although there are vocal and ardent devotees of each approach, it is suggested by other social work educators that both approaches are needed in setting appropriate educational objectives. For example, certain tasks require special knowledge and training, that is, clinical diagnosis or administration of a complex organization. On the other hand, when both the baccalaureate-trained worker (BSW) and the advanced-degree worker (MSW) are involved in the same area, such as policy and planning, the activities of the BSW worker would more likely be in direct service, such as gathering data, analyzing the needs of clients, and the delivery of services for gaps and overlaps. The BSW worker's perceptions would be primarily of clients and worker activity. Moreover such analysis would be only a small portion of his or her overall workload. The MSW worker, on the other hand, would spend a greater percentage of his or her time in policy and planning, and his or her activities would be more complex and less direct-service related (for example, program analysis and formal policy development or research activities). Furthermore, perceptions would be sought of the program and service delivery, and they would come from the community and other professionals rather than clients.

BASIC GUIDES TO EDUCATIONAL OBJECTIVES

The CSWE curriculum policy statement serves as a basic guide to the development of educational goals in advanced social work training, and the accreditation guidelines serve a similar purpose for undergraduate programs.[7] While they outline the requirements that must be included in the curriculum for accreditation purposes, there is considerable room for creativity and innovation in their application by individual schools, as well as in the individual outcome goals suggested above. When the educational objectives are set forth in explicit terms, they can be assessed more definitively. Moreover, learning is facilitated when everyone is clear about the expectations.

In developing educational objectives, the work of Ralph Tyler can serve as an invaluable guide. He argues that educational objectives constitute the criteria by which materials are selected, content is outlined, instructional procedures are developed, and examinations are prepared. Tyler believes that education involves significant changes in behavior. Therefore, "objectives should be a statement of changes to take place in students," and must prescribe the kind of behavior the student is expected to acquire.[8]

How the objectives will be evaluated is the topic of the next chapter, but clear explication of objectives which reflect the total curriculum must come first.

BEHAVIORAL OBJECTIVES AND COMPETENCY-BASED CURRICULUM

The heart of the concept under discussion has been aptly termed *performance-based curriculum* or *competency-based curriculum* whereby the components of instruction are identified by behavioral objectives. The model is referred to by Armitage and Clark as a contemporary extension of the work of Ralph Tyler and the argument is that "since a key feature of any profession is practice, social work education cannot function without a vision of practice that can be described in terms of what social workers should do."[9] Reminding us that the adequacy of any professional program in social work is based on the practice competence of its graduates, the authors list three major assumptions of the competency-based curriculum.

1. The ultimate purpose of a profession is practice.
2. The purpose of professional education is to effectively teach practice behaviors.
3. Practice behaviors can be specified as the operational objectives of social work education.[10]

A Taxonomy of Practice Skills

Since the behavioral objectives outline the instructional content of the curriculum, Armitage and Clark suggest that the traditional divisions of the social work curriculum into foundation courses such as human behavior, social policy, research, methods, and field practice may no longer be relevant. An alternative is to "... describe the curriculum components according to a taxonomy of behavioral objectives or areas of practice skill."[11] Drawing from Stuart, they outline seven categories of skills believed necessary for direct human services.

1. Observational skills
2. Problem-formulating skills
3. Skill in the functional analysis of behavior
4. Skill in interpersonal management with relevance to the processes of inducing, maintaining, and terminating client participation in treatment through persuasion (including cognitive restructuring and techniques of interpersonal social reinforcement)
5. Skill in treatment assessment
6. Skill in the analysis and change of agency and organizational variables which facilitate or impede service delivery
7. Business skills such as benefit-cost analysis and record keeping[12]

If this taxonomy of skills is adequate for capturing the central behavioral objectives of social work education, Clark and Armitage suggest that learning experiences (which I believe are the major content of field work) would ". . . cut across and selectively include elements from each of the former foundations-methods-field divisions of the curriculum."[13]

Translating Skills into Behavioral Objectives

Listing areas of skills is not sufficient. Skills must be described as practice behaviors and translated into behavioral objectives. According to Mager, an objective must contain three attributes to be considered behavioral.

1. The behavioral objective must contain a description of observable behavior or an observable consequence of behavior (i.e., a product such as a paper) that will demonstrate mastery of attainment of the objective.
2. The behavioral objective must specify the criteria that will be used to evaluate the adequacy of attainment of the objective (exactly how the behavior is to be judged as adequate or inadequate).
3. The behavioral objective must specify the conditions under which the behavioral objective is to be demonstrated (time, place, other people, physical setting).[14]

A Social Work Competency Scale

The Montana Social Work Competency Scale is a major effort in the evaluation of competency-based curriculum. The procedures and problems in its development are well documented and critiqued in the

CSWE publication *Competency-Based Education for Social Work.*[15] Although evaluation and curriculum issues are its primary concern, the setting of educational objectives is intrinsically included. A set of seven competence criteria generally recognized in the literature as the basic areas for evaluation stand as their working definition of social work practice and the criteria base for assessment. They are: the organizational context of practice; the community context of practice; problem identification and assessment; formulation of an intervention plan; implementation of the intervention plan; evaluation and feedback; and the professional context of practice.

Each of the competence criteria synthesizes a collection of relevant practice skills which are spelled out under each subheading. For example, "knowledge of the agency" is the first subheading of "the organizational context of practice," and in this regard the student worker should be able to: (1) explain the purpose of the agency; (2) demonstrate working knowledge of agency policies and procedures; and (3) identify services provided and state limitations of service.[16] Such expectations of practice behaviors are spelled out for each of the subheadings in the seven competence criteria.

In comparing the two sets of core behavioral objectives, the Stuart taxonomy is more limited as all of the areas of practice designated by Stuart could be subsumed under the Montana scheme, but the reverse is not possible. In the context of this chapter it is clear that the Montana Scale criteria reflect practice knowledge, values, and abilities which emanate from the total curriculum. Furthermore, many of the competencies could be learned and utilized in the classroom, the skills lab, the integrating seminar, and the community at large, as well as in the field setting.

Both of these points substantiate the basic thesis of this chapter, yet a cautionary note must be made regarding a pure competency approach to curriculum development and evaluation. It undoubtedly grew out of the demands for accountability in the 1970s, and while the notion of clearly delineated and more readily assessed objectives is to be applauded, there are still questions to be answered. For instance, one major dilemma is in training for practice effectiveness when the parameters of the profession continue to widen. Another lies in the difficulty we have defining the nature and purpose of social work itself which must precede the definition of *competent* social work practice.[17] Through the competency-based approach, it is as if the social work profession has again perfected a process while remaining less than clear about content.

Analytic and Interventive Skill Objectives

Another notable exception where field objectives tend to reflect much of the total curriculum is the first-year instruction program at Tulane

University where analytic as well as interventive skills are stressed and students are expected to apply them to all client systems from the individual to the community. These learning objectives include the following: relationship skills; interviewing skills; differential use of self; expanded role concept (nontraditional settings); management and administrative skills; assessment and analytic skills; group leadership skills; policy formulation and planning skills; legislative and political-process skills; and knowledge-building skills.[18]

When basic skill areas are selected, as in these three taxonomies, they are intended to be the core of professional practice and should provide a working definition of social work practice for a particular program. This core of professional practice skills would be acquired through learning experiences in the classroom, the field, and the community and demonstrated by the student through practice behavior—that is, behavior that exemplifies professional practice. Whether or not such objectives and the subsequent learning experiences would cut across the typical divisions of the curriculum and eliminate them as separate entities, or whether the traditional components of the curriculum would still be formally articulated, would be a matter of individual choice by schools. The schools, of course, would follow the patterns set by the curriculum policy statements and accreditation standards established by the Council on Social Work Education.

Another approach was taken by Gregory M. O'Brian and colleagues at Case Western University in 1973. Although their purpose was to assess curriculum and provide a more effective means of equivalency determination for students with different educational experience and background, their decision to use behavioral objectives as units of analysis offers an enrichment to our discussion.

Educational objectives were defined by O'Brian's group as "explicit formulations of the ways in which social work students are expected to be changed by the educational process. That is, the ways in which they will change in their thinking, feeling, and actions. In systems terms, objectives are statements specifying educational outputs."[19]

The use of behavioral objectives was seen as advantageous because it provided:

1. A better data base for communication
2. A better means for the translation of the competencies that incoming students brought with them
3. Greater freedom for faculty in pursuing different modes of teaching, different models, different methods, and even content which could be related to the same outcome objectives[20]

In their approach, behavioral objectives were set forth for the total curriculum, and then various specializations and sequence objectives were derived from the general curriculum which were to be achieved in sub-units. The final step in this process was the identification of specific course objectives which would combine to achieve the earlier stated specialization and total curricular objectives. This "top-down" or pyramid approach was considered ideal for a major curriculum revision.

For more frequent curriculum refinements, as opposed to redesign, O'Brian and colleagues suggest that schools begin by identifying and defining the curriculum and sequence objectives being achieved through the courses and field opportunities currently available to students. The purpose here is to find out whether each course actually accomplishes what it was intended to and which objectives are being pursued to achieve the outcomes being obtained. This approach allows for "curriculum drift," knowledge explosion, and changes needed due to manpower demands of the field.

The authors suggest that once course and sequence objectives are either "set" or "obtained" in behavioral terms, they can be used to revise or to reinforce course content and used further as baseline data for future reviews. It is necessary, of course, to obtain feedback on how well the objectives are being achieved from the perspectives of faculty, students, and alumni.[21]

Decisions will have to be made as to which approach schools wish to take regarding the development or revision of curriculum through the setting of core and/or course objectives. Educational objectives for developing professional practice skills provide a basis for sound curriculum development and a way of evaluating whether or not the school is fulfilling its purpose of turning out competent practitioners. Furthermore, when the educational objectives and practice skills are linked directly to specific parts of the curriculum, it provides a means of knowing which components of a program contribute to the achievement of the objectives.

A FRAMEWORK FOR DEVELOPING EDUCATIONAL/BEHAVIORAL OBJECTIVES

It may be helpful to the reader to outline a framework which provides major steps to be taken in developing curriculum objectives. The logical place to start is to compose a statement of mission which reflects the philosophy of the program. If such a statement already exists, it surely needs to be reviewed and revised as all else flows from it. In addition, it is the current faculty who will have to implement, teach from, and assess the educational objectives established from the outcome goals. Far better that it be a joint, original, and current effort.

Assumptions Associated with the Framework

In constructing a framework for developing social work curriculum objectives, the following assumptions are made.

1. All parts of the curriculum, whether human behavior, social policy, or research, are construed as social work practice just as much as methodology is so regarded. That is, when one is engaged in social-policy development, for instance, one is engaged in social work practice. Therefore, social-policy content should be taught as practice.
2. A workable compromise will have to be reached between having too great a specificity in the educational objectives and having them too abstract. The first can lead to inordinate length and a mechanical approach, while the latter can be so global as to be amorphous.
3. The framework will lead to a working definition of social work practice that is unique to a particular school. No single model can serve all programs.
4. The working definition of practice that is developed will need to be an open and flexible one that will allow for dynamic change over time.
5. The framework has the potential of linking the desired practice skills to various components of the curriculum, so that content and structure of the program can be assessed in terms of outcome.
6. The educational/behavioral objectives serve as guidelines for instruction as well as criteria for evaluation.

A word of caution. A framework can only provide the broad outline of the work to be done. It doesn't indicate the time that must be invested or the hard decisions that must be taken if social work programs are to achieve quality field instruction.

Steps in the Development of Education/Behavioral Objectives

It is helpful to follow the suggested steps below in developing program objectives.

1. Broad decisions regarding the mission and philosophy of the school
2. Outcome goals unique to a particular program for the BSW and/or the MSW graduate
3. Educational objectives for the BSW and/or the MSW graduate
4. The translation of these objectives into:
   a. Identifiable components of specific content

    b. Core behavioral objectives
    c. Course behavioral objectives
5. The decision as to where content, or which parts of it, can better be taught and learned—in the classroom, the field, or both
6. The decision as to where the behavioral objectives, or which parts of the practice behaviors, can better be taught and learned—in the classroom, the field, or both
7. The development of appropriate, meaningful learning experiences which are carefully planned and clearly tied to the total curriculum
8. The plan for evaluation of the behavioral objectives

For our discussion here, it is assumed the school will have made the difficult decisions regarding the mission and philosophy of the school and set down the outcome goals for their graduates.

The educational objectives will enable schools to delineate components of specific content, and, within those areas, decide on individual courses. Each of the courses will have their own behavioral objectives, which in turn come from the original set of educational objectives.[22] The set of core objectives or competencies, such as proposed by the Montana Scale[23] or the skill areas proposed by Lipscomb,[24] may be used alone to develop areas of curriculum content as suggested by Armitage and Clark[25] or in conjunction with specific course objectives. The more closely the educational objectives and practice skills or competencies are tied to specific parts of the curriculum, the more readily can content and structure of the program be assessed in terms of outcome.

The next part of the process involves decisions about where the particular areas of content can best be taught, learned, and reinforced, and, quite specifically, which behavioral objectives will relate to the classroom, the field, or both. The objectives of the field, therefore, must be embedded in and derive from the objectives of the total curriculum; but they must be set in behavioral terms.

Finally, in setting behavioral objectives, the progressive thrust of the university must be incorporated yet tempered by the realistic needs of current professional practice. The responsibility and leadership for this kind of balance must come from the university, but the right balance cannot be achieved without active involvement of the field.

NOTES

1. Council on Social Work Education, *Official Statement of Curriculum Policy for the Master's Degree Program in Graduate Professional Schools of Social Work* (New York: Council on Social Work Education, 1962 and 1969).
2. Bernece K. Simon, "Field Instruction as Education for Practice: Purposes

and Goals," in *Undergraduate Field Instruction Programs: Current Issues and Predictions*, ed. Kristin Wenzel (New York: Council on Social Work Education, 1972), pp. 63–79.

3. Lilian Ripple, *Report to the Task Force on Structure and Quality in Social Work Education* (New York: Council on Social Work Education, 1974).

4. Michael S. Kolevzon, "The Continuum in Social Work Education: Destiny Not So Manifest," *Journal of Education for Social Work*, Vol. 13, No. 1 (Winter, 1977), 83–89.

5. See, for example: Kolevzon, *Ibid.*; see also Morton L. Arkava and E. Clifford Brennen, eds., *Competency-Based Education for Social Work: Evaluation and Curriculum Issues* (New York: Council on Social Work Education, 1976); *Undergraduate Programs in Social Work: Guidelines to Curriculum Content, Field Instruction, and Organization* (New York: Council on Social Work Education, 1971); and Robert T. Constable, "Preparing for Practice: Field Experience and Course Work in the Undergraduate Social Work Program," in *Teaching for Competence in the Delivery of Direct Services* (New York: Council on Social Work Education, 1976).

6. See, for example: Kolevzon, *op. cit.*; and William C. Sze and Robert S. Keller, "Differentiation among Three Levels of Social Work Education and Practice" (Paper presented at the 21st Annual Program Meeting of the Council on Social Work Education at the Palmer House in Chicago, March 2–5, 1975).

7. Council on Social Work Education, *op. cit.*; and *Standards for the Accreditation of Baccalaureate Degree Programs in Social Work* (New York: Council on Social Work Education, 1974).

8. Ralph W. Tyler, *Basic Principles of Curriculum and Instruction* (Chicago: University of Chicago Press, 1950), p. 27.

9. Andrew Armitage and Frank W. Clark, "Design Issues in the Performance-Based Curriculum," *Journal of Education for Social Work*, Vol. 2, No. 1 (Winter, 1975), 23.

10. *Ibid.*, p. 23.

11. *Ibid.*, p. 23.

12. Richard B. Stuart, *Implementing Behavioral Programs for Schools and Clinics* (Champaign, IL: Research Press, 1972), p. 27.

13. Armitage and Clark, *op. cit.*, p. 24.

14. R.F. Mager, *Preparing Instructional Objectives* (Palo Alto, CA: Fearson Publishers, 1962).

15. Morton L. Arkava and E. Clifford Brennen, eds., *Competency-Based Education for Social Work: Evaluation and Curriculum Issues* (New York: Council on Social Work Education, 1976).

16. David E. Cummins, "The Assessment Procedure," in *Competency-Based Education for Social Work.*

17. Frank W. Clark, Morton L. Arkava, and Associates, *The Pursuit of Competence in Social Work* (San Francisco: Jossey-Bass, 1979).

18. Nell Lipscomb, "The Teaching-Learning Setting in a First Year Field Instruction Program," in *The Dynamics of Field Instruction* (New York: Council on Social Work Education, 1975), Table 1, p. 75.

19. Gregory M. O'Brian, Tom P. Holland, Robert I. Lazor, Robert O. Washington, and Jon L. Bushnell, "An Objective Oriented Approach to

Curricular Self-Evaluation and Planning" (Paper presented at the 20th Annual Program Meeting of the Council on Social Work Education, Atlanta, 1974), p. 12.

20. *Ibid.*, p. 3.
21. *Ibid.*, p. 11.
22. *Ibid.*, Appendix A.
23. Cummins, *op cit.*, p. 65.
24. Lipscomb, *op. cit.*, Table 1, p. 75.
25. Armitage and Clark, *op. cit.*, p. 24.

Evaluation of Field Teaching and Learning

E. Clifford Brennen

Field instruction is the soft underbelly of social work education. This stark and impolite conclusion derives not from controlled observation but from colleague regard. It is of some note, therefore, that the major attempts to uniformly assess student learning should have emerged from those faculty and agency personnel assigned field instruction responsibilities.[1]

Further examination of this curious turn of events enlarges the paradox. While no other sequence in the social work curriculum draws as much evaluative effort, those who put forth such effort tend to be the most reluctant to do so. Field instructors are squeamish about assessing student performance and compromise their efforts with undue leniency.

The twin roots of this paradox are exposed when we recognize that educational evaluation has the double function of *teaching* and *grading*. It is the latter that poses the problem. While evaluation is ongoing and wed to a variety of teaching techniques, it is often regarded as occurring only during periodic formal sessions scheduled for this purpose. An examination of several volumes devoted to field instruction reveals that evaluation is seen as a solemn affair requiring preparation of the student to allay anxiety, and the reader soon detects that it is not only the student who is anxious![2]

It is the thesis of this chapter that the teaching and grading functions of field instruction have a common destiny. To the extent that one goal is pursued to the neglect of the other, achievement in both will be undermined. The collection of data and the rendering of judgments solely for grading purposes is a hollow venture not likely to be executed with diligence, and, as a result, the summary evaluation and grade may not accurately mirror performance. Obversely, the exclusive focus on teaching can lead to a cavalier use of an assessment procedure which in turn may result in biased conclusions timidly shared with the student who is thereby provided with a weak rationale for learning and change. The sections to follow discuss the foundations of this thesis and implications for the improvement of field instruction. Let us turn first to the reluctance to evaluate.

THE VICISSITUDES OF EVALUATION

Social work educators are at once educators and social workers, much to our credit but sometimes to our undoing. The professional norms which govern the helping role spill over into teaching, which is seductively similar. As social workers, we are taught not to "judge," and the Biblical admonition is brought into play as evidence of our Judeo-Christian heritage. Further, as part of our humanistic-egalitarian ethos, we feel uncomfortable in helping roles which involve the use of authority. For years social workers have expressed doubts about practicing in authoritarian settings such as those found in corrections, and the link between authority and evaluation has been well documented.[3] Also, our function is to help rather than to harm, to encourage rather than discourage, and to assist the "helpee" achieve desired goals including (it would seem) entrance into the profession.

The teacher-student relationship which most closely approximates the worker-client relationship is found in field instruction, and it is not surprising that the professional norms are more intrusive here. Every profession has its "segments,"[4] each with a subculture of its own, and in social work education it is likely that the "field culture" stems from its instructors being strongly aligned with practice and having close relationships with students.

Field instructor sensitivity leads understandably to lenient grading. In the Montana study discussed in Chapter 4, mean ratings on the Montana Social Work Competency Scale were significantly lower than the mean supervisor scores on a similar form ($p < .01$).[5] The writer found that, of a combined total of 463 grades awarded first- and second-year graduate students in field instruction courses in a school of social work during the 1976–77 academic year, less than 1 percent of such grades were "C" or below (a few "incompletes" and "withdrawals" were registered). Similar reports of lenient evaluations are found in the research by Schubert[6] and in the Educational Testing Service review of the reference vouchers submitted by supervisors for certification of graduates to the Academy of Certified Social Workers (ACSW).[7] The resistance to evaluating students for grading purposes is not restricted to American social work. A British social work educator writes:

> There are indicators from the recordings I have seen, from the writings of others, and from my own experience with student training that the role of assessor is a most difficult one for social work tutors and supervisors alike. The job of the supervisor is to *teach*, not to "accept," her student. . . .[8]

This is a serious problem, for the most valid and reliable evaluation instrument designed will have limited utility in the hands of an unwilling rater. And it is a shunning of task which receives less condoning from students than is realized, if we may equate their attitudes with those held by agency workers. In a nationwide study in which several hundred social work supervisors and supervisees completed lengthy questionnaires, Kadushin reported that a major source of supervisee dissatisfaction was revealed in statements such as, "My supervisor is not sufficiently critical of my work so that I don't know what I am doing wrong and what needs changing."[9] The failure to be appropriately critical may be a reflection of instructors meeting their own needs more than the needs of their students.

Field-instructor resistance is not the only barrier to evaluation. The agency may not provide sufficient instructional time or range of assignments for proper evaluation to occur. This is more likely to hold if a rigorous attempt is made to incorporate classroom content and if a comprehensive rating instrument is employed. Also, the school or department may inhibit evaluation in several ways. First, the coordination of liaison activities may be so loose as to invite only minimal compliance with educational standards. Second, the school faculty may not involve agency field instructors sufficiently in the design and implementation of the evaluation process, with the result that the forms are perfunctorily completed and the narrative summary is based on idiosyncratic criteria. Included here would be the failure to provide rater training for the instructors. Finally, by not regarding field instruction as a course and field instructors as educators (as well as "our colleagues from the world of practice"), the school or department engenders the self-fulfilling prophecy. Field instructors who are not regarded as educators may perform with matching self-regard, with the expected consequences for performing the evaluative function. This is an empirical question worth exploring for it involves a variable which is easily controlled. It is a matter of defining people on the basis of what they *do*, not where they are employed.

In shifting our attention to the teaching function of evaluation, we encounter a more positive description of field instruction.

EVALUATION AS DIRECTED LEARNING

Evaluation is necessary in an educational milieu primarily because it gives direction to learning. When the student is chided for spending too much time in the initial interview explaining how the agency can help and not enough time listening to what the client wants, the evaluative comment gives focus to the twin objectives of identifying the problem and interpreting agency function. Objectives by themselves are inadequate to the task of helping students understand what they should learn to know and do.

While evaluation also benefits the agency and its clients, it is the student as learner who is of interest here. Admittedly, evaluation is ongoing and cannot be separated from regular supervision or peer review. The raised eyebrow will give one pause in the midst of a phone call, while an approving nod will spur one on.

Each time the student is told that a practice activity missed the mark a bit, he or she also hears indirectly what *might* be done to achieve the desired outcome. It is only through evaluation that the student learns more specifically what one needs to do to successfully carry out an assignment. *Through a succession of evaluations and corrections— some salient, some trivial—the field instructor helps the student transform knowledge into understanding and understanding into doing.* Evaluation also informs the student how far he or she has come in achieving a particular learning objective and what remains to be worked on.

As noted in the previous section, field instructors shun assessment when the purpose is visibly linked to grading. The discomfort is similar to that described in the practice literature of the 1950s relating to the "forced marriage" of teaching and administrative functions and its effect on agency supervisors.[10] As a consequence, agency supervisors and field instructors alike have sought to cloak their evaluative role with a collegial stance and a corresponding language. In the only observational study of field instructor–student interaction known to me, Nelsen analyzed taped supervisory sessions. The following quotation is illustrative:

> The field instructors' questions seldom conveyed the message, "I am testing you to see if you know this"; it was much more often, "What do you think, because we have to decide this together?" or "What do you know about this, because I want to help fill in what you don't know so you can help the client more effectively?" The field instructors seemed more interested in knowing what the students thought in order to put their ideas together or to help the students become more knowledgeable, rather than to evaluate.[11]

Such subtle evaluation techniques may seem admirable at first glance, but the decision not to consciously engage the student in a mutually recognized evaluation conference denies both parties access to an instrument regularly and openly used to measure student progress. *It is my contention that the most pervasive learning problem encountered by social work students in the field is that they do not know what is to be learned.* The regular use of an evaluation form throughout the duration of the placement is one concrete way to delineate expected learning outcomes and to advance field instruction one more step from the apprenticeship model. But before an evaluation process and instrument are designed, there are some choices to be made.

ISSUES AND CHOICES

Several issues in performance evaluation seem particularly germane to field instruction,[12] the first being *what* is to be evaluated? I am familiar with state merit examinations for entrance-level social work positions, ostensibly heavily weighted with social work content. Yet, social work majors have at times received lower scores than have recent graduates in other fields on the same tests. Apparently certain assessment items may be more a measure of general intelligence than of social work knowledge, and this may be true as well of evaluations of field performance (e.g., how well one writes process recordings). Also, some assessment items seem to relate more to personal traits than to what was learned or demonstrated. No good evidence exists in the psychotherapy research literature as to the efficacy of such traits, including the Rogerian variables (e.g., empathy, warmth), for client improvement.[13] Particular personality characteristics may be helpful, detrimental, or innocuous depending on the type of client, interactional context, or other factors.

A related conceptual issue, which apparently has been resolved pragmatically in social work education, is whether to use *outcome* or *process* measures. Given the state of the art, it may not be wholly fair to evaluate students on whether their clients improve or the extent to which their community-planning activities bear fruit. Further, the difficulties involved with evaluating outcome in the helping professions may argue against the present feasibility of such an approach, although experiments in this direction should hardly be discouraged. Process, or second-order, criteria refer to whether the student can apply relevant knowledge and follow professionally acceptable procedures in practice activities. Ideally, both types of measures (outcome and process) should be utilized in the assessment of performance, and in the following section we will examine selected instruments.

In the broadest sense of *what* is to be evaluated, the question is whether assessment of field performance is to be restricted to a separate field curriculum[14] or whether it will embody integrated classroom content. The paradigm in Chapter 1 argues for a single practice framework for both class and field. Evaluation properly follows objectives and is fashioned by the curriculum design.

A second issue concerns the *source* of data. Researchers recognize that differences in perception exist among such respondents as the client, persons close to the client, the supervisor, external judges, and the change agent in his or her self-report. Because of the strategic position of the field instructor for observing process and socialization, almost total reliance has been placed on this source of data. However, since evaluation is typically based on the student's recordings or oral accounts, to a substantial extent *self-report* is a data source. Direct observation or unobtrusive methods such as audio or video recording are still not employed to any appreciable extent. So in addition to the usual concerns with rater bias (see below), we have the problem of accurately gauging the student's self-report. On at least one dimension, self-report data in social work invites caution. Wilkie compared tapes against process recordings of caseworkers in a research-oriented, psychiatric setting and observed significant omissions.[15]

By employing an evaluation procedure that specifies the attainment of specific competencies, rater and self-report biases can be reduced. As a rule, the more general the guidelines for evaluation, the more opportunity for subjective factors to intrude.

The final issue to be discussed here involves the *number of observations* of student productions to be made for a fair and accurate assessment of performance. Since evaluation tends to be ongoing and largely for the purpose of teaching, formal evaluations occur usually once or twice a term. It can be said that the field instructor's time is best used focusing on the student's weaknesses, with areas of demonstrated strength receiving only cursory attention. Yet Schubert concluded:

> Whatever means may be used in examining the individual student's performance, in several cases, no clear pattern of case performance emerges. Students can be more easily grouped by the mean and median scores of their cases . . . If each student's total case load is examined item by item, almost all students show gross inconsistencies. For example, most students offered a highly appropriate form of reassurance to some of their clients and either omitted the activity or offered it inappropriately in other cases.[16]

Not only may good initial performances by students on selected dimensions create a rater "set" for those dimensions on later assignments, the perception of good performance on some items may lead the field instructor to judge that the student has done well in other areas (halo effect). More critically, early judgments based on fragmentary evidence can lead to an overall judgment which then determines how the field instructor rates specific items on an evaluation form. We may be correct in attempting to view the student holistically (the whole person), but to err in timing is to turn virtue into vice. An adequate sampling of the student's practice activities is essential for accuracy in judgments.

It is necessary to make a distinction between the frequency of sampling performances, as we are discussing here, and the frequency of supervisory conferences. Students can file regular reports on their activities, perhaps daily, but have formal appraisal conferences scheduled less often. Both procedures, however, should be carried out with some frequency. In a large-scale study, in which some of the subjects were members of related helping professions, frequency of performance sampling and appraisal were each found to be related to supervisee satisfaction.[17] The teaching function of evaluation may be enhanced as well. Kendall reported that residents in a general hospital were anxious to have frequent evaluations, "for without this they cannot readily increase their knowledge or improve their skills."[18]

THE NEED FOR STRUCTURE

Effective evaluation requires three types of instruments or documents, covering student productions, assessment of productions, and evaluation procedures. The literature in social work does not link these three components in any explicit manner. Yet the need for such documents and a systematic format for their utilization would seem imperative in a profession where student (and practitioner) activities have relatively low visibility. While visibility can be increased through greater use of observational strategies and a reconsideration of just how much confidentiality is needed to "protect" clients, it will be assumed here that field instructors will rely heavily on after-the-fact reports, written and oral.

As for student productions, there would seem to be a need for a recording instrument which would require specific statements on the client(s), the situation, and the actions taken. Statements which lack discriminatory power and, therefore, seem to fit most people most of the time (e.g., "Mrs. A tends to feel uncertain in new situations"), contribute little to the assessment process.

Kadushin presented three summaries of actual case histories to sixty agency field instructors (all MSWs) attending an institute on educational supervision at a school of social work.[19] Each field instructor was given one of three cases, with a fabricated universal (fits anybody) diagnostic summary attached. The summary bore no relationship to any of the three cases and was supposedly written by a student. The subjects were then asked to evaluate the quality of the alleged student's diagnostic ability, and each group of twenty respondents receiving one of the three cases gave a mean rating of 5 on a 7-point scale, the equivalent of "slightly above average." In fairness, the raters probably exercised good judgment, for the three-hundred-word summary was abstract enough to fit almost any case—and that is just the point.

On the other end of the evaluation process, the assessment of student productions, similar consequences can be expected. Heavy reliance on holistic impressions of the student's performance can result in abstract evaluative statements which say little and sound very much the same, student after student, year after year. A field coordinator, after having read numerous evaluations of first-year students, and inspired by the study noted above, composed the following universal student evaluation which reflects meaningless statements often found about student performance.

> Whereas originally the student tended to focus on her perceived needs in any given situation and consequently her own goals for improving it she can now look at the situation more clearly from the client viewpoint. Hence, she can now truly begin where the client is and accept him better on his own terms.
>
> Previously held conflicts about being in the profession seem to be nearing resolution. These have been discussed with me in conference and she now sees the profession as having a more specific and worthwhile contribution to make to society. She is, therefore, more relaxed in her work, has gained strength from her identification with the profession, and is able to represent the agency well publicly.
>
> The student has presented two cases for psychiatric consultation and did a nice job, though naturally was a little nervous. The presentations were well focused and questions appropriate. Summary recording tends to be a little lengthy at this point but is of good quality. Any lack of organization may be due to the complexity of the problems—but the degree of her understanding of the dynamics involved is appropriate to this stage of development.
>
> This student brings to her field work practice qualities consistent with the profession. She is interested in people, usually establishes relationships easily, generally uses good judgment, and strives to be objective.
>
> She is eager to be of help and has found it easier to offer concrete or practical help than to explore and help in the emotional area. The reluctance in the latter area may be a projection of her own fear of hurting the client. She has been able to move in this area following support and guidance and has shown increased self-understanding as well.[20]

RECORDING STUDENT PRODUCTIONS

Urbanowski identifies the problem and solution when she says, "The student needs structure and guidelines to help him reach his goals, and the field instructor needs clear evidence of the level of the student's performance; recording can provide both."[21] She adds that process recording may be useful in the initial stages of learning to further self-awareness, but more explicit guidance is needed if the student is to develop a disciplined approach to the problem-solving process.

However, such a framework for recording would have to be kept rather simple. It is an administrative axiom that organizational members—such as students and their field instructors—tend not to maximize, but to *satisfice*.[22] Bluntly put, people frequently do only what is minimally needed to complete the job; perhaps even in academia we should not expect heroic behavior. Then there is the matter of time. To tap the student's every attitude, perception, and action with a research-length questionnaire following each interview would be to give supreme credence to the cynical observation that teaching interferes with learning.

The Problem-Oriented Record (POR) developed by Weed for teaching and auditing purposes in medical practice has received attention in social work.[23] Recording in our profession has focused on history-taking and diagnosis rather than on planning and action, and any recorded worker's plans have not been consistently linked with specified problems. At times it seems that a student's announced intention to "offer support" or "let the client test reality" is compatible with innumerable problem situations, and it is not always clear what such actions can be expected to accomplish. The four components of POR are highly congruent with any list found in the literature of stages in the problem-solving process: collection of data, problem identification, development of an intervention plan, and implementation.

The data base would differ according to the setting and the problem or primary mode of helping (e.g., community development). Without sufficient data, problems cannot be accurately identified. The problem list serves as an index to the record, and all actions must be justified in relation to it. All entries following the baseline data would include subjective information obtained from client or group, objective information (e.g., records or own observations), assessments drawn from the data, and plans. The four steps have come to be referred to as SOAP (Subjective, Objective, Assessments, Plans). With the POR, the worker (student) is forced to justify all actions in relation to a specific problem. For teaching purposes it would seem highly desirable to go beyond this step and require the student to provide a detailed rationale for actions and make reference to a practice principle whenever possible.

Let us take a foster care situation in which the student is developing a contract with the neglectful single parent to care for her only child, a preschooler, on weekends. The baseline data are already on record, and the most recent entry might read:

Subjective information: Mrs. L. reports she has no transportation to foster home and insists worker arrange for delivery and pickup of Nancy.

Objective data: Mrs. L. has no car, but city bus will bring her three blocks from foster home and her income is enough to cover fare. In past foster parents have been willing to provide transportation for child in placement.

Assessment: Mrs. L. continues to depend unnecessarily on others. Giving in to her demands now may perpetuate problem. To do for client what client can do for self encourages dependency. Also, rewarding client's demanding behavior reinforces it.

Plan: Negotiate with Mrs. L. to take bus on own with foster parents agreeing to drive Nancy only in heavy rain or agency-approved emergency.

In the Weed system, auditing (evaluating) medical records involves four major questions: 1. Is the data base complete and appropriate? 2. Have the problems been fully identified? 3. Is there an appropriate plan of action for each problem? 4. Is there any indication that the plan has been carried out? In an educational setting, the field instructor should also ask, Does the student provide a professional social work rationale for the intervention plan? In the fictitious case described above, the primary problem is child neglect. Foster care was the intervention but resulted in a "service" problem of denying the mother opportunities to practice child-care behavior. The foster care plan itself provided more data, calling for additional plans.

An instrument for recording student productions which follows the POR format excels in helping the student decide what are significant data (must be related to a problem) and in focusing attention on what the situation requires, as opposed to "being helpful." But the POR will not provide much direct evidence of relationship skills. As is true of process recording, oral elaboration is needed and direct observation would be highly desirable.

A major strength of the POR format, in keeping with the theme that evaluation is directed learning, is the emphasis on problem solving. When new material is placed into an organized behavioral pattern, as is true in the POR, learning is enhanced. This is perhaps the finding of greatest certitude after several decades of research on learning.[24]

ASSESSMENT OF STUDENT PRODUCTIONS

The use of a rating scale, at least for research purposes, was suggested by Mudgett as early as 1930.[25] On the whole, the development of rating instruments has been parochial, with each program designing its own. One of the major contributions of Schubert's landmark research was to distinguish between the goals of professional practice, as defined in a variety of assessment items, and a systematic description of actual student performance.[26] The level of skill was found to be lower than had been believed—a depressing prospect as we move toward more rigor. A second feature of her work, and one not consistently followed today, was the use of a framework. Schubert chose the *motivation, capacity,* and *opportunity* approach (MCO) developed by Ripple.[27]

While there has been some experimentation with assessment, and a national symposium sponsored by the Council on Social Work Education,[28] advancement has been modest. One is hard put to find mention of the evaluation of student field performance in the latest edition of the *Encyclopedia of Social Work.* The first attempt to combine the evaluation of field performance with a comprehensive exit examination on the full curriculum was undertaken on the baccalaureate level at the University of Montana.[29] At this writing it is too early to assess the impact of this research on field instruction.

Until such time that continued research results in a rating form that can be uniformly adopted on the order of an ACSW examination, departments and schools will need to draw upon existing instruments (Chicago, Michigan, Minnesota, etc.) or fashion their own. The Montana instrument (MSWCS) incorporates components of the student's broader curriculum in social work and employs categories that reflect the ubiquitous problem-solving activities of individuals through concepts ingrained by the selection of practice texts which feature a problem-solving approach. Because these two features are consistent with the themes expressed in this volume, the MSWCS suggests itself as a possible model.

Upon examination of a number of practice texts currently in use, I have found that their authors tend to utilize a sequential presentation of content that parallels the stages of problem solving encountered in research and other endeavors.[30] Two decades ago, Perlman faced the same task in attempting to find the common elements of casework (i.e., social work practice) and concluded that its operations are essentially those of problem solving.[31] This process includes: problem identification and assessment, establishing a contract with the client, collecting information, designing an intervention plan, implementing the plan, and evaluating the outcomes.

Given the above, perhaps the evaluation instrument should be in accord with the mental processes engaged in by the student in practice situations. In fact, this very point was emphasized at the CSWE symposium by an invited speaker with expertise in learning.

> Unless learning involves differentiation and integration of old and new responses into a problem-solving type of mental process or an organized behavioral pattern, it has little permanence or value. . . . When test items approximate the situation in life in which the learning will function, each item is not only an excellent test item, but a good teaching question as well.[32]

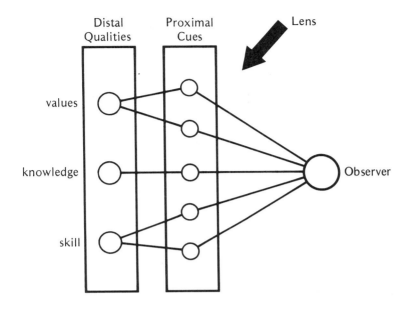

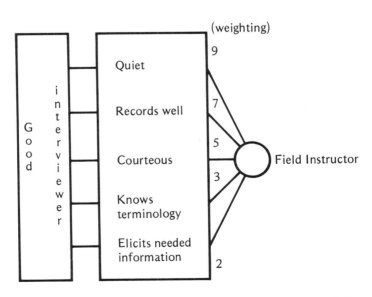

FIGURE 5.1 Egon Brunswik's Lens Model. (*Used by permission of Egon Brunswik. Adapted from management training materials developed by Teleometrics International, P.O. Drawer 1850, Conroe, Texas.*)

Under each general category on the instrument there would be a brief listing of major competencies; for example, in the Montana Social Work Competency Scale under "Utilization of Community Resources," the student would be asked to identify several local resources relevant to the client's situation. The field instructor could read from the "Problem-Oriented Record"* and ask the student: When it became obvious that Mr. T. required someone to look in on him daily, what was available for this elderly and infirm man? The student would be expected to know about the Senior Citizens Center Telephone Reassurance Program, even though the presence of a caring relative obviated the need for such a program at the time.

Note that the student was asked about a service which was relevant and that the question called for an "observable" response. The student's knowledge of community resources cannot be tested directly; the instructor must rely on *indicators* (in this case, identifying a specific relevant service). The selection of effective indicators is a crucial step in the design of a rating instrument. Depending on what indicators we use, our assessments will be either good or poor predictors of subsequent practice performance. Let us examine what occurs when a field instructor prepares to evaluate whether a student is a good interviewer. The Lens Model, attributed to Egon Brunswik, helps to describe the process. (See Figure 5.1.)

One cannot observe "good interviewing" even if it is in full view, for it is an abstraction. Much like the boastful clod who claims the ability to judge integrity by a man's firm handshake or whether one looks him straight in the eye, we all employ indicators in our assessment of qualities in others (and in objects). The field instructor in the fictitious illustration in Figure 5.1 judges the student's interviewing ability (the distal quality) on such proximal cues as whether the student is quiet, records well, is courteous, knows the terminology, and elicits the needed information. Implicitly, weights are also attached to these variables. Being quiet may imply that one listens well—a requirement for good interviewing. The only fairly objective and relevant variable, eliciting needed information, may be rated low. In this deliberate characterization, the field instructor may wonder if the student regarded "getting the facts" as more important than hearing the client out, forming a relationship, and coming to a tentative diagnosis. The "lens" we use determines what we see.

The recommended approach for determining whether a learning objective (knowledge or skill) has been achieved is to list several behaviors (indicators) which would lead you to agree that the objective is being met. For example, the student knows how to "refer" when he or she:

---

* The Problem-Oriented Record was not utilized in the Montana study.

1. can identify the specific service of the agency which matches the client's expressed need;
2. phones the agency to alert them of the client's arrival;
3. accompanies the client to the agency when rejection is anticipated;
4. is able to empathize with the client's sense of confusion regarding the social service network.

Item 4 is what Mager[33] calls a "fuzzy," because you cannot *see* empathy. You must either select another indicator in its place or transform the statement into a set of behaviors, one of which might be: "Explains to the client how the selected agency can offer the desired help."

In addition to the categories representing stages in the problem-solving process, related categories may be included to reflect the application of classroom knowledge in policy, research, and human behavior. Further, categories might be added to cover socialization items such as abiding by agency regulations, keeping appointments, and the like. Here, as elsewhere in the evaluation process, parsimony and feasibility should be the watchwords. It might be possible to design an instrument with several hundred detailed items, all found to be solid predictors of practice competence, but who would use it with diligence?

Throughout we have focused on process evaluation, and a word needs to be said about assessing outcomes. A few ambitious field instructors, apparently acting on their own, have adopted a version of the Kiresuk and Garwick Goal Attainment Follow-up Guide (see Table 5.1).[34] The student, with help as needed, lists the problem to be worked on at the top of the column, then sets a reasonable outcome. In Scale 1, the student (worker) in a mental health outpatient clinic aims toward helping the client develop an interest in employment within the next twelve months if training is not required. Getting the client to accept the likelihood of even a brief period of training is considered to be more than expected success. On the other end of the scale, if after counseling the client merely tolerates the idea of going to work "someday," this is less than expected success. Not only does the model help the student to focus on goal attainment, it aids in learning goal setting. Teaching and evaluation center on the student making adjustments in the problem definition, the objectives, and the intervention plan through a problem-solving model with feedback loops. A scoring system is provided for those so inclined.

There are several other models of outcome assessment, generally employed in behavior modification. However, the treatment schedule requires numerous observations of client progress, and the analysis can be complex.[35]

TABLE 5.1
Goal Attainment Scale

Scale Attainment Levels	Scale 1: Employment (interest in work) self report ($w_1 = 10$)	Scale 2: Self-concept (physical appearance) patient interview ($w_2 = 15$)	Scale 3: Interpersonal relationships (in training program as judged by receptionist—do not score if he does not go to training program) ($w_2 = 5$)	Scale 4: Interpersonal relationships (report of client's spouse) ($w_4 = 8$)	Scale 5: ($w_5 =$)
a. Most unfavorable treatment outcome thought likely	Client states he does not want to ever work or train for work.	Client (1) has buttons missing from clothes, (2) unshaven (but says he is growing beard), (3) dirty fingernails, (4) shoes unshined (if wearing shoes needing shine), (5) socks don't match.	Never spontaneously talks to anyone. May answer if spoken to.	No friends and no close friends (i.e., "close" equals friends with whom he can talk about serious, intimate topics and who he feels like his company).	
b. Less than expected success with treatment	Client states he may want to work "someday" (in year or later) but not now, and wants no training.	4 of the above 5 conditions	Spontaneously talks to his own therapists or caseworkers, but to no other clients.	One person who is a friend or acquaintance but not a close friend.	

c. Expected level of treatment success	Client states that he might be interested in working within the next 12 months, but only if no training is required.	3 of the 5 conditions above	Spontaneously talks to therapists, caseworkers, and one other client.	Two or more persons who are friends, but not close friends.
d. More than expected success with treatment	Client states that he might be interested in working within the next 12 months and training for no more than 30 work days.	2 of the 5 above conditions	Spontaneously talks to therapists, caseworkers, and 2 to 4 other clients.	One close friend, but no other friends.
e. Most favorable treatment outcome thought likely	Client states that he might be interested in working within the next 12 months. Will train for as long as necessary.	One of the above 5 conditions.	Spontaneously talks to therapists, caseworkers, and 5 or more other clients.	One or more close friends, plus one or more other friends or acquaintances.

* The weight for each scale is identified in parentheses (e.g., $w_1 = 10$). Scale 5 may be defined and weighted by the person administering the scale. Source: Thomas J. Kiresuk and Geoffrey Garwick, "Basic Social Attainment Scaling Procedures," in B.R. Compton and B. Galaway, eds., *Social Work Processes* (Homewood, IL.: Dorsey Press, 1979), p. 414.

Much remains to be done in the design of rating instruments in social work and other helping professions. Although certain schools have differing criteria or levels of expectation for baccalaureate, first-, and second-year performance, no consensus exists. The plethora of specializations and their varying curriculum patterns suggest that sections of the field instrument will need to be specially tailored. Items specific to methods other than casework are less well developed, although Rothman and Jones have contributed substantially to community organization and planning in an imaginative way through incorporating simulations, programmed instruction, and other laboratory exercises.[36]

Finally, there are external complications: the as yet untested limits allowed in the 1969 CSWE Curriculum Policy Statement,[37] the increasing impact of baccalaureate social work education on master's-level curriculum, and the uncertain consequences of the CSWE House of Delegates actions on *base content* taken in 1976. And in all cases, program objectives, type of student body, and range and quality of field placements need to be considered.

EVALUATION PROCEDURES

As noted earlier, procedures have not been developed for linking the collection and the analysis of assessment data for evaluation. Typically, the student records in detail (or keeps a log or submits a project), using a rather loose guide, and at the appointed time the field instructor reflects on selected happenings during the term and completes a rating sheet and narrative summary related to the student's activities and reports. The assessment items may show only moderate correspondence with points raised during the regular supervisory sessions and are not arranged in a manner which enables students to work toward their achievement as they think through and record what they are doing on field days. *It is essential that students know from the first day of placement exactly what they are required to learn and that the written and oral reports furnished for ongoing evaluation be designed to provide learning opportunities for the achievement of these competencies.* Field experiences in themselves fall short of creating such learning opportunities for the same reason that classroom lectures do not provide enough guidance for the writing of term papers or simulated research projects. Instructions are needed on what learning is to be demonstrated through the assignment.

Prior to the first week of field instruction, and in active collaboration with agency-based field instructors, students should be instructed in the use of a format for recording, keeping logs, or submitting projects. This format, which preferably will incorporate the advantages of the Problem-Oriented Record, should be in close correspondence with the evaluation form also handed to the student at the time (with suitable explanation).

During the regular supervisory conferences the field instructor can comment on the student's productions, relate them to the evaluation form, and enable the student to make the required changes in how he or she performs as a professional social worker. While this teaching process takes time, there may be room for it if the "supervisory hour" is used more effectively than it is now. Time consumed by the rambling accounts students offer on their activities can be reduced considerably through structuring the reports. Further, some of the time now spent on what is termed "development of self-awareness" is more accurately an exploration of why the student departed from acceptable professional procedures with a client. If the procedures to be followed in practice are made more visible to students from the outset, self-awareness may be enhanced!

The running account which the field instructor keeps should help substantially in completing the assessment instrument when the time arrives for a comprehensive evaluation. Further, it may be easier to cite specific instances ("I gave you an 'above average' here because of the way you were able to quickly develop a contract with Mrs. A and with the Y family; you did not get an 'excellent' because you assigned yourself some of the tasks they could have handled themselves").

Concurrent with the student orientation, field instructors will require parallel sessions on how the recording and evaluation forms are to be used. The amount of rater training required for the evaluation form will depend in part on whether the items have anchor statements that describe what "average" and other ratings mean on any dimension. While differences in rating behavior among field instructors can be reduced only so much through training, in the Montana study the inter-rater reliability (amount of agreement) was found to be high.[38]

When the evaluation session is finished, the student should receive a copy of the rating instrument and the summary statement. The next field instructor (if there is to be one) should receive a copy as well. If the evaluation is to have a teaching function, both the student and the field instructor will need to refer to it.

EVALUATION OF FIELD INSTRUCTION

Field coordinators have several potential sources of information available for evaluating field instructors and liaison faculty, including the following:

1. group meetings and individual conferences;
2. records, such as the field-performance rating sheet and summary statement;
3. student evaluations of the placements, field instructors, and liaison faculty;

4. reports from advisors and other faculty members;
5. reports from liaison faculty on field instructors;
6. reports from field instructors on liaison faculty;
7. informal and official commentary from agency personnel.

While there is much to draw upon, it is unlikely that such material is utilized extensively for evaluation purposes. Field coordinators are quasi-administrators and adhere to the professional norm of *review* rather than the bureaucratic norm of supervision. In practical terms this means that it is assumed all is well unless problems arise. Field instructors new to the program may be observed closely for a year or two, then the usual assumption comes into play.

The literature on the supervision of field instructors attests to this reluctance to evaluate their performance; there are no known studies of it in social work, to my knowledge, and even the anecdotal literature is sparse. But if agency-based field instructors are to become accepted as teachers, then we must accord them the scrutiny they deserve.

SUMMARY

One major contribution of field instruction to social work education has been the development of instruments to systematically assess student performance. However, due to the reluctance of field instructors to evaluate students with these same instruments, the assessment process has not been fully exploited. The twin evaluative functions of teaching and grading are mutually supportive, and the resistance to grading inhibits student learning. Evaluation primarily is directed learning and must accompany the setting of objectives if learning outcomes are to be achieved.

Evaluation items must be designed with care if rater bias is to be reduced and if learned behavior, rather than intelligence or personality traits, is to be measured. Frequent monitoring of student productions is necessary for accurate evaluation since the quality of a learner's performance in live situations is not consistent.

A structured format is necessary for collecting data on performance, and the Problem-Oriented Record, expanded to include a statement of rationale for worker activities and augmented by an oral report, is particularly suitable because it places content to be learned into an organized pattern and reflects the sequence of thought processes. The assessment instrument should correspond to the data-collection instrument, and the selection of relevant and observable indicators is essential for accurate perception by the rater. Structured evaluation procedures are required to link data collection with data analysis and to provide a cognitive map for the student. The most pervasive learning problem in field instruction is that students are not sufficiently aware of what it is they are supposed to learn.

Field instructors must be trained in the use of recording and assessment instruments. The evaluation of field instructors is a barren area in social work education.

NOTES

1. Useful reviews of evaluation in field performance can be found in: Merlin Taber, "A Sampling of Techniques for Evaluative Research in Field Instruction," *Social Work Education Reporter*, Vol. 15, No. 3 (September, 1967), 22–25, 33; Solomon H. Green, "Educational Assessments of Student Learning through Practice in Field Instruction," *Social Work Education Reporter*, Vol. 20, No. 3 (September-October, 1972), 48–54; Alfred Kadushin, *Supervision in Social Work* (New York: Columbia University Press, 1976), Chapter 5; and Morton L. Arkava and E. Clifford Brennen, "Quality Control in Social Work Education," in *Competency-Based Education for Social Work: Evaluation and Curriculum Issues*, eds. M.L. Arkava and E.C. Brennen (New York: Council on Social Work Education, 1976), pp. 3–21.

2. See, for example: Rosemary Reynolds, *Evaluating the Field Students* (New York: Family Service Association of America, 1946); and Dorothy E. Pettes, *Supervision in Social Work* (London: George Allen and Unwin, 1967).

3. Sanford Dornbusch and W. Richard Scott, *Evaluation and the Exercise of Authority* (San Francisco: Jossey-Bass, 1975).

4. Rue Bucher and Anselm Strauss, "Professions in Process," *American Journal of Sociology*, Vol. 56, No. 4 (January, 1961), 325–334.

5. David E. Cummins, "Examination Results," in *Competency-Based Education for Social Work*, p. 88.

6. Margaret Schubert, "Field Work Performance: Suggested Criteria for Grading," *Social Service Review*, Vol. 32, No. 4 (September, 1958), 247–257.

7. See Kadushin, *op. cit.*, p. 288.

8. Bessie Kent, *Social Work Supervision in Practice* (Oxford: Pergamon Press, 1969).

9. Alfred Kadushin, "Supervisor-Supervisee: A Survey," *Social Work*, Vol. 19, No. 3 (May, 1974), 288–297.

10. See Pettes, *op cit.*, p. 19.

11. Judith C. Nelsen, "Teaching Content of Early Fieldwork Conferences," *Social Casework*, Vol. 55, No. 3 (March, 1974), 147–153; see also its continuation entitled "Relationship Communication in Early Fieldwork Conferences," *Social Casework*, Vol. 55, No. 4 (April, 1974), 237–243.

12. A comprehensive review of evaluation issues is provided in Martin Bloom, "Analysis of the Research on Educating Social Work Students," *Journal of Education for Social Work*, Vol. 12, No. 3 (Fall, 1976), 3–10.

13. Julian Meltzoff and Melvin Kornreich, *Research in Psychotherapy* (New York: Atherton Press, 1970), pp. 310, 335.

14. Margaret Schubert, "The Field Work Curriculum: A Search for Descriptive Terms," *Social Service Review*, Vol. 42, No. 3 (September, 1968), 297–313.
15. Charlotte H. Wilkie, "A Study of Distortions in Recording Interviews," *Social Work*, Vol. 8, No. 3 (July, 1963), 31–36.
16. Margaret Schubert, "Field Work Performance: Repetition of a Study," *Social Service Review*, Vol. 34, No. 4 (September, 1960), 286–299.
17. Dornbusch and Scott, *op. cit.*, p. 167.
18. Patricia L. Kendall, "The Learning Environments of Hospitals," in *The Hospital in Modern Society*, ed. E. Friedson (New York: Free Press, 1963), p. 200.
19. Alfred Kadushin, "Diagnosis and Evaluation for (Almost) All Occasions," *Social Work*, Vol. 8, No. 1 (January, 1963), 12–19.
20. Dorothy E. Gibson, "Letter to the Editor," *Social Work*, Vol. 8, No. 3 (July, 1963), 127; a more detailed universal evaluation can be found in Kadushin, "Diagnosis and Evaluating." I selected the Gibson version because it was composed by someone with field responsibility.
21. Martha L. Urbanowski, "Recording to Measure Effectiveness," *Social Casework*, Vol. 55, No. 9 (November, 1974), 546–553.
22. Herbert A. Simon, *Administrative Behavior*, 2nd edition (New York: Macmillan, 1961), p. xxiv.
23. Rosalie A. Kane, "Look to the Record," *Social Work*, Vol. 19, No. 4 (July, 1974), 412–419.
24. Jerome S. Bruner, *The Process of Education* (Cambridge: Harvard University Press, 1960).
25. Mildred Mudgett, "The Place of Field Work in Training for Social Work: Its Educational Content," in *Proceedings of the National Conference of Social Work, 1930* (Chicago: University of Chicago Press, 1931), pp. 562–568.
26. Margaret Schubert, "Field Work Performance: Achievement Levels of First-Year Students in Selected Aspects of Casework Service," *Social Service Review*, Vol. 32, No. 2 (June, 1958), 120–137.
27. Lilian Ripple, "Motivation, Capacity, and Opportunity as Related to the Use of Casework Service: Theoretical Base and Plan of Study," *Social Service Review*, Vol. 27 (June, 1955), pp. 172–193.
28. *Field Learning and Teaching: Explorations in Graduate Social Work Education* (New York: Council on Social Work Education, 1968). This is a report of the symposium held in New Orleans in October, 1967.
29. Arkava and Brennen, *op. cit.*, pp. 62–82.
30. E. Clifford Brennen, "Classifying Base Content" (Working paper prepared for the West Virginia Undergraduate Social Work Curriculum Development Project, 1976); a fuller treatment of the pervasiveness of the problem-solving approach can be found in Martin Bloom, *The Paradox of Helping* (New York: John Wiley, 1975), Chapter 11.
31. Helen H. Perlman, *Social Casework: A Problem-Solving Process* (Chicago: University of Chicago Press, 1957).
32. Melvin L. Gruwell, "Development of Tools for Educational Research," in *Field Learning and Teaching*, pp. 68–92.
33. Robert F. Mager, *Goal Analysis* (Belmont, CA: Fearon, 1972).
34. Thomas J. Kiresuk and Geoffrey Garwick, "Basic Goal Attainment Scaling Procedures," reprinted from a Department of Health, Education, and Wel-

fare project report in *Social Work Processes*, eds. B.R. Compton and B. Galaway (Homewood, IL: Dorsey Press, 1975), pp. 388–401.

35. An example can be found in Bloom, *Paradox of Helping*, Chapter 17.

36. Jack Rothman and Wyatt Jones, *A New Look at Field Instruction* (New York: Association Press, 1971).

37. Council of Social Work Education, *Manual of Accrediting Standards for Graduate Schools of Social Work* (New York: CSWE, 1971), pp. 55–60.

38. Cummins, *op. cit.*, pp. 85–89. The raters were not formally trained but developed norms through considerable practice in team evaluation.

Part III
ROLES AND RESPONSIBILITIES IN FIELD INSTRUCTION

Part III is concerned with the rights and responsibilities of the key actors in field instruction (e.g., dean or program director, field director or coordinator, placement agency, student, and client) as they influence the ability of the field instructor to become an effective teacher. It is important that the reader not only recognize the roles each perform but also examine the linkage between them. Problems in field instruction exist as often in the linkage among actors as in the performance of any single actor.

A field instruction program can only reach its fullest potential if the dean or program director has an in-depth understanding of and commitment to supporting field instruction as an essential component of the curriculum. The creation of a supportive environment from the top administrative level in a school or program is prerequisite to achieving a high quality field instruction program.

In Chapter 6, "Responsibilities of the School: Administrative Support of Field Instruction," Fellin examines the important function of the school and dean or program director in providing adequate resources and giving personal leadership to the field instruction enterprise. This involves seeking sanction from within the university and maintaining sound working relationships with the practice community. It also involves finding an approach to field instruction which is compatible with the objectives and resources of the program. Finally, it involves securing competent staff, allocating sufficient staff time, and providing an organizational structure which will accomplish the goals of field instruction.

Fellin discusses administrative activities which support a good field instruction program. Some of these are provision of a role for field instructors in the governance of the school, the engagement of field instructors in classroom teaching, the provision of workshops

and other educational opportunities for the growth and development of field instructors, and a carefully planned use of university-
paid faculty in the field liaison role.

Speaking from the role of a field director or coordinator, Gordon
discusses the responsibilities of the school for maintenance of the
field program in Chapter 7. In this material Gordon makes abundant-
ly clear the enormous time and energy it requires for a school to
maintain a good program of field instruction.

Complimenting Fellin's chapter, Gordon elaborates on the role of
the faculty field liaison. She goes on to describe supports the school
might offer which help the field instructor become a good teacher,
discusses school-agency relationships (including contracts between
them), and concludes with a suggested outline for a field manual.
Throughout this chapter the reader will find a unique sensitivity to
the difficulty of this task, yet a consistent expectation that field
education be accomplished with an expectation of a high quality
educational experience.

In Chapter 8, Selig discusses field instruction from the viewpoint
of an agency. He discusses the reasons agencies invest staff time
and other resources in the education of students. The material recognizes the inevitable tension that exists between student learning
and agency service responsibilities which must be kept in balance
and stresses the importance of a carefully planned orientation of
students to the agency. Finally, Selig discusses the agency as a part
of the learning environment and especially stresses its important
role in the socialization of the student to the profession.

In Chapter 9, "Responsibilities of the Student in Field Instruction," Judah emphasizes the shared responsibility of field instructor
and student in field education. She emphasizes the student's responsibility to actively participate in the learning endeavor, and to
practice within the values and ethics of social work. Judah specifically refers to the role of the student in defining specific learning
objectives, offering service to clients, and evaluating learning and
service activities. This material should help both students and field
instructors clarify responsibilities for both the learning and service
functions.

Randolph concludes Part III with a provocative chapter, "The
Rights and Responsibilities of Clientele in Field Instruction." He
examines the role of clients in student learning and recognizes the
risks the clientele face when served by a novice worker. Randolph
raises the difficult, and often neglected, question of the right of
clients to receive quality services and to determine if they want to be
served by a student social worker. He then offers a plan for
approaching this problem and discusses the active role clients can
(and sometimes do) assume in the student's education.

Responsibilities of the School

Administrative Support of Field Instruction

Phillip A. Fellin

The development and maintenance of learning experiences for students through field instruction require strong administrative direction and support. Along with an in-depth understanding of the central role field instruction plays in a program's success in providing a sound education for its students, this support is crucial in providing for positive relationships between education and practice. However, the fact that social work education is frequently criticized in terms of a gap between education and practice suggests the need to reexamine the administrative responsibilities of the school.[1] We will introduce an administrative perspective concerning a number of aspects of field instruction, with our focus on the roles that key school personnel, particularly the dean or program director, must play in order to enhance student field learning.*

RESPONSIBILITIES OF THE PROGRAM DIRECTOR

General direction for the development of field instruction and the involvement of the program director in this part of the curriculum can be found in the Council on Social Work Education's *Manual of Accrediting Standards*.[2] The manual states that the "social work practicum is an essential component of professional education for social work."

* We have used the term *program director* throughout the chapter to refer to a dean or director, of a school or program.

Criteria established for practicum learning experiences call for "availability of qualified field instruction." Specific standards state that the school shall assume responsibility for the development and administration of field instruction, and planned cooperation and coordination between the school and field agencies are regarded as essential to this endeavor. The primary responsibility for field instruction is clearly and precisely placed with the social work program of the college or university. At the same time, there is a strong expectation that positive education-practice relationships will prevail to support educational objectives.

The program director seeks to follow these guidelines by ensuring that practice is adequately recognized as a part of the educational system and that personnel in the social work program carry out essential roles vis-à-vis field instruction. The program director's role in this area is derived from a general responsibility "to develop an organizational structure and administrative policies and procedures which coordinate and use faculty resources effectively to attain the educational objectives of the school."[3]

There are several crucial areas in which the program director can influence the quality of field instruction. The director determines, with faculty consultation, the amounts and kinds of program activities necessary to accomplish the program's overall educational objectives. Decisions are made regarding the efforts administrative and faculty members will devote to field instruction, such as staff time, activities, commitment, and the allocation of material resources and funds. These decisions should be made in the context of total program curriculum objectives and in light of the effectiveness and efficiency expected of the various field instruction activities.

The program director's participation in the specification of educational policies will provide a foundation for making operational decisions regarding field instruction efforts. The program must be conducted within available resources which will include contributions and involvement of personnel from within the educational institution and from practice. As a particular model of field instruction is developed, the administrator considers the budgetary and personnel allocation requirements of the model. Thus, a program that uses school-employed field instructors makes an investment which is considerably different from a program that relies entirely on agency-based personnel. Under either agreement, high-quality field consultation requires a significant contribution of the school's resources. As a particular model of field instruction is designed in the developmental stage of a program, the director can take steps to assure that sufficient resources are assigned to field activities. For example, the size of student enrollment may have to be limited in order to assign an appropriate portion of the resources in support of field instruction. The number and types of elective courses may have to be curtailed, or the size of classes increased, in order to allow faculty time for field-related tasks.

The program director has several options in regard to resources; that is, to seek out additional resources, to reallocate resources, or to limit the program to available resources. Making decisions in regard to these options requires a determination of the effectiveness of the program's field instruction model in relation to educational goals. For example, if the educational objectives call for field placements which include experiences with several modes of intervention, a review of student field tasks will indicate whether or not the agencies being used are appropriate learning sites. If they are not, increased resources may be needed to consult with field personnel or to develop new field placements. In some cases, the school will employ different models for field instruction and will seek to determine how effective they are in assuring specified practice experiences and how they compare in terms of the resources expended. There is no set formula for investment of school resources in field activities; however, there are some essential personnel activities which must be carried out in order to assure quality field experiences.

The program director is responsible for establishing the organizational structure under which field instruction activities can operate properly and effectively. Graduate and undergraduate levels both require a faculty member assigned responsibilities for administrative direction of the field program. In the developmental stages of a program which relies on field agencies for practice-skill instruction, a considerable amount of time must be devoted to selection and approval of field sites and instructors. Procedures must be established for the assignment of students to field agencies, and decisions must be made in regard to the ways in which liaison activities will be managed between the field and school personnel. In the developmental stage, the field coordinator must have support for the preparation of written materials for the field such as a field manual. The program director must establish an appropriate workload arrangement for the field coordinator in keeping with the size of the student body, the activities of other faculty members in field-related activities, and the workload requirements of the college or university. A minimum of a half-time assignment is desirable for the field coordinator of a small program. Larger programs with fifty or more students in placement each year should have a full-time field coordinator.

There is an increasing demand for formal commitment of resources to be established by the program director in regard to field instruction. This includes a specific assignment of workload credit for field activities and a specific description of the duties of individuals with responsibilities related to the field practicum. Thus, in addition to a field coordinator, a program using agency personnel as instructors should make time available to faculty members for liaison duties. This includes time for conferring with students regarding their field placements and time for consulting with field and class instructors about student performance. Workload commitments should be made to faculty who engage in activities related to the field, and fiscal commitments, such as funds to meet, travel, phone, and meeting expenses, must be established by the school.

A circumstance in which special resources are needed is the use of field sites where instructors do not possess the MSW degree. Social work programs are guided by accreditation standards in this regard, as the learning experience must have a social work focus and, when appropriate, faculty backup for non-MSW instructors. The program director seeks to assure this by formal commitment of time for the faculty representative to assume the social work instructional activity. This would normally require at least a weekly meeting with the student.

Given the specification of some of the efforts which go into field instruction, the program director can assist in the effectiveness of these efforts through formal recognition of these activities in workload computations, in the criteria for promotion, and in the determination of yearly salary levels. Recognition should be based on written guidelines and in communications from the program director to individual faculty members. In order to evaluate the efforts devoted to field instruction, the director needs information. This information may be obtained through a variety of evaluation techniques and should include as sources the field instructors, agency executives, students, and faculty. Evaluation with regard to individual performance, as well as overall functioning of the field instruction component of the program, is necessary. Such evaluation requires staff time and commitment on the part of the administrator in order to assure an assessment of effectiveness and efficiency of the field operation.

Obstacles to Positive Relationships

We have identified some of the activities the program director engages in, in order to create sound conditions for field instruction. At the same time, it is useful to note some of the obstacles which seem to interfere with positive education-practice relations and, hence, with student learning. The program director should pay particular attention to the creation and support of arrangements that will minimize or eliminate adverse effects of these obstacles.

First, there are numerous variations in the field settings and, therefore, in the nature of the students' learning. As Rothman observes, there are at least four patterns of education-practice relationships: where integration of classroom theory and skill development in the field is relatively complete; where class and field supplement each other, and some integration may occur through efforts of instructor and student; where class and field seem to be unrelated; and where class and field seem to be in conflict.[4] When class and field learning are unrelated or in conflict, the program director and staff are involved in remedying the situation or withdrawing students from such settings. The identification of these four patterns highlights the fact that we cannot make the assumption that complete integration exists or that it is easy to achieve. There are a number of factors that impinge on the achievement of integration of class and field, and the educational program staff must be alert to these as they seek to carry out activities to improve integration and to minimize conflict and unrelatedness.

The most commonly mentioned problem in education-practice relationships is the role strain on the individuals involved. The practitioner must provide services and is accountable to his or her organization to give primary effort to reaching service objectives. These service obligations place a strain on the individual who also engages in the role of educator for the social work student. The practitioner may not have sufficient time and effort to handle both roles. Field instruction may not be the primary task of the practitioner, nor is it usually the primary task of the educator. The faculty member's goals in education are often heavily weighted in favor of presentation of theoretical knowledge and of knowledge development through scholarly work. When the teacher is called upon to engage in activities related to the field learning situation, such as liaison work, there is a strain created by time pressures, individual interests, academic requirements, demands for publication, and so forth. Thus, in the majority of instances, there seems to be a situation where neither the field instructor nor the teacher has as a primary task and interest the instruction of students in practice skills. Such a circumstance places on the student the major responsibility for integration of classroom knowledge and field learning experiences.

Another factor which may interfere with the students' field learning is the discrepancy in the nature of the knowledge available to and taught by the classroom teacher and the field instructor. The teacher's knowledge is likely to be highly theoretical, whereas the field instructor's knowledge is likely to be more practice oriented. While teachers and field instructors make efforts to keep up with both areas of knowledge, the different emphasis of these individuals with regard to knowledge may inhibit integrative learning for students. A common problem arises from the introduction of new knowledge in the classroom before that information has been transmitted to field instructors. This "transmission lag" is not inevitable, but it is highly probable at a time when there is such a rapid rate of knowledge developmennt in the social and behavioral sciences.

A major obstacle to education-practice relationships comes from inadequate rewards and benefits for the individuals involved in field instruction. Despite the fact that most field instructors do not derive an extra financial reward for field instruction, there are benefits associated with this instructional role. Some of these include: opportunity to work with students, usually described in terms of stimulation provided by students with energy and new ideas; opportunities to relate to classroom instructors and to obtain consultation from academics; pleasures associated with teaching and observing students increase their leaning and practice skills; and achievement of personal goals and values regarding service through the efforts of students. On the other hand, when benefits are limited and recognition is absent from the agency and/or the social work program, this circumstance is likely to have a negative influence on the student's field learning.

The work of the CSWE Task Force on Social Work Practice and Education provided a useful review of differences between education and practice, some of which act as barriers to positive relationships.[5] The task force noted that the decision-making processes in practice and education differ, with agencies structured along hierarchical lines and educational institutions having a mixture of collegial and hierarchical arrangements. Mandates for the two types of organizations differ as well as the systems of accountability. There are various degrees of autonomy in the organizations vis-à-vis their funding sources and constituencies, and social workers and educators have different degrees of autonomy in their respective roles. At times these differences become barriers to interdependent and cooperative relationships, and we should keep them in mind as we explore ways of improving the interchange between practice and education.

Guides to Improving Relationships

Given the nature of the conditions under which field instruction is offered to students, it is useful to consider ways in which social work programs can minimize and/or overcome these obstacles. We start with the premise that education and practice, through field instruction, share in the goal of preparing competent practitioners. The ingredient most often mentioned in attempting to reach this goal is the integration of class and field learning. In order that education and practice do not attempt to prepare practitioners in isolation from each other, there must be adequate communication, cooperation, and coordination. This includes creation of reciprocal opportunities for personnel in the educational program and practice settings to influence each other. Just as faculty members will have interactions with personnel in field settings in order to influence the educational experiences of the student, the educational program must allow for practitioners to influence the total curriculum.

The educational program has several alternatives for building positive relationships between education and practice and thereby facilitating student learning. Better communication is the most frequent request of practitioners serving as field instructors. It is essential that a faculty member acting in a liaison role become acquainted with the field instructor through periodic personal contacts. It is also desirable for the faculty member to know personally the agency executive. This form of communication occurs mainly through the fact that students have been placed for field instruction in the social agency. In addition, the program director should create opportunities to meet field instructors and agency executives, so that the director's perspectives on social work education may be conveyed to those individuals and so that the individuals may develop a personal acquaintance with the chief administrator. This may be accomplished by meetings at the university, such as at an annual luncheon with a speaker on a topic of common interest. Visits by the program director to the field are another way of reaching these goals. This kind of interpersonal relationship among administrators, faculty members, the field instructors provides an opportunity for making clear the expectations of the social work program and provides a communication base for positive relationships.

Communications with field personnel are often carried out by secretarial and administrative staff. The program director has the responsibility of arranging adequate and competent secretarial support for field instruction activities. Staff members maintain a crucial type of contact with field personnel through proper handling of phone conversations, requests, and messages; through accurate record keeping; and through timely written correspondence. The coordination of field activities is highly dependent on the skills and competence of the program's support staff.

The kinds of communications we have been referring to can be expected to minimize some of the consequences of role strains on faculty and practitioners and to create an improved learning environment for the student. Equally important is the development of modes of participation through which practitioners can influence educational policy. It is unlikely that a single mode will be sufficient to engage and involve the full range of agency executives and field instructors. Yet, a combination of several modes, some formal and others informal, can help in reducing some of the strains between practice and education and, most significantly, provide practitioner input into the total program curriculum. As we mention these various approaches to involving field personnel in curriculum building, we should keep in mind that all of the efforts require a commitment on the part of the program director and faculty. The decisions regarding communication—that is, what, when, and how much—are important since communication is costly. Thus the efforts need to be evaluated periodically to ascertain the extent to which they are effective and efficient. It is the responsibility of the program director to assure that evaluation of this type takes place.

While the major focus of contacts between faculty members and field instructors is on the performance of a student in field placement, these interpersonal contacts can provide an opportunity for practitioner input into educational policy. In the liaison role, the faculty member should make an effort to engage agency practitioners and executives in discussions about issues and changes in the social work program curriculum. The faculty member is in a position to introduce ideas from these discussions into the deliberations of the school policy committees. This approach has the potential for bringing a wide range of opinions from the practice field to bear on the determination of curriculum structure and direction. Its influence is informal and indirect and should be supplemented with more formal arrangements.

Another way of reaching a large number of field personnel is through school-sponsored meetings for field instructors. These meetings may serve several functions, such as providing for description of school programs, presentation of new theoretical approaches to practice, and social interchange. Properly structured, these meetings can allow for significant input from practitioners on current educational issues. This requires joint education-practice planning in a manner that allows time for practitioner input and assures that faculty members are involved in the process.

The use of an advisory committee of field personnel is yet another way of obtaining practice input. Such committees have been criticized by groups such as the Family Service Association of America as being pro forma, not continuous and not involving decision-makers.[6] However, when the program director chairs an advisory committee and involves key school personnel in its membership, as well as a mixture of agency executives and agency instructors, such a committee can have a powerful influence on school policy. It is particularly important that the names of members of such an advisory committee be known to all agency executives and field instructors so that the membership can be influenced by field personnel. This mechanism for communication will probably not be worthwhile unless strongly supported by the program director.

There are, of course, many variations of advisory committees. For example, it may be useful to have joint practice-education task forces operating in the development and implementation of federally sponsored training grant projects, such as in child welfare, community mental health, and alcohol and drug abuse. Practitioners may be invited to join interdisciplinary university-wide committees on special training areas, such as a committee represented by law, medicine, and social work relating to child abuse and neglect. Another example is the development of ad hoc practice task forces in communities interested in continuing-education and extension course offerings. These formal arrangements offer opportunities for practitioner input into these educational programs even though the number of participants may be limited.

One of the most potent forms of practitioner input into the school's curriculum is through classroom teaching. This may occur with the assignment of a practitioner as a part-time lecturer for a course, or through special lectures by practitioners as part of regular course offerings. These arrangements serve to close the gap between education and practice and to improve relationships between them. Another example of this mechanism is the faculty-field staff exchange wherein individuals exchange places for a term or an academic year. The practitioner as exchange person participates in ongoing committees and faculty deliberations and provides a practice input into these activities. All of these teaching arrangements require the active involvement and support of the program director.

Membership on school or program committees provides for another formal and powerful mechanism for meaningful participation of practitioners. Most social work programs make use of committees for areas such as curriculum, admissions, field instruction, and personnel matters; and it is usual to find formal arrangements for student and faculty membership. Membership of field personnel on school committees is infrequently used as a method of facilitating practitioner involvement. Lacking any kind of organizational structure, field instructors are not accustomed to "demanding" participation, as are students, nor are they generally anxious to spend the time demanded for most committee work. Yet, through the special efforts of a program director, field instructors could be enticed, even paid, to contribute to social work education policy through formal committee membership.

These are but a few of a number of mechanisms for involving practitioners in educational program activities, which, in turn, will have a positive effect on field learning. There are several other efforts a program can make to recognize and reward the role of the field instructor. The most challenging task for social work programs remains the provision of recognition of the faculty role of field instructors. Faculty titles are in many instances controlled by the larger university which may limit the options open to a social work program. An option used frequently is to modify a regular faculty title with the term *adjunct*, as in *adjunct professor of social work*, or with the term *clinical*, as in *clinical professor of social work*. The privileges that go with the titles vary but usually include issue of a faculty identification card, library privileges, use of recreational facilities, bookstore discount rates, and so forth. These titles may allow for a vote on the governing faculty of a program, but this is uncommon. Of course, the title of field instructor is used by many programs and often carries the privileges of the adjunct professor. Whatever the title, a listing of the names of the field instructors in the school catalog is a significant public recognition of the faculty role of the practitioner. Considering the major investment the field instructor makes, a social work program should establish some form of service award for continuous service of five years or more as a field instructor.

Perhaps one of the most costly, yet most beneficial, contributions the social work program can make to the field instructors is to offer educational opportunities for them. Most programs arrange special instruction for new field instructors with a focus on educational supervision. There are, in addition, many regular courses which field instructors would benefit from as well as advanced courses, extension courses, and courses in other college/university departments. The program director is the person who is in a position to negotiate with the university for admission of field instructors to these courses with a waiver of fees. The school also keeps field instructors current with the knowledge being offered in the classroom through special institutes where instructors review course content and provide course bibliographies. There are also a number of occasions when faculty members provide consultation to agencies in specialized areas, such as consultation regarding group work in agencies having staff without this expertise. In all instances, we are speaking of efforts on the part of education to recognize, reward, and collaborate with social-agency personnel to promote improved education for students. An unmentioned and rarely used reward is money, either in the form of a token stipend or something more substantial. Considering the fact that student tuition is collected by the university for credit hours granted to field instruction, it is appropriate to consider the use of part of these funds as stipends for field instructors.

While we have mentioned a set of activities and interactions between school and agency personnel which are somewhat formal, we should recognize that the informal, interpersonal relationships are most significant. The CSWE Task Force on Practice and Education hearings of 1974 revealed that educators and practitioners placed high value on knowing each other and interacting in a variety of ways. In keeping with this notion, with a limited amount of funds, the program director can hold social functions connected to meetings of field instructors and sponsor other on-campus social affairs, such as lunches. Signs of appreciation extended to individuals involved in field instruction serve the school and agency relationship well.

ROLES OF PROGRAM PERSONNEL

Throughout our discussion we have made references to the various roles assumed by faculty in regard to the conduct of the field instruction program, such as program director or dean, field coordinator, and faculty liaison. These roles are essential in the management of field instruction offered by agency-based personnel. While some writers would maintain that the school has little control over the field practicum, it is our contention that a considerable amount of control can be exercised by faculty when sufficient attention is given to carrying out these roles. It is useful to briefly note some of the field-related activities involved in each of these roles and to consider how the roles allow for quality field instruction.

We have already indicated some of the responsibilities of the program director with regard to field instruction. It is useful now to highlight the basis for the director's unique role. The chief administrative person has a leadership role with faculty members in relation to curriculum development, although curriculum decisions are likely to be the jurisdiction of the total faculty. Granting all the implications of academic freedom, the director has an authority relationship with faculty in terms of personnel matters, work assignments, and compensation. As chief administrator of the program, the director or dean has a management role which involves influence over selection of personnel for administrative assignments, such as the field coordinator. The director has a consultative role, as faculty members frequently defer to the director's judgment in educational matters and operations. The director has an evaluative role, being in a position to make judgments about the performance of individual faculty members. The director represents the program to higher university officials and provides communication links between them and the program. These characteristics give the director the potential for considerable influence over the total social work program, and this includes capacity for a high degree of control over activities related to field instruction.

In this presentation we have highlighted the responsibilities of the program director in regard to development of quality field instruction. It it clear, however, that the major assignment of field activities in most social work programs is carried by a faculty member serving as field coordinator.[7] In fact, standards for undergraduate social work programs require a field coordinator with an MSW degree. The field coordinator carries many roles, from participation in educational curriculum planning and policy making to management and public relations functions. The role in an emerging program includes development of policies, preparation of materials, coordination of faculty members assigned to field activities, selection and approval of field placement locations and instructors, assignment of students to field placements, and service as a problem solver and troubleshooter. In an established program some of these functions may be carried out by the field coordinator and others by faculty members. A major responsibility of the coordinator is to be sufficiently acquainted with the agencies and instructors, from the viewpoint of the kind of learning experiences provided, to evaluate them and assure that they meet standards for quality field instruction.

The field coordinator can assist in developing positive relationships with the practice field in a number of ways, such as identifying and/or creating educational opportunities for new field instructors and arranging workshops and special meetings with faculty and field instructors on topics of mutual interest. The coordinator can serve as a consultant to field instructors and to faculty members on practice-skill issues but must be cautious not to take over the liaison functions of other faculty members. Within the social work program, the coordinator will participate in committee work, particularly curriculum planning, in order to assure appropriate attention to field issues.

The field coordinator can take a leadership role in the development of field instruction as a curriculum unit and in the design and implementation of assessment and research activities in this area of the curriculum. This person must be the guardian of an educational focus in field instruction, which requires considerable curriculum development activity and responsibility for linking class and field instruction. In addition, this person plays a major role in helping field instructors recognize their role as educators. It is important that the coordinator's role be specified and evaluated by the program director in order to assure performance of these activities.

One of the most demanding parts of the field coordinator's role is the handling of conflicts and disputes between students and faculty liaison persons and/or field instructors. In instances where the faculty liaison is unable to resolve conflicts, the field coordinator attempts to handle the situation. The field coordinator frequently serves as a person to whom a field instructor can go with complaints about faculty behavior, and students may also seek out the coordinator with complaints about the field situation. The field coordinator may serve as the receiver of grievances regarding field instruction prior to matters being brought to the program director's attention.

As will be noted in Chapter 7, on maintenance of the field program, the faculty-field liaison provides the single most important linkage between class and field. Most often, the liaison person gives the field grade and is the individual expected to have the overall understanding of a student's progress and performance. Under ideal conditions, the liaison visits the field agency and confers with student and field instructor at the beginning of the field experience, at appropriate intervals (every three or four weeks), and at the end of the field assignment. Since in many instances the location of the placement will not be in close proximity to the college or university, visits represent a considerable time investment for the faculty member serving as liaison. This arrangement requires administrative support in terms of time and workload credit in order to assist the faculty member in carrying out this role. The program director is also responsible for having an adequate number of faculty members to allow for a reasonable number of liaison assignments. The program director must have a system for receiving feedback on the faculty member's performance as liaison (from students and the agency) and for evaluating that performance. The program director supports the role by clearly specifying the rewards of good performance in terms of promotion and compensation. The field liaison is in a position of observing and evaluating the quality of the field placement and of assisting the instructor and the student to engage in a positive learning experience.

Faculty liaison patterns vary with programs. Some make use of all faculty and attempt to make assignments by virtue of individual faculty competencies and the nature of the agency. Others use a few faculty with a major responsibility in liaison work. Differential use of faculty for liaison work may be desirable since instances occur wherein some faculty members have little facility for such activities.[8] However, involvement of all faculty in field instruction can lead to a greater appreciation of field teaching and better integration of classroom and field instruction. Faculty members who engage in liaison activity enjoy rich opportunities for keeping current with social work practice.

The use of individuals paid by the educational program to engage in full-time field instruction activities has been in effect in a limited way in most graduate schools of social work and in an exclusive way in a few schools.[9] At the undergraduate level, this is not a common practice although it occurs in some programs which use federal funds, such as Title XX, for this purpose. A chief impetus for the pattern of faculty field instructors was the federal funding provided for social work education from the 1950s onward. Grant funding typically provided for employment of instructors to have units of students in areas where personnel were not available for instruction and in areas of priority to federal programs such as mental health, aging, corrections, and schools. One model of this type occurred when some schools used only faculty members to provide instruction for all first-year students. Another model of use of faculty as field instructors is found in situations wherein a school takes over an agency operation. Still another model involves faculty members who devote their time partly to field instruction and partly to classroom instruction. In the models where faculty members spend a substantial amount of time in the field, the faculty frequently report a feeling of second-class citizenship. This is sometimes due to individuals not being on "tenure tracks." When they are on the track for tenure, they sometimes have difficulty getting promoted due to their lack of attention to publication requirements. Clearly, there are opportunities under the faculty-paid field instruction plans for the individuals to link education and practice. Most graduate schools have not invested their university resources in this way, choosing to enroll more students and take advantage of the services of agency personnel. It is reasonably clear that faculty field instruction is an expensive proposition, but some would contend that such an investment is the most appropriate way of assuring quality education. Few undergraduate programs have deployed their resources in that way, and they have depended almost entirely on agency personnel. Unfortunately, data on the use of school-employed field instructors is scarce. Studies have not demonstrated a clear advantage of this model over others although it has been asserted that integration of learning is enhanced by it.

SUMMARY

Recognizing the complexities of achieving educational objectives which deal with the learning of practice skills, we have nonetheless explored some of the administrative roles and responsibilities that can contribute to quality field instruction. We have assumed that most social work programs are not in a position to completely staff and/or control the field learning of students and that, therefore, a positive education-practice relationship is desirable and in need of administrative involvement and support. There are, of course, other ways in which a social work program can define its responsibility for the teaching of practice skills. Rothman advocates increased responsibility through the provision of campus-based instruction in the first year of the master's program and field-based instruction in the second year.[10] He anticipates that such a first-year plan would increase integration of theory and practice skills, and the second year would allow for the field to supplement classroom learning. Many of our ideas about administrative support would still pertain under this model. There are, on the other hand, models for which our comments would be less relevant such as an approach offered by Schutz and Gordon.[11] This plan would reallocate responsibilities of schools and agencies, with complete control over all degree-related instruction assumed by the school with the objective of "preparing for" practice, followed by agencies taking graduates for "training in" practice in an internship or residency situation.

It is debatable whether or not schools and social work programs will choose to allocate sufficient resources to practice-skill instruction to allow for modes such as those suggested above. Even if such plans are economically feasible for a program, they may not be adopted due to educational philosophies which point to the more traditional approaches. In our discussion, we have not been concerned with reallocation of the responsibilities of the various groups involved in the traditional field instruction models. Rather, we have advocated the need for clear definition of responsibilities and for substantial improvement in the performance of school personnel in field-related activities. This is not to say that quality field instruction does not occur today in social work education; there is ample testimony that social work surpasses many other professional education groups in its ways of handling development of practice skills. We are saying, however, that when problems of unevenness, lack of integration, lack of coordination, or "gaps" in the education-practice relationship are prevalent, a renewed emphasis on school responsibilities is required. We have especially noted the need for increased investment and commitment on the part of administrators and faculty members in social work programs to the field course component of the curriculum.

NOTES

1. See Betty Lacy Jones, ed., *Current Patterns in Field Instruction* (New York: Council on Social Work Education, 1969); Kristen Wenzel, ed., *Undergraduate Field Instruction Programs* (New York: Council on Social Work Education, 1972); *The Dynamics of Field Instruction* (New York: Council on Social Work Education, 1975); Ralph Dolgoff, *Report to the Task Force on Social Work Practice and Education* (New York: Council on Social Work Education, 1974).
2. *Manual of Accrediting Standards* (New York: Council on Social Work Education, 1971). Graduate standards are cited here because of their specificity, but the principles are applicable to baccalaureate programs as well.
3. *Ibid.*, p. 25.
4. Jack Rothman, "Development of a Profession: Field Instruction Correlates," *Social Service Review*, Vol. 51 (June, 1977), pp. 297–299.
5. Dolgoff, *op. cit.*, pp. 18–23; Jerome Cohen, "Selected Constraints in the Relationship between Social Work Education and Practice," *Journal of Education for Social Work*, Vol. 13, No. 1 (Winter, 1977), pp. 3–7; Elmer J. Tropman, "Agency Constraints Affecting Links between Practice and Education," *Journal of Education for Social Work*, Vol. 13, No. 1 (Winter, 1977), pp. 8–14.
6. *FSAA Statement on Issues in Social Work Education* (New York: Family Service Association of America, 1974).
7. See Helen Cassidy, "Role and Function of the Coordinator or Director of Field Instruction," in *Current Patterns in Field Instruction*, pp. 147–155; Ruth Werner, "The Director of Field Work—Administrator and Education," in *Current Patterns*, pp. 157–164.
8. Elizabeth Navarre and Edward Pawlak, *Guidelines for Deployment of Faculty Liaison*, mimeographed (University of Michigan, 1967).
9. See Alex Gitterman, "The Faculty Field Instructor in Social Work Education," in *Dynamics of Field Instruction*, pp. 31–39.
10. See Rothman, *op. cit.*
11. Margaret Schutz and William Gordon, "Reallocation of Educational Responsibility among Schools, Agencies, Students, and NASW," *Journal of Education for Social Work*, Vol. 13, No. 2 (Spring, 1977), 99–106.

7

Responsibilities of the School

Maintenance of the Field Program

Margaret Schutz Gordon

The maintenance of a quality field program is an extremely sensitive, difficult, and time-consuming task. It is primarily the responsibility of the field coordinator,* but it also involves quite a few other faculty and staff members in the school. This is not always fully recognized either by social work deans and program directors or university administrators. Once sanction has been given for a faculty member to serve as field coordinator, and knowing that the major day-to-day field teaching activities are handled by agency staff members, administration may assume that everything is taken care of in the field sector. Not true! A great many ongoing activities are necessary throughout the year if a quality field program is to result.

It must be remembered that field teaching (except for the small number of university-paid faculty field teachers) is usually a voluntary, unpaid service, taking much time, thought, and physical and emotional energy. It often goes unrewarded within the agency. Rarely does a worker receive more salary or special accolades for being a field teacher; and sometimes absolutely no time is released from regular job duties for a worker to spend in field teaching. For some, the challenge of teaching and the opportunity that teaching presents for self-learning—

---

* I have used the term *field coordinator* throughout the chapter to refer to the role of field instruction director or coordinator as it is performed in either graduate or undergraduate programs.

116

most field instructors speak of the tremendous amount they learn while serving in this role—is enough. But, usually, even those instructors are found to require considerable support and backup—maintenance, if you will—from the school. Support is needed if the experience is to remain both meaningful enough for field teachers to devote their time and progressive enough to meet the changing needs of the educational institution. Giving this support requires considerable time and effort.

The important maintenance activities described here are required in addition to the essential "usual" administrative duties of the field coordinator which are assumed, since unless the usual duties are successfully carried out, none of the additional "maintenance functions" can make the program effective. The usual duties of the field coordinator include:

1. identifying, assessing, and selecting agencies to be used as field educational sites;
2. selection, upon recommendation from agency executives, of the persons to serve as practicum instructors;
3. determining qualifications for field liaison and giving guidance to faculty serving in that capacity;
4. recommending policies and procedures for carrying out the field program;
5. actually "placing" students in the field or "matching" students to field placement settings.

Assuming these administrative tasks are satisfactorily carried out, what then are some of the ways a sound field teaching program can be adequately maintained and field instructors sufficiently "nurtured"? Although any suggestions can only be a partial list of possible things that might be done, they can serve as a start. The following recommendations are not intended to be in order of importance except for the first, adequate liaison work, which does seem to be the most essential element. For the others, importance will depend on the particular situation—size of school, numbers of agencies and field instructors involved, and so on. Some may say the field manual, containing the basics for the school and agencies working together, is most important. But even the best manual needs interpretation, to say nothing of constant update, so it does not serve in lieu of adequate faculty liaison work though it is an important adjunct to it.

Some suggested ways to maintain a good field program are:

1. adequate faculty liaison work;
2. ongoing class or seminar for new field teachers;
3. meetings between field faculty and class faculty on a regular basis;

4. special seminars or workshops geared to field teaching, held by outside "experts";
5. written communications between school and field teachers—as an adjunct to communications between faculty liaisons and field instructors;
6. openness and availability of a coordinator to agency executives and field instructors—and to faculty liaisons and students;
7. meetings of participating agency executives with deans and department heads and directors of field instruction;
8. field instruction manual and contracts.

ADEQUATE LIAISON WORK

As the most continuous link between school and field, the faculty-field liaison carries the major responsibility for making any field situation "work" once it has been determined that it satisfactorily meets the criteria for a suitable field site for students. Often, the original "checking-out" visit, usually made by the coordinator, seems to promise considerably more than actually happens after students get into the setting, so that assignments thought possible are not forthcoming for students. Who must help? The field liaison. Or, if the field teacher expects student(s) to be more knowledgeable and skilled than they are, and makes a too difficult early assignment, who can help? The field liaison.

The Role of the Field Liaison

A clear definition of the role might help but is difficult because there are no absolute or generally accepted expectations of the field liaison. All we are sure of is that it is a very sensitive role in many ways. Field-liaison duties are always intended as collegial rather than supervisory work with agency field teachers. Yet, since the school is offering a "course" in the field and is, therefore, ultimately responsible for its outcome, the liaison can not responsibly stand back and serve merely on call or as a consultant (one who gives professional advice upon request, knowing the advice may or may not be taken). The field liaison is required to monitor the agency field teaching sufficiently enough to be sure the school's requirements are being met and eventually to assess the adequacy of the field site and of the field teachers there; thus, there is always an evaluative element, whether openly recognized, formally structured, or not.

The liaison should be available to help field teachers develop their teaching skills to help ensure the students' getting a quality experience. Since field teachers are selected for demonstrated superior competence in their practice (as well as meeting other school criteria, usually even harder to measure than competence), it is not always easy to help such persons recognize gaps in their practice which may be uncovered during the teaching of field students.

Field teachers may have basic differences with the school in some aspect of philosophy or practice and may attempt to make students carry out goals which are tougher or narrower than, or otherwisely different from, the school's. Well, one might ask, why not just pull the students from such places and replace them in a setting more compatible? It is recognized that most field teachers want to do a good job, but in their new role they also want to appear competent, adequate, and smart to their students and the school. So, if they goof or are anxious, scared, and unknowing, they may find it difficult to ask the field liaison for help. However, if help is offered skillfully and in a timely manner, they can make good use of it and move on to become excellent field teachers. We cannot give up easily even though we may have some differences. Also, with the high turnover in field teachers, for reasons of job changes, attrition due to family responsibilities, and so on, it is essential to work with and develop as many good field teachers as possible among those expressing interest.

Finally, if a field teacher does a poor job and has received no help from the school, even if none was asked for, there is a tendency to want to be relieved of that role the next year, and a good potential field teacher is lost for lack of sufficient intervention by the field liaison.

Delicate and sensitive as the task is, the field liaison must continuously keep on top of the situation, offering help, though not hovering or pushing too hard, and doing far more than saying, "Call me if you need me." New field instructors, like new students, may not know when they need help, or by the time they do know, it may be too late to be of maximal use.

Extreme sensitivity and objectivity is required of the field liaison when problems arise. In the spirit of the collegial relationship, the liaison must make every effort to "hear" the field teacher in disagreements or entanglements with students. The liaison faculty must hear the students fully, too, and thus may well find themselves in a mediating role, wherein neither field instructor nor student is all right or all wrong, and must help them both sort out the pieces so that they can work productively together again. The field liaison must be accessible both to students and to the field teachers and must maintain sound and objective judgment on matters in which the two differ.

The role is tough, too, because the field liaison represents the school and must be current on curriculum matters, objectives, expectations, and changes. Since field objectives, except perhaps in rare instances of true competency-based curricula, are rarely "tight" and are, therefore, subject to individual interpretation, the field liaison must be certain to represent them within the parameters of the school and be willing to object when they are not being met. For example, if student performance objectives are not being met, the field liaison can then work with the field teacher to alter the type of assignments; decisions must be made on whether the student will be failed or other appropriate plans will be made. New agency field teachers sometimes give grades that are too high, which is natural since they want to be able to point with pride to how well their students have done. Then, there are those few who seem to want to fail almost any student because the student is "just not good enough to be a student of mine." Field teachers making either of these errors can probably be nurtured and helped to grow and change by the field liaison.

There is an additional important but subtle "influencing" aspect to this role. For example, if a school has a broadly based generic curriculum for its beginning level and expects the field to provide learning experiences consistent with it, and if the liaison then finds an agency field teacher who is not abiding by that curriculum, the liaison can often help the teacher move a bit beyond his or her preferred limits, noting that there are indeed ample possibilities in the setting which the teacher has not tapped. Out of this sometimes (but not always and never as a goal) can come not only the necessary desired field learning activities for the students but a broadened base and perspective for field teachers which may help them develop an expanded approach to their practice.

Field Liaison Activities

What makes the liaison work "go"? First, we fall back on one of the backbone concepts of our profession—relationship. If a trusting, productive, helpful relationship is formed between the faculty liaison and the agency field teacher, then each can learn from and teach the other such that a true collegial relationship develops. At the same time, that relationship must recognize the relative responsibilities of each—the faculty liaison, the student, the field instructor, the agency—so that their differences can heighten rather than reduce the effectiveness of the experience for all. A field teacher who is terrified over teaching for the first time or a faculty liaison who doesn't know or understand biofeedback as it is practiced in the field can admit these concerns and become a learner if sufficient time and investment are given to carrying out the liaison role. Since the field course emanates from the school, it seems reasonable to expect the field liaison to take the initiative in beginning the relationship, though it must be clear that the relationship is a two-way street. It seems shortsighted for both schools and agencies to fail to allow sufficient time for this kind of relationship to develop when, without doubt, most of us single out our field experience as the most significant aspect of our learning experience. Should we not all strive to devote enough time and skill to making that experience the absolute best it can be? Remember, not only will our students suffer but all our future employers and clients, too, if we have not done our job well!

Another specific measure that can make the situation go better is for the faculty liaison to visit the field agency very early in the semester to become acquainted, to decide on the way the liaison and field teachers are going to work together, and to take up any questions each may have. This can occur before students come or, in any case, soon thereafter; and a joint meeting with all three quite early on is desirable to establish an open and honest way of dealing with mutual concerns. In this way no one will seem to be acting behind another's back. That is not to say there will never be conferences between just two members of the triad—there may indeed be with good reason—but some joint conferences surely tend to make for less concern about "secrets." The number of visits to the setting is, of course, highly dependent on factors beyond our control, such as distance, but there seems to be no ideal number. The trick is for the liaison to be available when needed and to visit quickly at such a time. It is also essential to visit before problems arise so the liaison is not viewed merely as a troubleshooter, though she or he clearly carries that role in addition to others.

After good relationships are developed, well-placed phone calls can help but cannot substitute entirely for agency visits. Telephone calls tend not to pick up the more subtle concerns or difficulties; they do not enable the field liaison to become known at the agency or better acquainted with its functions, or allow him or her an opportunity to read records, meet with the executive, or convey true interest in the agency's operations. A specified three visits per semester, or one hundred visits a year, will not automatically create a good situation. What the liaison puts into the situation early and genuinely in the way of helpfulness and responsiveness will help determine the number of visits. However, it is impossible to do the job without any visits, so early planning must be established to decide what the agency needs and wants and how the agency and liaison will work together.

Another important point to remember is that the agency executive is a significant person in the whole operation. Usually, specific planning is carried on very early with the executive who obviously wants students in the setting and is willing to have the agency comply with the policies of the school before students can be placed there. The executive should be kept informed of what is going on and given the opportunity to tell the liaison of pleasure, concern, or doubts about the field program. Frequent visits with the executive do not seem essential, but some amount of contact is.

A final point: the availability of the field liaison to the agency when needed is very important. Great frustration is expressed when a field instructor calls a field coordinator indicating that he or she has tried and tried to reach the liaison but could not and so is calling in desperation. All agencies with whom the liaison is working should know how to reach the liaison; and when and if the liaison is especially hard to reach, telephoning at home should be suggested. Also, the liaison must be sure to return calls—as with clients, that is one very tangible way of showing interest.

ONGOING CLASS OR SEMINAR FOR NEW FIELD TEACHERS

Moving from the role of practitioner or administrator to teacher involves quite a shift in perception. Attention as a teacher must now be focused on the student as learner, not as the means of getting help to the agency's clients and not as a producer of the agency's services. While students do both of these jobs, the teacher must approach the task with the students' learning as the foremost objective. In order to help achieve this, a class or ongoing seminar for new field teachers seems essential. It must be more than a two-hour "orientation" to field teaching if it is to be effective and must engage the field teachers themselves as learners in this new role. Although offered by most schools originally to benefit their own students—that is, to ensure that their field teachers provide the experiences and skilled teaching promised by the school—it is not by accident that many secondary benefits accrue directly to the field teachers themselves.

For one thing, the seminar enables them to keep in touch with trends in social work education. What does current curriculum look like? Is education moving toward or away from specialization, and if toward, what forms do the specializations take? What are students being taught about ethics and about current values in the profession? What approaches to practice are being emphasized? If the approaches originate outside social work, how are they being incorporated into our profession? How are some of these new methodologies being evaluated? Do schools know which methods are most effective for which situations? Is management by objectives useful to social agencies, as business teaches it, or does it need adapting? How is operant conditioning being taught within social work, and under what circumstances might it profitably be used by a social worker? Even though the emphasis is on the *process* of field teaching, it is important for field teachers to be well informed on the class content and the ordering of knowledge, both to reinforce and to know when to supply new information not currently in the curriculum. For example, if a student is in an agency serving clients who abuse drugs and the school offers no course content in that area, it will be obvious to the field teacher that knowledge in the general understanding of drugs and drug usage must be offered in the field. Since social work covers such a broad field of endeavor, there will be a lot of areas like this. No school can afford to have in its curriculum specialized courses on every field of practice in which students might have field placements, but the field teacher will need to know where the lacks are.

Another benefit for field teachers is that they find a "ready ear" from the school's seminar leader for some of the concerns, gripes, and suggestions they want to convey to the school. As they become acquainted with the school's program, they tend to evaluate it from their own perspective and in the seminar begin to develop a sincere group feeling as they realize their concerns are being shared by others. The seminar leader becomes a ready transmitter of those concerns back to the dean or program director, curriculum committee, admissions committee—whoever has appropriate responsibility. Thus, although the school may not immediately change to meet the criticism, the field teachers know they have been heard and sometimes gain a different understanding about why something is as it is. Likewise, the seminar provides opportunity for field teachers to let the school know what they particularly like about the total program in a way that may have more force and meaning than a single field instructor telling a single field liaison.

Sharing among field instructors—beyond the planned content—is another gain from the seminar. Field teachers get to know practitioners from other agencies. Not only do they discover quite different practices and policies being used in agencies similar to their own, but they broaden their knowledge of resources in the community and find some exciting new opportunities for their clients. Then, too, learning to know practitioners from other agencies personally, instead of only by phone, is a great positive often expressed. And this is all in addition to sharing the realization of the many ways social work can be taught in the field as well as perhaps the most significant sharing—of their selves—to become a group in which they can admit lack of knowledge, risk themselves, examine their own practice in a way that may no longer be done in their agencies, and thus share a meaningful growth-producing experience which enhances their professional practice well beyond the limits of the field-teaching experience itself.

Admittedly, such a seminar or class is a sensitive area since the learners or "students" are all competent, experienced social workers who may think there is no reason for them to participate; and if the seminar is required for all new field teachers, as I believe it should be, the requirement adds another negative dimension. The similarity between new field teachers and new students entering a social work program is striking in that few want to admit their ignorance or even that there are a few things they don't know. With the field teachers, this feeling is even stronger since they all do know social work. This, of course, must be acknowledged and reinforced with recognition that the seminar is to assist them to take on a new role within social work—that of enabling students to become knowledge- and value-guided professional practitioners and of transmitting their specialized knowledge and skills to students, sometimes students who themselves come with considerable prior experience in the field. Don't we all know of the bright new field teacher, 25 years old, two years out of her MSW, eager to help a "new" student learn, who is assigned a 45-year-old student with at least fifteen years in social welfare, the last five as a supervisor? Of course that's rough, but it can work out well. One "secret" in this situation would be to help the field teacher focus on what she knows that the student does not—and she will soon realize these areas are numerous enough that she can be comfortable in finding some areas in which her student knows considerably more than she. No one says field teaching cannot be a mutual teaching-learning experience, and herein lies another lesson—to help field teachers realize the field-teaching process will indeed be a learning experience. They will have many opportunities to think through and defend their knowledge, techniques, values, and agency policies and procedures, and in the process, they may consciously learn some things they had taken for granted and see areas of their practice that need change.

There are many ways such a seminar might be dealt with and a variety of content areas and ways of packaging them. Some of the topics commonly discussed are:

1. helping the student begin—the student as adult learner, the practitioner as teacher;
2. assumptions about learning and teaching—implications for field instruction;
3. learning objectives—the student, the field instructor, the work of the agency, the expectations of the school;
4. assignment building—the social work tasks to be performed and the skills that have to be mastered in the performance of those tasks;
5. the supervisory conference—focus, process, the use of process recording in teaching and learning;
6. struggles encountered in the teaching-learning relationship, e.g., authority and dependency;
7. evaluation of the student's performance.

Packaging is likely to be diverse among the schools. With films, games, video and audio recordings, drama, role play, good old-fashioned reading, lecturing, paper writing, and testing available, quite a variety might be used. Certainly for this group experiential learning seems most useful and perhaps a natural. However, experience with this indicates that field teachers are just as ambivalent about it as social work students. One might expect them to accept the idea of bringing to class an audio recording or videotape or process recording of their own conferences with a student for discussion and critique by fellow learners, or to engage in role play of real situations they are encountering. Although professing to want to "do it ourselves" some field instructors are really seeking didactic how-to material in the seminar and become angry or frustrated when expected to risk themselves. Reminding them that whether they like it or not they are role models for the students, sometimes but not always helps.

In the seminar, focusing attention on the field instructors as learners rather than only on the students, who are the reason for the seminar in the first place, is essential. But first, the field instructors need help in realizing that they are both learners and teachers. It is important to treat field teachers as "super" adult learners (à la Malcolm Knowles*), yet recognize there are a number of areas of new learning required of them in this new role. Of course, they should also utilize a great deal of what they learned earlier in becoming social workers, now shaping and viewing it a bit differently. Everything a field teacher knows about relating to a client can be utilized in relating to a student, and it is clear that relationship is a big must for effective field teaching, though not sufficient by itself. While it is essential that field teachers learn not to treat students as clients, nothing prevents their knowledge of human behavior from being applied, only differently in this context.

One final suggestion: If possible, allow the seminar to take place over a sufficient period so that field teachers can see evidence of progress and change in their own practice. That experience is a tremendous boost to their learning and to good field instruction!

REGULAR MEETINGS BETWEEN FIELD AND CLASS FACULTY

Although both adequate faculty-field liaison work and the seminar for new field teachers provide some "regular" meetings between classroom and field faculty, they are both on a more limited basis than we are speaking to here. The opportunity for ongoing interchange between field and class on all facets has great payoff for both, and seems especially meaningful for field teachers.

Clearly, if both class and field instructors are teaching from the same practice frame of reference, those who teach in the field should have the opportunity to meet with those who teach the same content and techniques in the classroom. Although sharing class outlines, bib-

---

* Malcolm Knowles, *The Adult Learner: A Neglected Species* (Houston: Gulf, 1973).

liographies, and other materials help, actual face-to-face encounters have great meaning for both field and class teachers and the students they both teach. With this, there can be true enhancement of learning, instead of competition for the students' loyalties! Even when the topics of the meetings are not of prime import to all teachers involved, such meetings still provide an opportunity for them to talk at coffee breaks, at meals, and in subgroups for special discussions valuable to both. It is not uncommon for a school to be criticized if its classroom-faculty contingent is small. The field teachers appropriately express real displeasure and a sense of being let down by the school when that happens.

Since generally the field teachers are asked to come to the school for these sessions and take time away from their primary jobs, it is essential that the meetings be focused on matters of import to them, as indicated in their feedback to the school. But what field teachers need and want encompasses a great variety of subjects. They want to hear detail about the curriculum—what is being taught, when, by whom, and why—and have a chance to react and make suggestions. They want to discuss specifics of field teaching—how to help a student pick up on feelings or become more self-aware, recognize his or her tendency to tell a client what to do, or learn that seeking personal information is not prying if done for a professional purpose and with professional skill. They want to consider the school's mission, how it was arrived at, if it is changing. In short, they are interested in many topics, consideration of which should, if possible, always include participation by both field and class faculty.

Certainly, if the meetings are directed toward meeting some of their needs, field teachers should help plan the sessions and ensure field and classroom teacher participation as appropriate. Working on these meetings together as well as presenting information together further solidifies the partnership notion of field and class teaching and helps everyone appreciate the strengths and particular concerns of each. Experience indicates that the most successful meetings are those in which small group participation is a part. Thus, in addition to a panel or formal presentation which might be given by field and/or class faculty and/or students, a chance to explore issues in small groups in rewarding both for the participants and for the school.

It is recognized that where schools are using field agencies hundreds of miles away such meetings cannot be frequent, but at least one or two per year seem well worth the time and expense. What number would be ideal? Again, no one knows, but perhaps once every month or two might be profitable if possible to arrange. Where distance is an obstacle, regional meetings taken to the field instructors by the school may provide a useful alternative.

SPECIAL SEMINARS OR WORKSHOPS GEARED TO FIELD TEACHING BY OUTSIDE EXPERTS

As an adjunct to regular seminars for new field teachers and periodic meetings of field and class teachers, it is highly desirable every now and then to have some special seminars or workshops devoted to field teaching, though never in lieu of the other meetings. We are all aware that an outside expert can sometimes say just what we do but get it across much more effectively. Additionally, an outsider can indeed bring in new knowledge, insights, or perceptions that can greatly enhance the field part of the curriculum. These meetings, held infrequently and usually not more often than once a year, may take many forms and deal with a variety of content. Sometimes the topic may be a substantive area—such as assessment, the aging process, termination, new developments in family therapy—with the focus on implications of the subject for field teaching. Other times, emphasis of such workshops may be on use of special tools for teaching such as audio or video recordings, role play, films, and games. Still other pertinent subject matter may be on some specifics of field teaching, such as how to set field learning objectives with students or how to help students learn to use confrontation with clients. In addition to focusing special attention on important topics by known experts and thus exposing the field teachers to additional knowledgeable persons, these meetings also expose the classroom faculty and administration to new and important developments in various areas significant to field instruction. One more gain might be that by bringing an outside expert on campus to focus on field instruction, the university administration will be further sensitized to the importance of field in the education of social work students.

Along with the obvious advantages of bringing in outside experts to address important concerns of field teaching, a possible disadvantage should be mentioned. Most field teachers, as competent practitioners, can, with the help of the school's personnel, work out and work through many of the questions and concerns they may have in this special role. Instead of struggling to do that, they may learn to prefer having the experts *tell* them what to do. Another possible danger is that an outsider may present an ideal situation that is totally unreasonable for a given school to achieve, yet may set up that expectation for the field teachers and make them unduly dissatisfied with things as they are at the school with which they work. The risk is usually worth it, however, provided the school selects the expert carefully and sets forth what they want of him or her—rather than simply inviting some "expert" who happens to be in the vicinity and allowing that person to expound on any favorite topic.

WRITTEN COMMUNICATIONS BETWEEN SCHOOL AND FIELD TEACHERS

Good field liaison arrangements, seminars for new field faculty, meetings between field and class faculty, and special workshops geared to field teaching are usually not enough to maintain sound field programs. There need to be written communications from the school to field teachers to give tangible evidence of recognition and appreciation, coming from the persons to whom the field teachers are ultimately responsible—the director(s) or coordinator(s) of field instruction and the dean or director of the school or department. It is important that field teachers get some kind of official letter from the dean or director appointing them to the post and recognizing their special contribution. In a system with no monetary rewards, it is nice at least to know the dean realizes field teachers exist and is aware of who they are and where they work. To ensure that the dean understands the full scope of the field program, it is indeed important that she or he know these people—the number, variety of agencies and sites represented, their geographic spread, and so on, in addition to the actual individuals involved.

If a school has a newsletter or a house organ, the field teachers should be a part of the house and regularly receive such communications and be invited to contribute. They collectively give so much time and talent to the school's teaching enterprise that, indeed, they should be considered Very Important Persons in the school's operation and should, at the very least, be regularly informed of happenings at the school.

In a small school or department, in which the coordinator of field instruction can maintain personal contact with each agency field instructor, it may not be so important to maintain written communications beyond those already mentioned, but in a larger school it seems essential that some communications go to the field teachers from the field director to show that he or she knows who and where the field teachers are and views them as the important adjunct faculty they are. Some statement of appreciation at the end of the year, some information noting changes in program and new developments, invitations to participate on field task forces or committees, opportunities to react to proposed field policy changes, and the like, are all ways field teachers can know the field director is continuously aware of them. Even though these communications must of necessity be form letters, it is possible to add a personal note if a field teacher has made a special contribution or has done an especially fine job.

OPENNESS AND AVAILABILITY OF THE FIELD COORDINATOR

Although some believe all personal contact between the school and the agency should be carried out by the field liaison, as long as roles are clear the field program may be enhanced by some direct communications with the field coordinator. It is essential that the field coordinator be open and available to agency executives, field instructors, faculty liaison, and students on matters involving field operations. There must be a genuine openness—a real willingness to listen to and to hear whoever initiates the contact, with recognition that there are always other parties involved in any situation involving the field. Caution must be taken not to jump to conclusions too quickly or to intervene without hearing the other sides of the situation. It is easy for a field coordinator to take over the faculty liaison role if a student comes to relate a very trying field experience and says that the field liaison cannot be located or that the field liaison "doesn't understand" him or her! Or, if a student's report suggests the field teacher is doing a poor job, it is tempting to step right in and side with the student without hearing the teacher's point of view.

Probably the most important phrases to use, after listening to students' complaints or concerns from the field are: Have you discussed this with your field instructor? and Have you discussed it with your faculty-field liaison? Often the student has not, so the field coordinator's job can be to enable the student to do that, with either one or both, as the situation may indicate. But even then, it is important that the student know the field coordinator will listen, is concerned, and can be called upon later if things don't work out. Most often, the field coordinator will never hear from such students again. On the other hand, a field instructor and/or a field liaison can at times handle situations poorly enough, though perhaps not intentionally, that intervention is necessary. Such *intervention* should occur only as a last measure and does not preclude early listening and understanding. While it is quite easy for a field coordinator to get caught in the middle, refusing to listen to a student, field instructor, or field liaison who seeks help is a greater risk. A ticklish situation, yes, but the chief administrative officer of field instruction can not appropriately avoid involvement. The trick is to learn how far to go, where to refer the situation, and from whom to get more information.

From the other side, if an agency employee—either field teacher or executive—calls to raise some question about the behavior of a student or the field liaison, the field coordinator must convey genuine interest and concern and in no way create the impression of being an advocate for either the student or the field liaison. In other words, the field coordinator's role is to convey to all parties concerned that they are all in this together, that each one is important, and that any matters of difference or difficulty must be settled in the way that seems best for the school, the agency, and all individuals involved. Students sometimes say they would not complain about something in the field because they assume the field coordinator would side with the field instructor. Similarly, field instructors sometimes say they would not bring up concerns regarding a student since they assume the field coordinator would be on the student's side. A response should always be, "Try me," since evidence indicates that all difficult decisions are made individually depending on the circumstances.

Open communication is difficult to consider because of the wide variety of concerns. Perhaps citing the most applicable generalizations will help. The field coordinator should hear all parties, refer the situation back to those most closely concerned if they have not yet dealt with it, and intervene only after other efforts at resolution have failed. He or she should then be prepared to move in quickly when the need has been established and attempt to deal with the problem as objectively as possible—a tough order but one worth striving to fill in the interests of effective maintenance of the field program.

MEETINGS OF AGENCY EXECUTIVES WITH DEANS OR DIRECTORS

Yet another type of meeting is essential for a good field program: periodic meetings of agency executives with the deans or directors of schools and departments. Since the ultimate responsibility for the field programs within the schools rests with their chief executive officer, and the ultimate responsibility for the field program within the agencies rests with their chief executive officers, it just makes good sense to give these people the opportunity to have face-to-face conversations even though most of the day-to-day field business can be carried on by their staffs. Again, with small programs this kind of meeting probably happens very naturally; in large programs, bringing these people together can be a major operation.

Agency executives who have to approve plans for student field placements must have periodic opportunities to tell the head of the school's program what they think of the program as reflected in the students—and in the school's graduates since the agencies usually are employers of the graduates as well. Such meetings are probably better handled informally, with ample opportunity for give and take about matters ranging from high level curriculum to mundane specifics about field instruction. Likewise, deans and directors need a forum to consider with agency executives the inefficiency of so much turnover in field instructors from year to year or of agencies not providing the variety of field learning experiences called for by the school's plan and promised by agencies earlier. The agency and school heads need to tackle up-coming concerns such as liability coverage for students and increasing transportation costs with decreasing agency support.

These and many other items seem appropriate subjects for discussion by agency and school heads, not only for the successful mainte-nance of the field program but for additional payoff's for both. Such meetings provide opportunities for discussion between practice and education, to which we all give lip service but too seldom carry out, to help each become more familiar with the other, its goals, problems, mutual or different concerns, and possible ways to work on them— together or separately. Additionally, such meetings ensure that neither deans nor agency executives get too far removed from the field pro-gram—important because support from both is essential.

In this connection, it seems wise that, in addition to the heads of agencies and schools, the meetings be attended by others in both programs carrying major responsibility for student training, as well as by selected others; however, all field instructors should probably not be included as that would change the character of the meeting and like-ly get it onto matters more appropriately handled in some of the other meetings described earlier.

FIELD INSTRUCTION MANUAL

Some would want discussion of the field instruction manual to come first as the most significant means of maintaining the quality of field programs since it indeed provides the "floor" or baseline information from which the agreements between the school and agencies are de-veloped and which form the basic "contract" between them, whether or not an additional document labeled *contract* is used or not. With-out a manual, all kinds of misinterpretation, misunderstanding, and downright violations of policies (usually unintended) are possible and do occur.

Any manual must be viewed as subject to change, and help must be sought from field instructors, field liaison faculty, agency directors, students, and field instruction coordinators, since they are in the best position to call attention to policies that are lacking, unclear, or not being followed in practice, and to suggest alterations and additions that will improve the understanding and carrying out of the field in-struction experience. (Since such change is a continuous process, a word should be said for having the manual in loose-leaf or unbound form to allow for easy change through page substitutions.)

Below is an outline of the field practicum manual at the University of Kansas,* which suggest's some of the areas to cover.

* Margaret Schutz Gordon, *Field Instruction Manual* (Lawrence: University of Kansas School of Social Welfare, 1980).

1. *Introduction*: the intent of the manual, as a type of "contract," along with an invitation to users to suggest changes and a word of appreciation to all who contribute to good field practice, especially to agencies giving their personnel and resources.

2. *Objectives of the Field Practicum*: the general objectives of the field practicum within the framework of the school. Greater specificity is desirable if a school has developed distinct objectives for each level and each "track" or "model" of practice; or, these specifics may be given only to those involved in each special unit.

3. *Selection of Practicum Settings*: what the school looks for in a setting and how, in fact, a practice setting becomes a practicum site for the school.

4. *Selection of Practicum Instructors*: the qualifications required of social work practitioners to become practicum instructors and the procedures taken to move them into this role.

5. *Responsibilities of the School*: what agencies and students can expect from the school in the way of supports, guidelines, instruments of evaluation. (Included in this manual—although it could be separate—is a job description for the faculty field liaison.)

6. *Responsibilities of the Setting*: a statement that indicates when agencies are expected to tell the school the numbers of students they will accept, that they are to provide a description of the setting for the student and school use, and specifies the kind of learning experiences they will provide students. Also included are the specifics of what is expected from practicum instructors, such as amount of time for conferences, establishment of some means for examining the students' work, (for example, process recording, or video or audio taping), and writing a semester-end evaluation on each student using the school's evaluation instrument.

7. *Responsibilities of the Students*: a description of the students' role, including provision of information about themselves for use by practicum instructors, development of a beginning learning plan, participation in their own evaluation and that of the setting, and adherence to the policies of both agency and school.

8. *Selection of Students for Placement*: how this complex procedure takes place (insofar as it is possible to spell it out) including the students' role in it.

9. *Evaluation of Student Performance*: the significance of evaluation, some guidelines for making it both a continuous process and an end-of-semester product, and what happens if there is disagreement between student and instructor. The school's evaluation instrument might be placed here, but was put in the appendix so that it can easily be removed for use and because it is likely to change frequently.

10. *Operating Policies of the Field Practicum*: specifics about hours expected, sick leave or other absences, participation in school governance if it occurs on field days, grading policies, and so on.

11. *Appendix*: the year's field calendar, the evaluation instrument used by students to evaluate the practicum setting and instructor, and the school's instrument for evaluation of student performance in field.

For reasons of focus, availability of information, and ease of change, the field manual should contain only matters related to field, thus leaving material about the school's mission, curriculum, faculty, and other matters to the annual school bulletin for use in conjunction with the field manual.

AGREEMENT

Let us consider formal "contracting" between the school and the agency in addition to the agreements the field manual represents. Contracts or formal written agreements are becoming more common, though with great variation in content. An example of an agreement used by one school serves to indicate at least some of the items a desirable contract should contain.

Agreement between the ABC agency and the XYZ University Social Work Unit for field placement of social work students.

The ABC agency agrees:

1. to furnish the necessary space with adequate furniture and equipment along with allied maintenance services;
2. to pay the students at the rate of 12¢ per mile for all travel in connection with servicing cases assigned to them by the agency and related responsibilities;
3. to require the students assigned to the agency to maintain the same attendance regulations as are in effect under the agency's personnel policies for all staff members;
4. to provide MSW field instructors who will have at least 1½ hours of conference with their students on a weekly basis;

5. to provide assignments limited and geared toward maximizing educational experiences.

The XYZ University Social Work Unit agrees:

1. to ensure that students going into placement are prepared academically with the required courses for placement;
2. to provide guidelines for the field practicum program;
3. to provide a faculty field consultant to assist the agency by:
   a. providing inputs that will make the academic content relevant to field practicum;
   b. assisting in helping students to design and meet their project requirement;
   c. serving as a resource for field instructors' meetings, workshops, etc.
4. to take ultimate responsibility for grading of students.

This agreement shall continue for an indefinite period from the date hereof, subject to the right of either party to cancel this agreement at the expiration of any semester (five calendar months) during the term of this agreement upon giving ninety (90) days written notice of such cancellation to the other party.

XYZ UNIVERSITY SOCIAL
WORK UNIT

ABC AGENCY

_____

Social Work Program Director

_____

Director

_____

(date)

_____

(date)

While contracts may be very useful, they seem of questionable value in ensuring a good field program. The idea has great promise and suggests protection for all parties. But can contracts live up to that promise? The generality of the language in the contract is often so great as to be almost worthless except to say what is already known—that the school will supply students to be "taught" in the agency and the agency will supply learning experiences and acceptable staff people as field instructors. Or, the degree of specificity may be so great that the contract is almost impossible to fulfill.

Unfortunately, some of the things we might hope a contract could do seem outside its limits. Can any contract produce suitable students for an agency if indeed the enrollment is less than expected, or can a contract prevent a field teacher's leaving the setting one montn after field instruction begins, leaving no qualified field teacher to take over? In one school's limited experience with contracts (they are not required, but a few agencies prefer to have them), over half the contracts were broken by the agency that initiated them. Perhaps a contract can remind both parties—the school and the agency—of the responsibilities each takes on, and in that sense is valuable, or perhaps more experience is needed in finding a contract that does guarantee important "rights" to both parties.

The possible dangers of contracts are that they may be too prescriptive and/or too dictatorial and often too static. In a recent study at the University of Kansas on field liaison work, a clear majority (61 percent of 118 respondents) were either "positive" toward or "interested in" moving into a contract system, but the over 32 percent who expressed doubt about it were more vocal about their objection, fearing the contract could destroy rather than strengthen the trust and sense of partnership already operating between the school and agency. Obviously, a contract need not do that, but the response suggests care must be taken in drawing up a contract to be sure it furthers the partnership rather than detracts from it.

CONCLUSION

Perhaps by this time you are thinking that if all these additional efforts are essential to maintaining an effective field program, forget it, it's not possible to do all that. But wait—no one started off with all these. We have learned of their importance over time, so each school and department must examine the suggested ingredients to see what seems essential or most important to them and then go to work to obtain them. Remember that even with all these present, one can have a poor field program if each is not carried out well with the spirit of mutual cooperation that any field program must have to succeed. And, a very limited program in the sense of not having many of these ingredients may be very successful because the *people* involved are so exceptional. So, the ideal is probably a combination of dedicated, hard-working people in both schools and agencies, working constructively together, along with as many of these support systems as possible, toward a common goal—to provide the best possible practicum situations to produce the most knowledgeable and well-trained social work graduates who will become the practitioners and field instructors of tomorrow.

⑧

Responsibilities of the Field Instruction Agency

Andrew L. Selig

This chapter presents a framework that field instruction agencies, schools of social work, field instructors, and students can utilize in planning, developing, maintaining, or evaluating the agency's role in field instruction. It is divided into three major areas: agency responsibilities, pros and cons of being a field placement, and common pitfalls experienced by agencies in field instruction.

AGENCY RESPONSIBILITIES

Commitment to the Educational Process

Strong commitment to the educational process is a necessity at all levels within an agency. Top-level management, including governing boards and administrative staff, needs to develop policies that support and encourage the training of social workers. Job descriptions for agency staff need to include field instruction as one of the expectations, and the staff should be rewarded for providing sound instruction. Recruitment of staff should include a commitment to hiring individuals who have the knowledge, skills, and motivation to help educate social work students. When such top-level administrative commitment is not present, it can lead to negative experiences for the students.

A first-year social work graduate student was placed in the legal aid agency. The social worker in the agency did not have the time to provide the student instruction, and, therefore, what "supervision" she received came from an attorney. She never developed an understanding for the social work role within the agency and had virtually no supervision or consultation about social work knowledge and skills. She began her second-year placement very discouraged about school, the role of social work, and the opportunities for learning to provide good-quality social work services.*

Managers, or middle-level administrators in an agency, should provide time for the staff to be involved in the instruction of students. This means time not only to meet with the students but also for observation of behavior, for attendance at agency and school meetings dealing with educational issues, for reading, and for skill development as a field instructor. Adequate space for the trainees is necessary. An agency must provide facilities for interviewing, telephoning, report writing, and communication with others; but space also symbolizes the importance the agency attaches to the students. The provision of basic equipment is also necessary to meet the expectations of the agency, such as dictating equipment, telephones, and so on. Management-level personnel must also help create openness for students to participate in agency process. This might mean, for example, including them in meetings and conferences dealing with agency programs and services. Excluding trainees from some meetings can limit their learning experiences and seem to communicate a negative viewpoint on student maturity and usefulness.

> Students from all disciplines were excluded from a staff meeting called to discuss staff morale, program, and objectives. Simultaneously, these students were told that they were mature and competent individuals who should think of themselves as part of the agency. (At times the students were exposed to conflicting interchanges between staff members which were then discussed further in the staff meetings which they were not allowed to attend.) Students appropriately complained that they had no formal input into the staff decisions and were unable to see the staff work out their conflicts. Over a period of time the staff were able to work out their difficulties and improve and enhance the relationships, but, unfortunately, the students missed the opportunity to participate in this process. The students accurately evaluated this experience by stating that although they were told by the agency to consider themselves mature and competent individuals, agency practice did not coincide with that position.

Finally, the front-line, professional-level staff needs to have the desire, motivation, knowledge, and skills to supervise and train. It is difficult, taxing, frustrating, and time-consuming to provide good instruction.

---

* All case materials in this chapter were developed from the personal experience of the author.

Unless the field instructor has a high investment in this process, much of its potential value will surely be lost.

In summary, a major responsibility for a field-work agency is to be committed to the educational process from top management to front-line workers. Policies that support and encourage the educational process should permeate the agency at all levels.

Provision of a Positive Educational Climate

The probability for positive student experiences directly increases when an agency encourages and supports the development of its own staff. Leadership that encourages personal and professional development and inquiry will help provide an agency climate of self-directedness, mutuality, and a respect for contributions from all. This agency climate increases the likelihood that students will be respected, encouraged, and stimulated to pursue their interests and develop themselves. If the agency can make resources available to both staff and students to attend workshops or to bring training sessions into the agency, the students gain a respect for the importance of continuing educational development.

Possibility of Adequate Learning Experiences

The agency has a responsibility to identify its own resources and potential learning opportunities for students. Agency representatives need to be clear about what opportunities exist within the agency and communicate this clearly to school personnel and prospective students. For example, an agency should identify the extent to which trainees can become involved in clinical work, research, program development, community involvement, and consultation. A clear understanding of potential opportunities is very important in contracting with students and should be part of a three-way contract between the student, the school, and the agency.

> Two second-year master's students were accepted at an agency which was primarily a center for evaluating children and their families, offering limited treatment opportunities. However, the students' interest in ongoing treatment experiences had not been adequately expressed or explored. After several months had passed, the students became concerned that they were not getting any ongoing cases for treatment.
>
> There had not been adequate discussion between the agency and the students regarding the agency's function or the students' main interests. The following year the agency developed more treatment opportunities for students but openly discussed with prospective students the fact that ongoing treatment might still be minimal. Emphasis was placed on what could be learned from the agency, and students were sought who were interested in attempting to develop more referral networks that would lead to more ongoing treatment. The agency accepted three students, two of

whom came with the intention of helping develop programs of an ongoing treatment and consultative nature. Combining the needs of the students with the possibilities at the agency provided a satisfying and productive experience for all.

PROS AND CONS OF BEING A FIELD PLACEMENT

A major incentive for the agency to engage in field work instruction is that through the experience fresh, "outside" viewpoints become available to the agency. Students as well as faculty from the school can ask questions and make statements that help agencies articulate their goals, clarify their current function, and identify where change is desirable. However, the agency must be open to these questions and willing to consider possible changes. Without this openness, the student is constrained and loses the opportunity to learn that every profession should constantly be alert to possible ways to improve agency functioning.

> In a mental health center two second-year social work students conducted a consumer feedback survey to evaluate clients' perceptions of services. The process and actual data gathered in this survey became very useful to the director and staff of the center. It led to very productive discussion about aspects of the program that needed changing.

Students can provide stimulation not only for the agency but also for the individual field instructors. The educational process encourages instructors to be more analytical about how social workers use themselves to help clients resolve social problems. This contributes to enhancement of the field instructor's own practice ability. Field instruction also helps the instructor to remain "intellectually alive" through the process of inquiry and discussion with students.

> A field instructor was preparing to present a seminar to trainees from many disciplines on the theory and practice of family therapy. The instructor discussed his ideas with two social work students he was supervising and through the discussion modified the presentation. They told him that many of the trainees questioned the usefulness of having children present when interviewing parents. Trainees were concerned that certain kinds of information would do harm to the children and questioned the value of including them during evaluative interviews. Armed with this information the field instructor was able to plan his presentation in a way that would address some of the major questions that the seminar participants had raised. During the presentation these issues were raised, and, because the instructor had a chance to anticipate them and prepare for them, he was able to much more adequately discuss the issues.

Serving as a location for field instruction is a way an agency can contribute to social work education and the development of a cadre of well-qualified social workers. Agencies, through their own programs and

staff, can also influence the knowledge, value, and skill development of future professional social workers and can influence the
direction and content of schools of social work by becoming actively
engaged in the school's decision-making processes.

> A child development agency, through its contacts with a school as a field
> instruction agency, was able to initiate discussions on incorporating con-
> tent on handicapped children and their families into the curriculum. Initial
> discussions with the school stimulated the development of collaborative
> continuing education programs throughout the state. Not only did stu-
> dents benefit from this interaction but so did many other social workers in
> that region.

Providing field instruction also helps to ensure the survival of the social work profession. Since practical experience is so basic to the social
work educational process, agencies that are willing and able to provide
good practical experiences for students are a critical link in that educational process. It is increasingly evident that the quality of social work
education in any school is partly related to the quality of its total program and agencies that are willing to supervise social work students.

Through the contact and interaction between the field instruction
agency and a school of social work, the agency is often in a position to
request and receive consultation that it might otherwise not have or
would have to purchase in the larger community. Schools of social
work have many competent faculty who often make themselves available to agencies for consultation in a variety of areas.

Last, but certainly not least, the agency can benefit by the quality
service that students usually can provide. Although providing services
should never be the primary motive to have social work students, once
they become accommodated to the agency and begin to master use of
self and social work skills they are usually conscientious and dedicated practitioners who bring a refreshing vitality to their work.

Although there are many advantages for an agency that provides
field instruction, conflicts between service goals of the agency and the
needs of education almost always exist. For example, it takes more
time on the part of the agency staff to provide the services. Adequate
field instruction involves observation, consultation, meetings at the
school, and other activities, and all these functions require time. The
more field instruction is considered a mandate of the agency, the less
the process will be conflictive. Sanction to provide instruction should
be part of agency policy. However, agencies receive no money for field
instruction; and in these times of shrinking human-service funding,
efficiency becomes a high priority. Schools and agencies should
periodically reassess whether or not the agency should continue as a
location for field instruction.

Other problems can also exist for agencies providing field instruction. Finding space and equipment for students is a common problem; if an agency's space and equipment are at a premium, it may be unsuitable for student placement.

Some agencies or staff have concerns that students will be harmful to clients. Issues can also arise around the sharing of information: Some agency staff members may believe that certain information and data should not be shared with students. When students are later asked to prepare papers or report in class on their practice experiences, that can become a sensitive subject.

Another area of potential conflict exists between student ideas and agency practice. There can be differences of opinion regarding the extent of the students' involvement in the agency. What information are they privy to? What meetings can they participate in? What tasks are appropriate? An additional area for conflict between student ideas and agency practice can develop when a student or group of students attempt to change an agency in a direction they believe it should move. Student efforts at systemwide change within their field-placement agency can be an extremely valuable experience. It can also be a very conflictive one, particularly if not everyone, or at least not those in authority, understands that the students' social action within the system is part of their learning experience.

There is also potential conflict between students and an agency over the scope of the social work role. Some take the position that social workers should be trained as specialists, developing knowledge and skills in a particular circumscribed area, while others believe social workers should be trained as generalists. The school contributes to this issue by requiring generalist and/or specialist learning experiences for its students. These differing positions are potential pitfalls and areas of conflict.

Finally, although I am unaware of any precedents, the legal responsibility of agencies for the behavior of their student trainees is a potential problem and an issue that raises several questions. What is the legal liability of a field instruction agency for the professional conduct of a student? What insurance safeguards should agencies secure for themselves when they provide field instruction? Should the students be required to have malpractice insurance before beginning field instruction? What is the school's responsibility in this matter?

Common Pitfalls Experienced in Field Instruction

Until they have actually had the experience, some people take the position that field instruction saves agency time by adding a "service person." As has been argued above, field instruction does not save time. In fact, it requires additional time, effort, and commitment. Another somewhat common misconception that some individuals have regarding field instruction is that knowledge of process is all that is necessary. Although a knowledge of the process of helping relationships is crucial to adequate field instruction, it is not sufficient by itself and needs to be supplemented and enriched by the field instructor's knowledge of social work theory and research as well as educational theory. The more able the field instructor and agency are to integrate their instruction with theoretical constructs, the more integration there can be between the field instruction process and the classroom.

Another common pitfall is for agencies and field instructors to assume too much responsibility for students. Clearly, agencies have major responsibilities for the educational process; however, as in any aspect of human development, the student needs to assume the major responsibility for his or her education. Although defining objectives and student tasks should be a joint endeavor, student responsibility and autonomy need to be an inherent part of the process.

> A social work graduate student was very unhappy with his field instructor in the beginning of the second year. His experience during the first year was with a field instructor who took the major responsibility of defining what he needed to know and how he needed to go about his learning. He was directly supervised in all his interviews and frequently checked with his field instructor before doing client-related tasks. The field instructor for the student's second year positioned himself differently and believed that the major responsibility for defining goals and for working the student into the system rested with the student himself. The instructor believed that (in addition to his direct practice with clients) part of the student's learning process should be integrating himself into the agency and developing his own caseload. This different approach to field instruction led to an increase in the student's anxiety and later to his complaining to the school's director of field instruction. After a conference between the student, instructor, and school coordinator, a satisfactory resolution was reached. By the time the student finished his placement in the agency he stated that the year had been extremely valuable and that he was very grateful for the push and encouragement to "make it work" primarily by himself. He stated he had gained a great deal of confidence through the experience and recognized his own tendency to want to provide leadership but yet look to others to depend upon.

As mentioned in the beginning of this chapter, some agencies take on field instruction without adequate discussion and commitment that this is an important function they want to pursue. Without this agency-wide commitment, problems such as those identified above can develop.

SUMMARY

Field instruction agencies have three major responsibilities. These are to make a commitment to the educational process at all levels within the agency, to provide a positive educational climate for staff and students alike, and to provide adequate learning experiences.

Being a field placement agency has both positives and negatives. Field instruction can make a major contribution to social work education, and serving as a field instruction agency can be a tremendous stimulus to the agency and staff. However, there are potential conflicts between the major service mandates of some agencies and the time-consuming tasks necessary to maintain an adequate educational environment and experience. Extra space and equipment are needed, and potential problems exist in the legal implications of any student's functioning.

Agencies have some common misconceptions about field instruction. One is the belief that providing instruction can save time by adding service personnel. In addition, some believe that adequate education can be provided by an instructor who knows a professional helping process but does not keep up with practice theory and research. Further, a field instructor must avoid assuming more responsibility for the educational experience than the students themselves and should be careful not to take on field instruction without sufficient agencywide commitment. There are also potential pitfalls when student ideas or school requirements conflict with agency practice.

Agency field instruction is a major priority in the social work educational process and a key to the survival of the profession. It behooves all social workers and social work educators to take it seriously, think it through, and develop it carefully.

Responsibilities of the Student in Field Instruction

Eleanor Hannon Judah*

A PARTNERSHIP SYSTEM FOR LEARNING

Quality field instruction requires a partnership with interlocking complementary roles and involving persons from school and agency, the clientele, and the student, each answerable or responsible to all the others for specific activities both in the achievement of mutually agreed upon goals and the smooth functioning of the system itself. The partners can be thought of as forming a social system in which relationships, while patterned, are dynamic, requiring flexibility to adapt to ever-changing situations found in real life. All system partners share responsibility in the educational enterprise, and the functioning of each individual member is contingent on the functioning of the others in the system. This requires that the roles, goals, and responsibilities of each must be clearly identified.

This system emphasis in practice and in field instruction departs from the older one-to-one model which dominated social work practice, supervision, and field instruction in the past. It focuses and objec-

* I wish to recognize the contribution in particular of Melinda Brecher, Annette Jolles, Charles Martel, and Wayne Pawlowski, all MSW, 1977, Catholic University students who met with me to discuss their ideas for this chapter, and also to many other students over the years for their helpful suggestions and candor.

tifies the still crucial relationship between student and field instructor and opens up the teaching-learning dyad to others, thus reducing both the isolation and dependence often found in the one-to-one model. Emphasis on a field instruction contract, discussed later, helps to focus on education and to avoid a "therapeutic supervision" which places disproportionate attention on the psychodynamics of the relationship between field instructor and student, or, worse, the intrapsychic states of the student.[1] The system or partnership model gives more adequate attention to other critical components, including the specific responsibilities of all involved in order to accomplish the dual educational and service components of field instruction. Further, this model, in its broader system focus, is an educational counterpart of the newer, ecological or integrated practice models which also use systems constructs.[2]

This chapter stresses that responsibilities of one member of a partnership system, with complementary and sometimes even overlapping roles and responsibilities, cannot be considered in isolation from the others. Consequently, it isolates for discussion one member of the partnership system, the student, to gain a format designed for overall clarity. Finally, it is critically important to observe that common sense and justice require that students *be given the opportunity* to assume their responsibilities in field instruction, especially if they are ever to be equipped to meet the increasing demands for autonomy of truly professional practice.

RESPONSIBILITIES: GENERAL AND SPECIFIC

The division of responsibilities in this chapter between general and specific is, of course, only one of many ways to organize the subject.[3] It was selected as one which might communicate the idea that the student is *no less* responsible on the first day of field instruction than on the last. Specific responsibilities, however, build on the general ones and differ depending on possession of knowledge and skill.

General Responsibilities

All students, once admitted to professional education, have three general responsibilities which must be fully assumed and which may be thought of as dispositions to act and as values as well as responsibilities.[4] These responsibilities are not dependent on the extent of the students' knowledge, skill, or experience but are related to the culture, norms, and values of social work and to the students' human qualities. They are the following:

    1. to learn (includes knowledge, values, and skills);

2. to participate as fully as possible in learning;
3. to act in a manner consistent with the ethics and values and other norms of social work.

To Learn. The students have the obligation to themselves and to the others involved in field instruction to learn (includes knowledge, values, and skills) as much as possible. Ironically, in the beginning they do not have enough knowledge about the profession or what they are expected to learn, nor about their own characteristics and capacities, to be very specific about what is to be learned. The student first must learn what is to be learned—to understand and then to learn it —to furnish the necessary core of knowledge. There is, theoretically, no outside limit to what students *may* learn, but there is a minimum they *must* learn, and this should be specified somewhere in the catalogue, field instruction manual, or other materials. Students must accept responsibility for finding out what learning is expected of them.

It is appropriate and desirable that students be somewhat general and open, or vague, about what they need to learn at the beginning. Openness is needed to gain knowledge. Students who are quite definite and specific from the beginning about what they want to learn are closed in that they have not allowed for the possibility to learn about new facets of their world or themselves. Premature choices demand from the student a sort of educational tunnel vision and are inimical to authentic education and analogous to the "premature closure" error in research.[5] So the students' choice of what to learn is limited in the beginning by their ignorance of what is required and of the options.

Needing to know and yet not knowing provokes anxiety. However, some anxiety is expected and natural in new situations and, when not excessive, is a useful stimulus to learning. The anxiety of not knowing can be turned to wonder and enthusiasm when the student can see it as an opportunity for discovery and for practicing serendipity, or for the unexpected reaping of insights or new knowledge in the course of an open-minded exploration.[6] Preconception of rigid learning goals is especially serious in field instruction, which is by nature unpredictable, because it closes out discovery of self and recognition of the unexpected in the field and agency.

Beginning students, especially younger ones, often will believe that they are expected to enter a program with fixed, specific learning goals, or they will set fixed goals for themselves because of excessive anxiety. In either case it is helpful to openly let students know that narrow, overly specific learning goals are neither expected nor desired, that education is an adventure into the unknown as well as the known, and that there are expectations for learning and for options about which they must become informed.

Clarity about learning goals and responsibility for setting them come gradually to open and growing students as knowledge of the profession, their options, and themselves increases. Certainly, as the student moves along, either beyond the BSW or into the second-year of graduate study, toward graduation and employment, the educational and vocational objectives should be much more focused but never solidified completely. For professionals, learning is ever new and never over; and the social worker's responsibility is to "keep on growing" through more learning and self-knowledge.

The general responsibility to learn, then, as knowledge increases, must gradually be channeled in the more individualized learning contract, discussed later, which includes both educational objectives and the learning experiences to achieve them. The progression of learning from general to specific is reflected as well in the movement from an emphasis on core or general knowledge for BSW or first-year graduate students to the stress laid on method, field of practice, or specializations such as administration and education for more advanced students.[7] It should be recognized, finally, that when students cannot, even with help, open up to new or revised goals in learning, they are not educable, at least at present, and this should be faced by all in the field instruction system.

In summary, the student's first general responsibility is to be disposed to learn and to be open and responsibly dependent to a continually lessening degree on others to map out the minimum of knowledge to be gained and the options that exist. As students master knowledge of social work and of self they can participate much more in setting learning objectives.

To Participate as Fully as Possible in Learning. In each program or school, there are certain general formats for learning or "rules of the game" from which role expectations for participants may be worked out. The student's participation in his or her own learning requires an assumption of responsibility to quickly learn not only what is to be learned but *how* (they are expected) to participate in their own learning. The "rules of the game" will reflect the culture of the profession as well as the norms and goals of the particular school or program and field agency. The hows of learning, like the whats, are largely prescribed for the student and can be found in the general format, or arrangements, such as the field instruction guidelines, liaison arrangements between campus and field instructors, courses to be taken, and agency services offered. Ideally, the "rules" are written in field manuals, school-agency agreements or contracts, or in other printed materials describing field responsibilities and expectations given to students before field instruction begins. However, such written guidelines are far from universal. Sadly, and too often, the rules are left implicit, which leads to different interpretations by different field instruction partners. Nonetheless, in every instance, hard as it may seem and regardless of the initiative which must be taken, the student must assume the responsibility to get the necessary knowledge from the field instruction office or other school partner. It may be necessary to have the rules and expectations clarified (for all partners perhaps) in order to participate fully and equitably in one's own education. Lack of clarity is almost certain to lead to problems later on for everyone, and in particular for the ones who did not understand or perhaps even know about these rules and expectations.

Another aspect of the hows of learning may be formalized in what has been called the "educational diagnosis," which is covered in Chapter 11, to recognize the personal and individual way each student learns best. It is obvious that there should be enough flexibility within the prescribed hows or guides to accommodate the unique learning styles. Examples are the student who may learn best through *doing* first and for whom minimal case discussion before an interview is indicated with fuller discussion later and another student who may learn best through an extended intellectual discussion before taking any action. Similarly, the greater exposure in recent years of social work educators and practitioners to andragogy, the study of adult learning, has resulted in greater awareness of the variety of ways in which adults learn. In addition, the student and consumer movements and protests of recent years have heightened awareness and provided methods to encourage more active participation of students in their own learning.[8] Social workers have traditionally been committed to the value of self-determination. This has been applied to clients and students both as a right and as a dynamic in growth, and this is reflected in the literature of social work education.[9] Andragogy, in particular, offers new ways to think about this, giving practical principles for helping students to self-actualization within the limits of the requirements of the profession.

In relation to this responsibility for fullest participation, the social work students studying Carl Rogers, Erik Erikson, Abraham Maslow, and others can vividly and usefully apply what they are learning about human growth and development to themselves as well as to their clients, especially the universal need to develop one's full potential. Thus, Knowles's principles of teaching and learning[10] can readily be applied to the field instruction situation from the point of view of the students' responsibilities there. For example: "The learners perceive the goals of a learning experience to be their goals"; "The learners accept a share of the responsibility for planning and operating a learning experience and, therefore, have a commitment toward it"; and "The learning process is related to and makes use of the experience of the learners."

In addition to enhancing the understanding and acceptance of students as adult learners, the past decade has also sensitized educators to students' rights and their capacity to be involved in new aspects of their education. These discoveries tend to allow more opportunities for students to be self-directing on an individual level through more elective courses, course and instructor evaluation, and the like, and on a program level in assuming a more active part in program planning and evaluation. Examples are students acting as voting members on curriculum and other committees, in judiciaries and grievance procedures, on board committees, admissions, and even, in some schools, on appointment and promotion committees. Similarly, students now have more to say about the agency in which they are placed for field instruction and at times find their own agencies. The amount and kind of student responsibility, not *whether* they can and should carry responsibility, in curriculum plans, selection of field instruction sites, assignments, and evaluations is a subject of reappraisal today; for if the past decade has taught anything it has been the basic soundness and justice in provision of opportunity for self-determination to all those a program aims to serve, including the students.

To Act in a Manner Consistent with the Ethics and Values and Other Norms of Social Work. This responsibility of the student refers to recognition of the authority of and a commitment to behave in the light of certain general standards of conduct jointly held by the professional membership and embodied in the Code of Ethics.[11] It is concerned also with the process of professional acculturation in which, in addition to gaining knowledge and skills, the students must internalize the values and develop the role perceptions and orientations which constitute the norms of the professional subculture.[12]

Full acculturation to the profession is not expected until graduation. Before then, however, the *actions* of the student must conform to the professional expectation in both service and learner roles. Thus, students must become thoroughly familiar with the Code of Ethics, realizing and acting to reflect acceptance that "the social worker should serve clients with devotion, loyalty, determination, and the maximum application of competence." They must gain knowledge needed for a particular case and use it consciously in order "to become and remain proficient in professional practice and the performance of professional functions." They must learn about available resources and their own biases in order "to retain ultimate responsibility for the quality and extent of service that individual assumes, assigns, or performs." Finally, they must realize that "the fundamental values of the social work profession include the worth, dignity, and uniqueness of all persons as well as their rights and opportunities" and that social work "fosters conditions that promote these values."[13]

While students in the beginning may not *feel* like professionals, they are required to *act* like professionals, to the limits of their ability to do so. To be sure, the ethics, values, and norms of social work are not internalized passively; the fullest participation of the students is called in for examination and questioning with professionals and peers these ethics, values, and norms, and their ramifications. Further, "professional responsibility does not demand a prescribed way of behaving. What it does require is that whatever methods are used have the presumption of being good for the client."[14]

Above all, it is the act of taking responsibility for his or her own learning and actions as partners in the field instruction system which may be in itself one of the best learning and professional growing experiences students will have in professional education. Truly, responsible functioning as a full partner in one's own education, acting in accordance with the ethics and values and customs of social work, and working with others toward mutually defined learning and service goals within specified limits is the essence of what he or she will do as a professional. This working together with others is common to all social work effort, and it is thought that this "real-life," full-partnership experience is the principal reason that time after time field instruction is cited by graduates as the most valuable experience of social work education.

These *general* responsibilities of the student persist and are values that underlie the specific responsibilities discussed below.

Specific Responsibilities

In contrast to the general responsibilities, which are assumed from the beginning and related to human qualities and values, the specific responsibilities, as defined here, are dependent upon the acquisition of esoteric professional knowledge and skill which must be developed over time. These specific responsibilities must, therefore, be gradually assumed and shared with others as the student moves toward professional autonomy. Unfortunately, this gradual assumption or responsibility toward autonomy has not always been the outcome of field instruction.[15] The list of specific responsibilities might be endless because of the variety in social work itself and in field instruction settings, but they fall into some categories under which similar ones might be subsumed. Among the *specific* responsibilities are the following:

1. to formulate with others specific learning objectives and experiences encompassing, but not confined to, the general objectives of the program (the learning contract);
2. to participate as a partner in goal-directed learning and related activities and tasks;

3. to offer services to and on behalf of clients with increasing skill and autonomy;
4. to offer service in consonance with the policies and practices of the field instruction setting and, as appropriate, seek to improve them;
5. to evaluate learning and service experiences and to seek to share these evaluations with those involved;
6. to assume other agreed-upon responsibilities which are unique to the educational program, field setting, or student, such as teaching, administration, research, and other specializations (optional).

To Formulate with Others Specific Learning Objectives and Experiences Encompassing, but not Confined to, the General Objectives of the Program. If the learning objectives and experiences of an individualized learning contract are to be realistic and thus appropriate, they must be based on knowledge of the realities involved. It is necessary, therefore, that the student gain increasing knowledge of the partners and the field instruction setting, the partnership system itself, the community, and the social work profession. Additionally, the student must gain self-knowledge to better identify appropriate opportunities for learning and learning objectives and experiences. While responsibility rests on the agency and school to provide orientation to the field, this too is shared, and the student should take initiative not only to gain knowledge of but to seek out possible learning resources and opportunities in the agency and community and not leave this all to the other partner. Every student, even the youngest and least experienced undergraduate student, has some initial knowledge and can begin to identify knowledge gaps, directions, and interest. It is important to realize also that the gaining of knowledge necessary to draw up a field instruction contract of objectives and roles may be seen as part of the process of contract negotiation itself. As mentioned earlier, the whats and hows of learning are prescribed in a general way for all. Within these bounds a specific and unique contract or working agreement must be achieved.[16]

The student's responsibility in negotiating a learning contract must of course be thought of in relation to the responsibilities of each person in the field instruction partnership. Indeed, one of the first and most basic responsibilities of each is to achieve a consensus on details of goals or objectives, roles, and responsibilities, including learning experiences and designating who will be responsible for what. They will work toward agreement on details of goals, roles, duties, tasks, and procedures. This working agreement, or the Contract for Field Instruction, will be renegotiated as new developments occur, new skills are developed, and new discoveries are made. These discoveries naturally include negative ones; for example, that original goals were unrealistic, specific experiences are not available, misunderstanding and/or new opportunities have occurred, and the like.

The Usefulness of the Contract. The resurgence of the idea of contract which requires the explication of norms for responsible participation of all partners in the field instruction system is timely, both because of past problems and current developments in social work and in the larger society. Past problems experienced by students and others in field instruction were known mostly through one's own or one's friends' experiences as student, field instructor, school liaison or advisor, and presumably as client; they were less known, until recently, through the literature. Thus, the search for norms and possibly the more legalistic nomenclature of *contract* is probably not coincidental, for as Robin Williams observes, "many rules for behavior seem to arise as a direct consequence of recurring problems that are found to be socially costly." Examples of such conditions of high cost (in terms of frustration, deprivation, and conflict) include persistent failures of coordination in important group tasks, mutual misunderstanding, chronic interferences in achieving consensus, and recurring interpersonal conflicts.[17] The increasing application of systems concepts not only to social work practice but also to field instruction requires the explication of norms of responsibilities for all involved in these rather complicated situations.[18]

Contracts are useful not only for students but for all partners. Williams observes that "persons in weak positions, fearing exploitation by the stronger, often favor predictable norms and sanctions. Persons in positions of authority and power often desire reliable conformity that is not dependent upon continual surveillance and coercion; they must therefore favor establishment of norms, even if their own caprices are thereby curbed."[19] Finally, all students have increasing ability over the course of field instruction to participate knowledgeably in the formulation (or negotiation) and reformulation of the field instruction contract. As with so much in quality field instruction, the objectives and processes have continuity in professional functioning designed to lead to the autonomous functioning of the fully professional social worker.

To Participate as a Partner in Goal-Directed Learning and Related Activities and Tasks. Once specific learning objectives and experiences have been identified (and to some extent during the process of identifying them) and the roles and tasks of the working agreement have been spelled out, the student participates with others in goal-directed learning activities, fulfilling as fully as possible all legitimate expectations. Learning activities are singled out conceptually here, but in actuality, service is a concomitant aspect of learning, and the two can be separated only in the abstract.

The student is not autonomous or independent, but his or her activities in learning from field instruction, to a far greater degree than in purely academic learning, depend upon complementary activity of others in the field instruction partnership system. Particularly since the client is one of the several members of the partnership system, the learning activities, although goal-directed, are not entirely predictable. Clients may withdraw, agency personnel resign, programs terminate, or a myriad of other surprises occur. This means that sometimes other activities and tasks will have to be substituted for the projected ones in order to reach the learning objectives. Because of the turn of events, students will have different activities and tasks than those originally planned. While the *objectives* of learning should not be relinquished easily, students must have flexibility in regard to learning activities designed to achieve the objectives, to see that there are many "roads to Rome," and to use imagination and goodwill in adapting to unanticipated situations. Another aspect of this unpredictability is that better learning opportunities often occur.

To Offer Services to and on Behalf of Clients with Increasing Skill and Autonomy. The ethical commitment of the student requires observance of the Code of Ethics, as mentioned previously, including responsibility for the quality and extent of the "service performed." The student is far from autonomous in offering service in the beginning, but experience tells us that most students wish to offer service to their clients in a skillful and effective manner, both for the client's welfare and for their own progress. In order to offer skillful and effective service, the student needs much help at first. Indeed, the feeling of responsibility in face of the reality of his or her lack of skill can often be a source of great stress and anxiety for the student. In a fascinating study, Amacher poignantly recounts in the students' own words their initial feelings of impotence and inadequacy, fear and lack of knowledge when faced with real clients who desperately need help. She cites the students' realistic dependency on others for help in their efforts to serve clients.[20]

Studies have shown that students' self-expectations tend to be too high[21] rather than too low. Paradoxically, this often contributes to poor service, a premature burnout, if you will, in the not-so-rare phenomenon of the neglect of cases or assignments by a student due to frustration or despair, or negative feelings aroused in attempts to help the client. It is critical that this phenomenon be anticipated as natural if it is to be faced; students, as well as their field instructors, must be alert for its possibility. Both must learn to recognize the signs and feelings of this turning away from service. Clues are withdrawal from the assignment in terms of contacts, either because the student does not schedule them or because the client does not "cooperate" (possibly because he senses rejection or because the service is so poor), and slow-ness or undue brevity in reports, dictation, or other media for discus-sion of the student's work. Students need to learn day-by-day what commitment to self-awareness, problem solving, and service mean—through example and by exercising with others the responsible be-havior that is instrumental in the ethical discharge of professional re-sponsibilities. They must learn that ethical behavior includes the cour-age to recognize their own contribution to problems as well as progress and the value of exploring together with others to reach an under-standing of the steps to be taken to bring about the conditions under which the client's right to service will be met. This learning process usually will involve the student identifying his or her problem with help, and seeking and getting supportive and supplementary help in the form of knowledge, skill, personal acceptance, and encouragement from others in the field instruction partnership system. As the stu-dent's self-knowledge and professional knowledge and skill increase, so will competence and autonomy in practice. It goes without saying that the other partners must not only permit but actively encourage the development of autonomy.

To Offer Service in Consonance with the Policies and Practices of the Field Instruction Setting and, as Appropriate, Seek to Improve Them. In contrast to the student's wish to offer services skillfully and impar-tially, the wish to offer service in consonance with agency policies and practices is more frequently a problem. This is a difficult area because, in spite of careful selection, field agencies range from good to unsatis-factory in their policies and practices. First of all, it should be stated that as a corollary to the student's commitment to ethical behavior, the school and agency are responsible for seeing that in offering service in a particular agency or organization, the student is not expected to violate his or her own ethics or the ethics of the profession in conform-ing to agency policies and practices. Much can be done through provi-sion of information and discussion to overcome any student biases. Agency staff and administration have biases as well and, more fre-quently, blinders. There are many gray areas, but assuming the good faith of agency and school, the student must be held responsible for offering service in accordance with the policies and practices of the set-ting. He or she may be simultaneously questioning them in discussion with field instructors and others and even working toward their change. In difficult cases in which the student's religious or other con-victions may interfere with carrying out service in consonance with agency practices, the student has the responsibility to make these be-liefs known early in the placement. His or her right to act as a profes-sional on his or her own ethical commitments should be safeguarded and upheld unless these beliefs and commitments are so idiosyncratic as to prohibit the flexibility needed to function in many agencies and roles of the professional social worker. As mentioned, these judgments are usually difficult to make.

The student's responsibilities as a professional found in the Code of Ethics include a commitment "to maintain and improve social work service," to "help protect the community against unethical practice by individuals or organizations engaged in social welfare activities." Further, social workers are charged to "work to improve the employing agency's policies and procedures and the efficiency and effectiveness of its services," and, finally, in a number of specific ways, to "promote the general welfare of society" through actions to prevent and eliminate unfair discrimination and to advocate for policies, services, and practices which improve social conditions and promote social justice." A student, therefore, must responsibly examine and question agency or organizational policies prior to or at the beginning of field work and work for change in the agency or organization as well as in the larger society.

Students' questioning and challenging of agency policies and practices, especially in the past decade, have offered a unique means of self-evaluation to professionals at both agencies and schools in forcing reexaminations and in sensitizing them to questionable policies and practices. In cases where it has been decided that the setting is not ethically satisfactory for field instruction and efforts to change the conditions have not been successful, the student must either be moved to a new setting or conceivably be permitted to exercise actions in conflict with the agency.

To Evaluate Learning and Service Experiences and to Seek to Share these Evaluations with Those Involved. Evaluation is a requisite of responsible action. Furthermore, it is an intrinsic function in charting both educational and service progress. Norms of evaluation are often ephemeral. Certainly the setting of objectives or goals for learning and service or "case outcomes" requires ongoing objective appraisals. This is inherent in contracting as well. Self-evaluation in relation to educational objectives and service norms is the responsibility of the student and the others in the field instruction partnership system. To be most useful, the basis for evaluations should require independent self-evaluation according to specifics identified from the beginning or very early on, and in a way that permits objectification. If self-evaluation is not demanded, the student should seek it out, as mentioned earlier, particularly in the roles and goals for all.

In evaluations of agency services and school programs, as in their implementation, existing channels such as forms or other feedback procedures should be used. Where none exists, students must study ways of proceeding based again on ethical behavior and strategy likely to produce the desired results.

Students should be given responsibility to evaluate all aspects of their field instruction, and all partners should be involved in this self-evaluation, including agency, school, client, and student, and strive for objectivity and mutual support. Specific recommendations for changes based on their experience should be made.

Examples of Responsibilities. The following are examples of students' responsibilities in the field instruction partnership system. This listing is by no means exhaustive.

Responsibilities to self:
1. to identify learning needs and objectives;
2. to be ethical in all activities;
3. to fulfill as fully as possible all legitimate expectations of the learner in the field and to go beyond them as feasible;
4. to apply self fully to learning and services—including realistic allotment of time to outside demands;
5. willingness to recognize the needs of the others in the field instruction partnership system and commitment to be helpful, if possible.

Responsibilities to school:
1. to maintain open, honest, and sharing communication for achievement of system goals and maintenance goals, which includes problem solving in the field instruction partnership system;
2. to complete all expected reports fully and on time;
3. to provide feedback from agency in the form of case illustrations for classes and sharing of knowledge gained in the field; to question and comment on the usefulness of concepts and methods taught in class in relation to field work;
4. to fulfill all educational requirements including spending the full time expected in the field as usefully as possible;
5. to work diligently to solve problems arising out of inadequacies or misunderstanding in the field instruction system, including evaluation of the system and its functioning in relation to its goals;
6. to work to improve ways in which the school functions with respect to field instruction through channels provided, such as committees, suggestions for improvements, and sharing in general;
7. to responsibly budget time to allow for adequate attention to both class and field and other student responsibilities.

Responsibilities to field setting:

1. to fully cooperate with field instructor and other partners in obligations of learning and reporting responsibilities including dictation, agendas for conference, identification of goals, problems, needs, and so on;
2. to carry out service and other field activities in compliance with agency policy and practices;
3. to help field instructor keep an *educational* focus, if this help is needed;
4. to question and evaluate agency policies and practices and work responsibly for their improvement;
5. to furnish all reports and other work required on time and fully, to devote the full amount of time expected in the field, and to be flexible when asked to change the specific hours worked for good reasons;
6. to discover how one's own learning experiences may simultaneously promote one's growth as a professional and augment the agency's capacity to function;
7. to enhance agency efforts, when possible, through extra service to clients, development of new resources, public relations contacts, feedback, sharing new learning, and so on.

Responsibilities to clients:

1. to practice social work in a disciplined manner and at the highest level of competence possible in view of time and skill limitations;
2. to work to maintain and improve social work service, of one's own and others;
3. to offer service promptly, courteously, and without prejudice, and in other ways to put the clients' interests first, before one's own convenience;
4. to respect the privacy of clients but also their right to opportunity to make use of service (outreach);
5. to never exploit clients in one's own interest and to share with appropriate persons the instances in which the agency and school policies or requirements collide with a client's needs.

To Assume Other Agreed-Upon Responsibilities Which Are Unique to the Educational Program, Field Setting, or Student, such as Teaching, Administration, Research, and Other Specializations. Some schools have specializations in particular areas, and in others this responsibility is optional. The special opportunity does not necessarily occur for each student. It is understood that it is a plus responsibility depending upon specializations offered and particular interests and skills of students and others.

Special Options. Many students are ready for and capable of seizing opportunities to assume special responsibilities beyond the ordinary. When this occurs simultaneously with a willingness on the part of the system partners to participate, exciting things can happen.

Examples of special options might be the opportunity to serve as field instructor to another student (probably a partial educational responsibility); to utilize some special skill or capacity in a new way, such as preparing and executing all or part of an in-service training program; and to combine special knowledge and skill in new ways in order to adapt appropriately to participate in agency services for special populations, such as the blind, certain minorities, and the addicted, or in new sites, such as work sites, pool halls, bars, and credit unions. The principles involved here are that:

1. These options are in addition to the minimal requirements as stated for students.
2. They build on some interest, attribute, learning, or expertise which the student brought to the field experience.
3. The activity utilizes the student's knowledge, capacity, or skill in a way that is in consonance with the function of the setting and the *values and goals of social work.*

Examples of inappropriate responsibility would be assignment of a student with musical skill to play the piano for an hour each afternoon at an old folks' home or assigning a student regularly to helping people fill out income tax returns. These skills might, however, be adapted within a social work context. For example, in the first instance the student might be helped to use his or her musical ability in program development as a tool in a resocialization group which he or she could help to develop and lead or in discovery of other ways in which music could be used to enhance program offerings. In the second, an income tax program might be used in reaching out to a neighborhood group, helping them determine the need of an income tax service and, if agreed on, helping the residents develop the necessary skills to launch their own program as a neighborhood development self-help project.

Particularly since students in MSW programs have had a solid social work base from a BSW program, and as people enter social work from other professions or at later ages, more extra opportunities will enrich and challenge the student, the field agencies, and the communities and client systems to be served.

SUMMARY

The student's responsibilities are elements within a field instruction partnership system. The partners are persons from school and agency, the clientele, and the student. They form a social system in which each partner shares responsibility in the educational enterprise, mandating the identification of roles, goals, and responsibilities for each member. For the student, three general responsibilities must be assumed from the beginning and are not dependent upon knowledge, skill, or experience in social work. They are: (1) to learn; (2) to participate as fully as possible in learning; and (3) to act in a manner consistent with the ethics and values of social work. Six specific responsibilities follow. They are: (1) to formulate with others specific learning objectives and experiences (the learning contract); (2) to participate as a partner in goal-directed learning; (3) to offer services with increasing skill and autonomy; (4) to offer service in consonance with the policies of the field instruction setting and, as appropriate, seek to improve those policies; (5) to evaluate learning and service experiences and share them with those involved; and (6) possibly to assume other agreed-upon special responsibilities.

NOTES

1. Aaron Rosenblatt and John Mayer, "Objectionable Supervisory Styles: Student Views," *Social Work*, Vol. 20 (May, 1975), 186.
2. Carel B. Germain and Alex Gitterman, *The Life Model of Social Work Practice* (New York: Columbia University Press, 1980); Max Siporin, *Introduction to Social Work Practice* (New York: Macmillan, 1975); and Allen Pincus and Anne Minahan, *Social Work Practice: Model and Method* (Itasca, IL: F.E. Peacock Publishers, 1973).
3. In the general sense, responsibility is "the duty and right of a person to be answerable to some one or some authority for his free acts and their consequences" (Bernard Wuellner, *A Dictionary of Scholastic Philosophy* [Milwaukee: Bruce Publishing Company, 1966]). It is "the state or fact of being responsible" (*The Concise Heritage Dictionary* [Boston: Houghton Mifflin, 1976]). In the *specific* sense, responsibility may be defined as "a person or thing that one is answerable for; a duty or obligation" (*The Concise Heritage Dictionary*). Further, duties are "tasks or assignments for which a man (*sic*) becomes responsible as a result of holding a particular job or office" (*The Encyclopedia of Philosophy* [New York: Macmillan and Free Press, 1976]).
4. A norm here is understood as "a rule, standard, or pattern for action—a cultural definition of desired behavior" (Robin Williams, "Values," *International Encyclopedia of Social Science*, Vol. 11 [New York: Macmillan and Free Press, 1968], 204). Values are "those conceptions of desirable states of affairs that are utilized in selective conduct as *criteria* for preference or choice or as *justifications* for proposed behavior." Williams agrees with Milton Rokeach that "values are closely related, conceptually and empirically to social norms; but norms are the more specific, concrete, situation bound specifications, values being the criteria by which norms themselves may be and are judged."
5. Abraham Kaplan, *The Conduct of Inquiry* (San Francisco: Chandler Publishing Company, 1964), pp. 70–71.

6. Jerome Bruner, "The Act of Discovery," *Harvard Educational Review*, Vol. 31 (Winter, 1961), 21–32.

7. Policy statements on Social Work Practice and Education and Structure and Quality in Social Work Education adopted by the CSWE House of Delegates, March, 1976; Curriculum Policy Statement for BSW and MSW Programs (draft) submitted at the 1981 Council on Social Work Education Annual Program Meeting.

8. Malcolm Knowles, "Innovations in Teaching Styles and Approaches Based on Adult Learning," *Journal of Education for Social Work*, Vol. 8 (Spring, 1972), 32–39; Knowles, *Self Directed Learning* (New York: Association Press, 1975); and Knowles, *Modern Practice of Adult Education* (New York: Association Press, 1975).

9. Charlotte Towle, *The Learner in Education for the Professions* (Chicago: University of Chicago Press, 1954); and Leonard Brown, D. Katz, and T. Walden, "Student Centered Teaching: The Analogue to Client Centered Practice," *Journal of Education for Social Work*, Vol. 12 (Fall, 1976), 11–17.

10. Knowles, "Innovations in Teaching Styles," pp. 52–53.

11. "The NASW Code of Ethics," *NASW News*, Vol. 25, No. 1 (January, 1980), 24–25. This revised code was passed by the 1979 Delegate Assembly, NASW. For the previous Code of Ethics, see "Profession of Social Work: Code of Ethics," *Encyclopedia of Social Work* (New York: National Association of Social Workers, 1971), pp. 958–959.

12. Eleanor Hannon Judah, "Acculturation to the Social Work Profession in Baccalaureate Social Work Education," *Journal of Education for Social Work*, Vol. 12 (Fall, 1976), 65–72; and Judah, "Values: The Uncertain Component of Social Work," *Journal of Education for Social Work*, Vol. 15 (Spring 1979), 79–87.

13. Quotations are from "NASW Code of Ethics."

14. Arthur Coombs, *Educational Accountability* (Washington, D.C.: Association for Supervision and Curriculum Development, 1972), pp. 37–38.

15. Laura Epstein, "Is Autonomous Practice Possible?" *Social Work*, Vol. 18 (March, 1973), 5–12.

16. See Pincus and Minahan, *op. cit.*, p. 92 and also "Negotiating Contracts," pp. 162–193; Anthony Maluccio and Wilma Marlow, "The Case for the Contract," *Social Work*, Vol. 19 (January, 1974), 28–38, Brett A. Seabury, "The Contract: Uses, Abuses, and Limitations," *Social Work*, Vol. 21 (January, 1976), 16–23; and Jessica Murtaugh, "Student Supervision Unbound," *Social Work*, Vol. 19 (March, 1974), 131–132.

17. Williams, *op. cit.*, p. 204.

18. Williams also notes that "the demand for norm is likely to arise from persons who find their interactions confusing or vaguely defined; for this reason, unstructured situations often create pressure for the development of new norms."

19. *Ibid.*, p. 207.

20. Kloh-Ann Amacher, "Explorations into the Dynamics of Learning in Field Work," *Smith College Studies in Social Work*, Vol. 46 (June, 1976), 163–218.

21. John Mayer and Aaron Rosenblatt, "Sources of Stress among Student Practitioners in Social Work: A Sociological View," *Journal of Education for Social Work*, Vol. 10 (Fall, 1974), 56–67.

10

The Rights and Responsibilities of Clientele in Field Instruction

Jerry L. Randolph

Few social workers would deny that the client, whether individual, group, or community, is an integral part of the teaching-learning endeavor in field work. The "practice" aspects of professional social work education continue to command 60 to 70 percent of the student's time in training on the graduate level.[1] While some changes in the field instruction format have evolved over the years, rarely have there been serious proposals that professional social work education would be complete without direct client contact.[2]

Consistent with the knowing-understanding-doing paradigm presented by Gordon and Gordon in Chapter 2, the "doing" in social work field instruction requires a client in some form. The student may work with the client directly or on behalf of a client system, but the client must exist. It can be argued that the client becomes the backdrop against which the student's knowing, understanding, and doing is assessed and the final link in a complex teaching-learning endeavor which also includes teacher, field instructor, and student.

Although students may be academically sound, they must also demonstrate a capacity to work successfully with a variety of clients, or it is unlikely that they will complete their professional education. The client is, then, a vital part of the student's training. Yet, to date, some aspects of the client's role in the field situation remain poorly defined, as do aspects of the client's rights. This is especially true where a student worker is involved.

While it can be agreed in principle that clients have a basic right to quality service, the reality is that they may receive less than quality service when they enter into a helping relationship with a student. Given this situation, should the client have the prerogative to refuse help from the student? Does the client, if made aware of the fact that he or she has a student social worker, take some responsibility for the student's education in dealing with the errors that may occur in their work together?

We will examine these issues and questions in detail, dealing first with client rights when being seen by a student and then turning to the complex question of the client's responsibilities in the field situation, an area which has received little attention in the professional literature.

CLIENT RIGHTS

The rights and responsibilities of a client in a helping situation are closely intertwined despite some dissimilarities. Simply put, a client whose rights are violated or not respected in a social work relationship cannot be expected to assume any responsibility for the relationship. Thus, a necessary precursor to a discussion of what responsibilities a client may have toward a student worker must include a clarification of the client's rights in the same situation.

Historically, social work's concern for client rights can be well documented in some areas. The profession's Code of Ethics calls for the practitioner to "not discriminate because of race, color, religion, age, sex, or national ancestry" and "to work to prevent such discrimination in rendering service."[3] Biestek's classic text, *The Casework Relationship,*[4] is another early example of concern for client rights with emphasis on issues of confidentiality, client self-determination, and individualization. In more recent times, social workers have been urged to take advocacy positions vis-à-vis the client when their rights have been violated, either by another agency or the worker's own.[5]

Thus, the concern for client rights in a student-client situation could be dismissed out of hand on the basis that a violation of client rights is so antithetical to social work practice that the client is automatically protected from such a possibility. A student is, after all, generally working in a social agency in which such behavior would not be tolerated on the part of a regular employee. It is assumed that the same behavior would be expected of the student and the protection of the agency would extend through supervisor to student and then to client.

However, such a view would not be realistic. While every client has the right to be told that he or she is entering into a relationship with a student, many are not. While every client should be aware that student workers may have gaps in their knowledge base or skills which may threaten the quality of their service delivery, this subject is rarely discussed. While the client should always maintain the prerogative of refusing help from a student (or worker), a variety of factors may prevent this right from even being extended to the client. In my opinion, these are primarily sins of omission and do not represent any systematic effort to deny the clients their basic rights in a relationship; they result from a poor understanding of the special nature of the student-client relationship.

THE RIGHT TO QUALITY SERVICE

Is it possible to guarantee quality service to the client of a student social worker? The obvious answer is no, nor could such a guarantee be extended by the most highly trained professional. Still, as a profession social work is faced with assuring, to the extent possible, that the client-student interaction is characterized by service delivery that, overall, consistently moves clients toward a resolution of their problems and, at the very least, does not hinder client progress.[6]

How can at least this minimal level of service be assured? Traditionally social work has posited that this assurance is offered in the form of the field instructor, a skilled professional who would support and closely monitor the performance of the student. Should the student-client relationship go astray, the supervisor would step in and right the situation.

This concept, however, rests on assumptions that are often less than tenable in the practice situation. It assumes that the field instructor is fully aware of what transpires between student and client. This is, of course, physically and cognitively impossible. Short of sitting in on every student interview, observing and video taping each interview, the supervisor must rely on what the student communicates verbally or records in writing concerning the client. The possibilities for distortion in communications of this nature are obvious. Kane speaks on this subject as follows: "Too often records have not been consistent or full enough to allow retrospective observations about effectiveness or even to permit factual statement about what the social worker did. The diplomat Talleyrand sagely remarked that language serves to 'conceal thought.' When social work records serve to conceal actions, such a concealment does a disservice to the practitioner's skills."[7]

Such a concealment may also mask considerable disservice to a client. In most situations a field instructor can only be partially aware of what transpires between student and client. To rest comfortably with the idea that the supervisory backup provided to a student will assure quality service delivery to a client is the first hindrance to the delivery of such service.

The usefulness of the student–field instructor support system is further undermined in instances where the client is not told that a student is to be the worker. And such instances are more common than is generally acknowledged. Lacking awareness that a student is providing the services and, therefore, awareness that a supervising field instructor is in the background, a client is less likely to ask for the instructor's intervention should an impasse develop in the relationship.

This could be viewed as the desirable state of affairs in the belief that what problems student and client may have should be worked out in the context of their relationship. It is sometimes suggested that the client, if made aware of the worker's student role, may refuse to engage in the relationship, seek to go around the student to the supervisor, and use the student's status as a means to undermine the relationship. This is often coupled with the argument that the student's capacity to work with the client will be hampered if the worker is presented as a novice—that this may suggest a lack of confidence in the worker on the part of the agency, foster doubts about the student's ability, encourage unnecessary dependency on the supervisor, and again wreak havoc with the student-client relationship.

While these may be construed as powerful arguments against telling clients that they are to be seen by a student, they are not powerful enough to seal off the fact that the client's right to be fully informed is violated in such instances. In addition, this practice may open the way to litigation as it has in several situations where professional trainees have been sued for negligence.[8] The issue in these cases was not specifically whether the student must identify him- or herself as a trainee but what standard of care could legitimately be expected from the trainee. The court concluded in one case that: "If individuals, such as students in a clinical training program, perform acts that fall within the area of professional service, the patient has a right to expect that these acts will be performed with the same degree of competence as if a professional person were performing them."[9]

The implications for social work students seem rather clear. Since they perform professional acts, they will in all likelihood be held to a reasonable standard of competence in the performance of these acts, whether or not they identify themselves as students. As a strictly nonlegal observation, to not inform the client of the training status would probably result in the student appearing even more negligent. There are possible legal ramifications for a student's supervisor also. Hershey concludes his article by stating: "Conceivably the nursing instructor who delegates duties to a student nurse for which the student has not been trained, or fails to supervise the student nurse's activities to ascertain whether she has reached the level of professional competence in the performance of the particular duties in question, could be held liable."[10]

Admittedly this court decision was rendered on a "clinical" situation. However, social workers are employed in clinical situations in large numbers, and the possibility of malpractice suits being filed in nonclinical situations is increasingly in evidence. To assume that social workers cannot be sued on the basis that they do not provide a clinical service is no longer viable.[11]

In this era of litigation and malpractice suits of every description, social workers can continue to expect an ever closer scrutiny of their activities. Aside from the ethical considerations in not fully informing a client that a student will be providing services, surely students and agencies will not want to incur the possibility of a law suit over this issue.

THE RIGHT TO REFUSE SERVICE

As with the question of whether the client is assured quality service when seen by a student, the question of whether a client has the prerogative to refuse service from a student could also be dismissed out of hand. Except in those few instances of the involuntary client, this right is supposedly extended to all social work clients. But is it, and especially is this so in the student-client situation? It is my contention that in many instances, we, as a profession, employ a variety of mechanisms to ensure that the client's right to refuse service will never become an issue.

Obviously the first mechanism to avoid this issue could be that of not informing the client that he or she is to be seen by a trainee. What doubts this might raise in the client's mind are, therefore, suppressed to a degree. What might remain are the normal doubts about receiving service which are perhaps easier to confront when the alleged competence of the worker is greater because of the expected level of training.

Beyond this, we often choose for our students those who are in some sense the most dependent of our clients and the least likely to raise questions about being seen by a student: the welfare client who knows full well where his check comes from and doesn't wish to alienate the worker; the client who wants desperately to tell her story to someone and doesn't question who provides the ear; and, frankly, those who are the least intelligent or most confused and unable to fully comprehend who they are being seen by.

No suggestion is being made that this is necessarily a conscious process on the part of field instructors. But field instructors are sometimes too much social worker and not enough educator. In a misguided effort to ease the student into direct client contact, the path of least (client) resistance is often chosen.

A PLAN

The social work profession might profitably utilize a system common to many legal clients where student lawyers are trained. Clients in these clinics sign a statement to the effect that: (1) They are aware that they are being seen by a student lawyer and (2) A supervisor will be monitoring the student's activities, and confidential information may be shared with the supervisor. A similar plan could be easily devised by most social agencies, and client and student rights would be better protected.

In conversation with a number of field instructors who make certain that clients are informed they are to be seen by a student, very few reported problems on this issue. Most said that clients seem less concerned with who they are to be seen by and more concerned with getting help with whatever problems confront them. This has also been my personal experience as a field instructor.

Aside from the legal implications of not fully informing a client that he or she will be seen by a student, to be consistent with social work values and ethics, we can do no less with the client than what has been suggested in the last few paragraphs.[12] On a more uplifting note, one student reported to me that she has been able to use her student status to good advantage. She always tells her clients that as a student she will have more time to work on their problems and really get to know them. Generally, the clients find this a cheering note, and they get along fine.

ANECDOTES AND RELATED PROBLEMS

Like most social workers who have practiced for any length of time, memories of those clients with whom I worked as a student have become progressively more dim. Some few, however, stand sharply etched in my mind because of their uniqueness (or personality or problem) or because at some level they were an integral part of my learning experience.

I remember with great clarity my first patient in the V.A. mental hygiene clinic where I was placed. He was an articulate, educated man, a longtime patient of the V.A. where he had been seen by a succession of workers. At our first meeting, after I mumbled through an explanation of who I was and what I thought my role to be, when I finally paused, he said, "Don't you worry, Jerry, I've helped train a lot of social workers." And, indeed, he helped to train me too. I have often used this anecdote in supervising students, I suppose to relieve their anxiety about initial meetings with clients or to suggest that we can and do learn from our clients, albeit without much thought about what we learn. Rarely, too, have I repeated this story to a colleague without him or her being able to relate a similar incident from past work. At some level all of us are aware that we do learn or are taught something by our clients, but that "something" remains difficult to pin down.

The reasons for this are varied and will later be examined in more detail, but one primary reason is certainly demonstrated in the vignette above. What we know about the client contribution to the student's learning remains primarily anecdotal in nature. I know of no systematic effort to investigate what the client may teach or the student may learn.

In large part this may be due to the profession having a different research focus in regard to client-worker interactions. We have been interested on one level in the reactions of clients to the helping process; that is, what did it feel like to be helped? Reports of this nature, while not plentiful, are available.[13] On another level, we have asked clients to reflect on what in the helping process seemed to make a difference in their progress or lack of progress.[14] But these questions are posed in the sense of asking the clients to respond to something they have experienced that is imposed from outside—a difference in worker style or technique or administrative arrangement for helping.[15] Thus, the order of the question is quite different when asking clients to reflect on what they have brought to the helping situation, what their participation has been, and what impact this may have had on the worker or agency. Yet sound thinking would suggest that the client system is not a static entity and that when infused with energy by a worker, reciprocity is involved. Energy flows between worker and client systems. Some of that energy exchange is a learning process, worker to client, and client to worker; but to date we have investigated only one direction of the exchange, worker to client.

The remainder of this chapter explores what responsibility a client may have, or assume, for the student worker in situations which (as I propose should always be the case) the client knowingly enters into a relationship with a trainee. The particular focus will be on the learning aspects of this relationship.

RESPONSIBILITIES OF THE CLIENT

What responsibilities a client may have towards the student in the helping process has received little attention in the professional literature. Some recent work in the area of formal contracting for services between worker and client spells out the client's responsibility for some aspects of the relationship. The client agrees to be seen for a certain number of hours at a specified time and perhaps even agrees to focus on specific problem areas.[16] Such activities can be inferred as part of the client's meeting his or her responsibility towards a student or worker.

In another sense the client has long been held to be responsible for certain aspects of the social work relationship, sharing pertinent information, truthfulness, a commitment to change, and similar factors to the extent possible. The client who is able to do so can be construed as meeting his or her responsibility, not only to him or herself but to the worker involved.

In a mechanical and somewhat philosophical sense, it can be demonstrated that the client has a responsibility toward a worker in a helping relationship. However, the carrying out of the responsibilities as described is as important to the client as to the worker. Implied in the above is the idea that as the client "gives" he or she will also "get." The client cooperates, shares, and enters into the relationship with a worker on the basis that by doing so he or she will get something from the worker—relief from anxiety, help with a marriage, knowledge of how to be a better mother, or an increase in welfare benefits. It is assumed that the worker, as a professional, has the knowledge, resource, or expertise that will benefit the client.

It is doubtful that the client enters into a helping relationship ever expecting less than maximum services from the worker. Yet, as has been suggested, this possibility exists when agency clientele enter a relationship with a student—a beginner in the helping process. A student, by definition, is not expected to possess all the knowledge, expertise, and skill necessary to carry out a professional role. Thus, an assumption can be made that the client, who knowingly enters into a relationship with a student, takes some responsibility for dealing with inevitable errors and may, to some extent, assume responsibility for a portion of the student's education.

On superficial examination, this concept sounds very correct. Few seasoned professionals would deny that as students they made numerous errors and that they learned a great deal from their clients. Given this situation, one wonders why the idea of students learning from clients has not been investigated in more depth.

Two explanations immediately come to mind. One being that this idea, as many others in social work, is thought to fall somewhere on the "art" side on the ledger.[17] While each of us could relate many instances in which we think a client has helped us learn a new skill, given us greater insight into our behavior, or made us aware of a liability, we have treated these experiences as essentially unique, to ourselves and to the particular client involved. As such, they become part of the lore of our own practice, exemplars to be passed along to the novice under our command or experiences to be shared with a colleague as we reflect on the richness of having learned something new and unique from a client.

A second explanation, which is tied very closely to the first, is as follows: Perhaps we have not investigated what students learn from their clients because we have lacked a conceptual frame for doing so. One simple construct which might aid such an investigation is that of reciprocity—as the student engages in the helping process with the client some learning is also taking place in both student and client.[18] Previously we have perhaps focused too much on what clients have learned that has enabled them to cope more effectively with and surmount their problems. If we were to focus as much on trying to extract specifically what it is that students learn from the client system, an understanding of the learning process between student and client could be moved from "art" to "science."

The knowing-understanding-doing paradigm is extremely useful in both guiding and assessing the student worker's field practice. This concept, coupled with a second idea in relation to the client system, can provide a means to understand the reciprocal learning process that takes place between student and client. The second idea is that the client rarely "teaches" the student anything at all. Teaching implies an intent to transmit knowledge, and except in rare instances, it is unlikely that the client system has this purpose. What the client system does do is to reflect where students are in terms of their affective and cognitive development. In effect, the client signals to the student (and supervisor) what new learning tasks or repetitions of tasks need to be undertaken and where the student is either deficient or competent in knowing, understanding, or doing in relation to the client's situation.

As an example, suppose a client complains repeatedly that the student does "not understand" the nature of their problem and this is reflected in a process recording or conversation between student and field instructor. The client may be signaling that the student is not as yet skilled in giving an empathic response which helps the client feel understood. A systematic investigation may reveal that the student has some knowledge of the concept of empathy (knowing) and grasps that the skilled use of the empathic response can facilitate a relationship (understanding) but is unable to respond accurately to client comments which call for an empathic response (doing). In this situation, the client has indicated where the student and field instructor need to do further work. It's equally possible for a worker and supervisor to find that the problem exists at another level, knowing or understanding, but the important point is that the format helps to specify in what area the student needs to do further work, and it does so concretely. It moves what the student is learning or needs to learn from art to science simply because a framework is available to explain the phenomena with which the student is grappling.

Even in situations where a problem in the student-client interaction does not point directly to an area of investigation, as in the example above, the understanding that the client system will reflect the state of the student's learning is still useful. Why do we, for example, assign a student to a family? Implied in the assignment are certain expected learnings, that is, that the student needs to know more about family roles, or communication styles, or developmental stages. Or perhaps the student is assigned a group where they may learn about group dynamics or group diagnosis. Other examples could be given, but the point is that there is something classifiable about each level of student-client interaction.

I think also that wittingly or unwittingly field instructors know that certain client systems may reflect more accurately the particular learning task that the student needs to confront. If a student has a low tolerance for ambiguity, where better to confront this problem than in working with a client system where ambiguity is paramount, such as the community. In a realistic sense, also, if the student is to learn about institutional behavior and bureaucracy he or she must at some time work in such a setting. The practice nature of our profession demands such experiences.

What the client's responsibilities are in those situations is very difficult to specify beyond the factors already mentioned. In the final analysis the client system probably does assume some responsibility for a student's education. However, this function may extend no further than a willingness to be seen by a student. Again, we must return to the issue that teaching implies an intent to transmit knowledge, which it is unlikely that the client has as a purpose. Thus, what the student learns from the client system is more accidental than purposeful and is reflected from client to student and, hopefully, to the field instructor.

While the fostering of the learning process on the part of the client system may be somewhat accidental, the understanding of the student participation in this exchange need not be a mystery. The conceptual framework suggested in this chapter can assist in extracting specifically what learning opportunities the client system is offering and to what degree the student is making use of these opportunities.

SUMMARY

The argument presented here in reference to what the client teaches the student is that the client rarely teaches the student anything new. It would be more accurate to say that the client reflects back the state of the student's learning development. However, within each client system there are certain learning opportunities for every student and these can become the screen against which a student's progress is assessed. The astute field instructor who has diagnosed a student's educational needs will realize that some client systems will provide better opportunities than others for the student to develop new skills or be exposed to new learning objectives.[19]

Although this chapter does not deal with either educational diagnosis or the selection of learning objectives for a student, it is suggested that these processes can be made more meaningful by a fresh consideration of the client's rights and responsibilities in the helping situation.

NOTES

1. Mark P. Hale, "The Parameters of Agency-School Social Work Educational Planning," *Journal of School Work Education*, Vol. 2 (Spring, 1966), 32–40.
2. See Jack Rothman and Wyatt Jones, *A New Look at Field Instruction* (New York: Association Press, 1971), pp. 46–47. The authors suggest that social work is at the second level of professional development where, " . . . skill and theory are given somewhat equal treatment."
3. "The NASW Code of Ethics," *NASW News*, Vol. 25, No. 1 (January, 1980), 24–25.
4. Felix Biestek, *The Casework Relationship* (Chicago: Loyola University Press, 1957).
5. See Ad Hoc Committee on Advocacy, "The Social Worker as Advocate: Champion of Social Victims," *Social Work*, Vol. 14, No. 2 (April, 1969), 16–22; also David Wineman and Adrienne James, "The Advocacy Challenge to Schools of Social Work," *Social Work*, Vol. 14, No. 2 (April, 1969), 23–32.
6. Professions increasingly are being pushed to define what constitutes at least minimal levels of service that may be expected by their clients. In instances where the profession has been unable or unwilling to do so, the legal system has stepped in to protect client rights to quality service. See Frank M. Johnson, Jr., "Court Decisions and the Social Services," *Social Work*, Vol. 20, No. 5 (September, 1975), 343–347.
7. Rosalie A. Kane, "Look to the Record," *Social Work*, Vol. 19, No. 4 (July, 1974), 413.
8. Nathan Hershey, "Student, Instructor, and Liability," *American Journal of Nursing*, Vol. 65, No. 3 (March, 1965), 122–123.
9. *Ibid.*, p. 122.
10. *Ibid.*, p. 123.
11. Richard S. Levine, "Social Worker Malpractice," *Social Casework*, Vol. 56, No. 7 (July, 1976), 466–468; Barton E. Bernstein, "Malpractice Future Shock of the 1980's" *Social Casework*, Vol. 62, No. 3 (March, 1981), 175–181.
12. For a discussion of the client's right to be informed, see Charles S. Levy, "On the Development of a Code of Ethics," *Social Work*, Vol. 19, No. 2 (March, 1974), 212.
13. Mary Overhold Peters, "A Client Writes the Case Record," *The Family* (November, 1945), 268–271; John E. Mayer and Noel Timms, *The Client Speaks: Working Class Impressions of Casework* (London: Routledge and Kegan

Paul, 1970); Alex Gitterman and Alice Schaeffer, "The White Professional and the Black Client," *Social Casework*, Vol. 53 (May, 1977), 280–291.

14. Mayer and Timms, *op. cit.*; James B. Taylor, "Doorstep Psychiatry in the Low Income Ghetto" (Unpublished manuscript, Topeka, KN: The Menninger Foundation Research Department, July, 1971); David J. Warfel, Dennis M. Maloney, and Karen Blase, "Consumer Feedback in Human Service Programs," *Social Work*, Vol. 26, No. 2 (March, 1981), 151–156.

15. Irvin O. Yalom, *Theory and Practice of Group Psychotherapy* (New York: Basic Books, 1975). Especially see Chapter 1, "The Curative Factors in Group Therapy."

16. For discussions of various aspects of contracting, see Anthony N. Maluccio and Wilma Marlow, "The Case for the Contract," *Social Work*, Vol. 19, No. 1 (January, 1974), 28–39; William J. Reid, "Target Problems, Time Limits, Task Structure," *Journal of Education for Social Work*, Vol. 8, No. 2 (Spring, 1972), 58–68; and Robert B. Rutherford, "Establishing Behavioral Contracts with Delinquent Adolescents," *Federal Probation*, Vol. 31, No. 1 (March, 1975), 28–32.

17. Elizabeth L. Solomon, "Humanistic Values and Social Casework," *Social Casework*, Vol. 48, No. 1 (January, 1967), 26–32.

18. I am indebted to my friend Dr. Hans S. Falck of the School of Social Work, Virginia Commonwealth University, who periodically reminds me that the very word *social* implies interaction and, therefore, reciprocity.

19. Alfred Kadushin, *Supervision in Social Work* (New York: Columbia University Press, 1976). See in particular Chapter 3, "Educational Supervision."

Part IV

THE FIELD INSTRUCTOR: BUILDING BLOCKS FOR GOOD TEACHING

In Part IV, the emphasis shifts to the tools available to the field instructor. The several chapters examine factors which serve as the basis for an effective teaching-learning endeavor. Siporin begins this section with a very tightly packed chapter in which both the teaching and learning processes of field instruction are examined.

Siporin approaches field education as part of a planned change process—a process directed toward helping the student change into a competent professional social worker. He appropriately describes field instruction as a "teaching-learning process" in which there is interdependence between the teacher and learner. Within this relationship there is a process of learning which is very similar to many problem-solving models used in social work practice.

The approach used by Siporin in Chapter 11 might be characterized as "peeling the onion." Beginning with the outer skin (i.e., a process conceptualization of field education), Siporin progressively reveals the characteristics of this process and the details to which the instructor and student must relate. These are finally translated into principles which can be followed to enhance this teaching-learning endeavor.

In Chapter 12, "The Structure of Field Instruction," Cassidy examines a range of alternative arrangements which might be used to structure field education. She discusses the importance of a structure to learning and cities learning theorists who relate to this viewpoint. The chapter is based on the premise that structure and sequencing can be planned to encourage the student's engagement in practice activities and, at the same time, promote learning.

Drawing on the experimentation used at Tulane University as a starting point, Cassidy examines structures developed to enhance field learning. She gives special attention to the training center

173

approach used at Tulane but also examines the strengths and limitations of other commonly used structures.

In Chapter 13, Shafer turns to an examination of the methods which might be used in field education. He identifies the important principle in field instruction of providing the student an opportunity to apply, validate, and integrate what he or she knows and values with the knowledge and attitudes of the profession.

Shafer recognizes the importance of selecting appropriate methods for the curriculum, the setting, the region, and the style of the field instructor. He helpfully discusses the strengths and limitations of a range of methods a field instructor might use (i.e., apprenticeship, tutorial, clinical treatment, group instruction, and team teaching approaches). Finally he suggests guidelines for the selection of structure and methodology by a field instructor.

In the final chapter of Part IV, "Integrating Field Instruction with the Total Learning Experience," Chambers and Spano focus on helping the student bring together learning from the field experience with learning from the classroom and from one's total life experience. They discuss factors which mitigate against this integration and describe ways a field instructor can help students deal with these impediments to integration. The importance of the student developing "cognitive self-consciousness" (i.e., becoming reflective in approach) is stressed as a mechanism for integration. Throughout the chapter Chambers and Spano identify the conscious use of knowledge as essential to the practice of social work.

11

The Process of Field Instruction

Max Siporin

Within schools of social work, students give high value to the field-work learning and teaching process.[1] The process conception of field work is associated with experiential and meaningful learning and carries with it a mystique and a heady emotional aura. Social workers have long shared Alfred Whitehead's view that "the process itself is the actuality."[2] In addition, though, an important concern for us has always been the product of the process—that the student become a competent social work practitioner.

In this chapter, a number of distinctive aspects of the teaching process in field instruction are identified. We examine significant characteristics of the teaching process and its relationship to the learning process. We also consider the distinctive dimensions, phases, and principles of field instruction. From this discussion, several implications are developed for improving the quality and effectiveness of both the teaching and learning processes in the field work courses. The orientation here is to field instruction as part of a planned-change process. The process is educationally directed to change the behavior performance and the development of the professional personality of social work students.

ON LEARNING, TEACHING, AND FIELD INSTRUCTION

In her classic book on learning and teaching for social work practice, Bertha Reynolds emphasized that the student learns as a whole person and that the "heart" of the teaching-learning process, whether in class or field, "is in a free access to what is to be learned and an interplay between the teacher and learner and between thinking and doing that is most active and reciprocal."[3] The interplay between teacher and learner, between the learning and teaching processes, is at the same time a source of strength and of some confusion in regard to field instruction in social work. The term *learning-teaching process* is used with a recognition of this reciprocal interdependence. It connotes the mutual experiential learning, the transactional interchanges, the educational games and dances that take place between student and teacher. It also should connote the important differences between them.

The ultimate goals and the criteria for success are the same for the teaching and learning enterprises: that the student achieve desired learning. But there are essential differences between the two sets of processes in terms of immediate objectives, tasks, role expectations, principles, and procedures. For example, a learning objective for a student may be that the student become effectively empathic in communicating with a hostile client. A related teaching objective is to demonstrate the attitudes and procedural steps of such empathizing in a role-playing rehearsal. The outcomes of this learning-teaching experience for the student and the teacher may be quite different. The student may learn a specific attitude as well as essential steps to follow. The teacher may learn some new aspect of the student as an intuitive learner capable of conscious and quick mastery of empathic procedures.

The two processes need to be complementary and to be expressed in an authentic dialogue between learner and teacher. The teaching should be sensitive to the student's readiness and need for instruction. When the procedures are discrepant and out of phase, when the needs and objectives of the learner and instructor are in conflict, one can expect difficulty and lack of progress in learning.

Learning

Learning is a process through which behavior is changed in a desired direction and which takes place through an individual's personal experience.[4] To acquire behavior, a learner needs to personally experience and make a mental connection between a specific behavior and a specific stimulus or rewarding consequence (which we call its reinforcement). The learner then can accept performing or developing the ability to perform that behavior. The acquired behavior abilities are stored in the body and mind and become what we call behavior potential or personality. All learning, therefore, consists of some degree of personality development and change in which knowledge becomes personalized, skill becomes individualistically stylized, and a vocational self and identity become part of one's ego identity. Also, learning involves existential, experiential interaction and relationships between the learner and teacher. As Dewey suggests, "All human experience is ultimately social . . . it involves contact and communication as well as adaptation and growth in the transaction between person and environment."[5] Since learning has to be inferred, the only way to demonstrate that learning has occurred is through the overt performance of targeted, desired behavior.

Teaching

Teaching (or instruction) refers to the deliberate, intentional "causation" of learning through influence upon the learner's experience in acquiring new, desired behavior.[6] It is true that one can "pick up" things in a contagious, incidental kind of learning; one can teach oneself to learn certain things; and the teacher can learn more of a subject matter in the teaching of it than a student does. Long-term social agency clients in particular do much teaching of social work students, often as a way of reciprocating for the help they receive from the agency. Social work students who present themselves as students are helped a great deal by such clients. However, there is a basic teacher-learner contract to the effect that the central objective of focused instructional effort is directed to the benefit of learning by the student and that the student's integrity and individuality be respected.

Field Instruction

Field instruction is a form of teaching done in a service situation in relation to learning experiences that concern services to clients, beneficiaries, or constituents. It is through the provision of learning tasks and experiences that teaching both "causes" and effects planned change in the behavior and personality of the student. Its influence may be primarily nurturing, enabling, directive, or authoritative. The teaching strategies may be oriented toward facilitating student personal growth, the mastery of specific knowledge and skill behaviors, or providing proper situational conditions, facilities, and atmospheres for learning. The teaching mechanisms may involve extinction, reinforcement, shaping, modeling, and feedback procedures.

Whatever the teaching procedures or techniques used, a definite content needs to be transmitted so that the student gains a specific mastery of desired knowledge, attitudes, and skill. The learning experiences need to have purpose, direction, and guidance and constitute a "growth-producing experience which will establish the conviction necessary for the skillful giving of professional help."[7] The service situation in which help is provided to a client then is turned into a teaching-learning situation. In this combined form, the service situation is beneficial to the client and also contributes to the student's acquisition and habituation of a new, desired behavior. The student's learning in the field is mostly a form of situational learning: knowledge content is introduced or sought and skills are obtained in response to the dynamic process and demands of personal experience in a life situation. Such situational learning takes place in response also to the demands for the competencies to provide service in the "type situations" (to use Reynolds's phrase) of social work practice.[8]

The relationship between the teaching and learning processes is a complex one; it goes beyond linear, stimulus-response, cause-effect relationships. Learning involves chosen, self-directed activity by the learner; his or her proactive conduct more than reactive behavior.[9] All learning, therefore, may be regarded in a real sense as self-education. The recognition of this fact has helped stimulate new trends for "self-directed" educational programs.

Field instruction should be distinguished from "educational supervision." The function of the latter, according to Kadushin, is "to help the worker learn what he needs to know in order to do his job effectively."[10] These role responsibilities are more limited than those of the field instructor. It is the field instructor who is expected to teach the student how to understand and to practice the art and science of professional social work. This means helping the student develop a high level of knowledge and of skill that is consciously based on theory and principles—a critical mind and a vocational identity. In addition, the student must be helped to commit him- or herself to a professional and humanistic value system, to ethical integrity, and to high standards of workmanship. These objectives are of a much wider and more professional quality than those associated with the job functions and services of a particular agency. There are, therefore, important advantages to maintaining the conception of field instruction as primarily a teaching function and role.

THE FIELD INSTRUCTION PROCESS

The field instruction *process* refers to the progressive phases and course of teaching activity through which teaching and learning objectives are achieved. We distinguish process from method, which refers to the "how" of skilled instrumental activity and systematic use of means and resources. Process is the "way" of the struggle for competence and its rewards, of role performance and task action, of the dynamics of the teacher-learner relationship.[11] It also is a flow of change through phases of time—a sequence of progressive movement from a beginning, through a middle, to a definite end. The general conception of the task stages and phases of the teaching process is akin to the models of interventive change that we use in social work practice: progression from a beginning in intake and engagement; through assessment, planning, implementation, monitoring and corrective action; to disengagement and termination.

As a planned-change-inducing activity, the teaching process has two basic goals. One is to promote the student's development of knowledge and abilities to help clients and provide services effectively. The second is to promote understanding and abilities that relate to a more personal, yet professional, internal growth and adjustment. The second goal refers to what we call process teaching objectives and behaviors. Thus, the student is helped to establish certain desired ethical attitudes and value commitments, for example, respect for the client's worth, dignity, and right to self-determination. Also, the student is helped to learn by doing and helping.

We make use of two kinds of developmental tasks in field instruction. One is of student learning. The second is of teaching.

Knowing the characteristic *learning tasks* at a particular stage, we can directly aid the student to cope. Thus, as Towle and others have identified, the initial stage in class and field for a social work student is marked by much anxiety and confusion in regard to initial learning and service tasks.[12] This anxiety and confusion may have personal sources and/or be related to the student's lack of knowledge, skill, and command over needed social resources. In either case, the student may respond with emotional constriction; overdependency or hostility; stereotyped, fragmented, and repetitive behavior; and ineffective service to clients.

Utilizing her developmental model of learning which emphasized integrative learning tasks and capacities, Towle identified a *teaching task* that applies to a lack of required knowledge.

> The educational task has become one of balancing giving and demanding, taking care not to give too much at once in too great detail. This entails giving first things first, with a realistic expectancy that they be mastered. It also implies helping the learner put them to use and holding him accountable for doing so .,. intellectual grasp is a first step in learning. The feelings of hope evolved by new knowledge may quickly bring depth of comprehension and integration.[13]

Towle then went on to formulate two teaching principles.

> It is essential to evaluate defenses in relation to the educational source of the learner's anxiety and in relation to their time, notably the age of the learner and his stage of learning . . . [Also] it is essential that educational measures widen the ego span through their positive nature, oriented to instill hope and to engender self-confidence whenever possible.[14]

One aspect of the process orientation, the development of process objectives, includes the student's development of a "social consciousness and social conscience" and the development also of a "learning process that will endure" to use Towle's phrases.[15] This means orienting the student to the profession's place in society; teaching him or her how to learn, to think critically, and to solve problems creatively; fostering a self-awareness of how one learns and relates to clients; helping to establish a self-renewing custom of learning so that the student thereafter travels through life "with a different view."[16]

Another process objective involves consciously "learning the ropes" about people, relationships, statuses, rules, work requirements, service operations; "achieving a measure of control over people and events"; and learning how to interact with people and negotiate one's way to a successful adjustment in a learning or work situation.[17] This includes learning how to cope with conflict behavior among clients or constituents, or with differences in practice theories and ideologies held by the field instructor, the school consultant, the advisor, and the classroom teacher. Still another objective, rarely mentioned though very important to students, is to learn how to make one's livelihood in what is seen as a "right livelihood" of social work. All of these learnings are only partially achieved during any one field placement or in the field instruction courses as a whole, and they require further learning following graduation from school.

These kinds of process learning objectives require appropriate instructional behaviors in how to carry on the teaching process. The field instructor is expected to model the democratic and ethical attitudes and behaviors needed for the student to gain emotional self-involvement and conscious, active participation in the learning program. The teacher also is expected to become involved in collaborative, consensual, as well as open, genuine, and empathic decision making and relationships with the student. The "process teacher" is further expected to model and directly demonstrate explicit and technical steps and tasks, to collaborate with the students in service and action programs with clients or citizens, and to make their shared experiences ones of mutual learning and growth.

These process objectives and instructional behaviors have important functions in stimulating commitment by the student for a specific learning program. Also, the process conception of field instruction expresses professional values in a very direct way. If offers certain ethical, teaching, and helping principles that social workers believe make the teaching and the helping process more effective. At the same time, the concern with process presents certain dangers. It can become an overriding preoccupation with the achievement of a mindless consensus and for an anti-intellectual, self-deceptive emotional experience. It may result in what Benjamin DeMott calls "a theatre of hypocrisy," in which there is a denial or derogation of power differences among participants, of conflict regarding different interests, of ambivalences and contradictions in desires and needs.[18] Other results may include a disinterest in the intellectual substance and complexities of human-life issues and a neglect of necessary outcomes and products, of just and beneficial results, and also of the need for direction and leadership in certain life situations.

The characteristic fondness of social workers for process conceptions of teaching has led to a long line of published efforts that describe the teaching-learning enterprise, including field instruction, in process terms.[19] These efforts have identified typical models of progression for student learning in classroom work and in field work. They map out the stages of task mastery, of what may be expected at different points in the year of placement, and give emphasis to the emotional ups and downs experienced by a typical student. Thus, a student may begin field work with much anxiety, confusion, and self-preoccupation, unrealistically high expectations of clients, and much dependency on the field instructor. The student may then move through the stages of muddling through or "sink or swim adaptation," a "cloud-nine" feeling of mastery, regressive depression, and self-doubt. Then there are the stages of "understanding the situation without power to control one's activity in it," followed by a sense of self-confident identity and relative competence, and finally to separation and termination.[20]

The idealized quality of many of these sequential stage presentations has made them useful in the inevitable games students and instructors play. At prescribed times, some students offer to the field instructor the desired and expected responses of successive anxiety, elation, depression, self-derogation, self-confidence, and so on. Some students include a presentation of November and April "slumps."

There are important advantages to having process conceptions of learning and of field instruction. We are provided with a development system model, a map or flow chart with which to understand the progressive history and maturation of a student.[21] Used as part of the frame of reference given by Gordon and Gordon in Chapter 2, we can chart the development of a student in terms of an orderly sequence of task steps, or how internal structures, abilities, and limitations arise and are realized.

A knowledge and application of process stages and tasks thus guides us in the choice of teaching objectives, procedures, and principles. Where there is a lack of student progress, this is identified by the noncompletion of stage-specific tasks. In this way, we are better able to locate the reasons for the impasse or the blocks to development and functioning. We are then better able to free the progressive forces in the student for further growth and to enable the successful matching of student and learning situation to function optimally.

PROCESS SEQUENCES, STAGES, AND PHASES

Now that we have demonstrated the importance of a process conception of learning and instruction, we must come to terms with the fact that we lack good models of the teaching process, let alone of the field instruction process. There are understandable reasons for this state of affairs. First of all, we still are struggling with the development of models of student learning. Robert Gagné has suggested that different types of content are learned in a cumulative process: content about signals, stimulus-responses, chaining, verbal associations, multiple discriminations, concepts, principles, and problem solving.[22] Second, our conceptions of human growth have become even more complicated than they were in the past. Instead of viewing development as a chronological, orderly stage of progression, the individual life cycle is now seen to involve a progression of a number of processes. A third source of difficulty in the development of teaching models is the fragmentation of class and field teaching. As a result, a proper differentiation of the field instruction process from the classroom instruction process, as well as their proper integration, is not easy to accomplish.

It is helpful, therefore, to turn to the cycle and character of the teaching process. In this regard, Jerome Bruner identified four features of a theory of instruction.[23] The first two concern the importance of motivating the learner and of providing an "optimal structure" of the knowledge to be learned. The third and fourth features concern process: the need to specify "the most effective sequences for presentation of the material to be learned" and to specify "the nature and pacing of rewards and punishments."

Malcolm Knowles has suggested a process design for instruction that offers a general model of process phases and tasks and that deals with a number of these process features.[24] His conception of the adult learning process is one of self-directed inquiry by the student, with the teacher acting primarily in the roles of facilitator and resource person and creator of optimal kinds of educational environments. We can include and adapt these design elements in a general sequence of instructional *stages and tasks* formulated in terms of our own social functioning frame of reference. This sequence takes place during the beginning and end of learning and teaching activity.

1. *engagement* between student and instructor and *orientation* to the placement, which includes the conscious setting of a psychosocial climate and a definition of the learning-teaching situation emphasizing humanistic ethical relationships and high standards of learning as well as of service.

2. *assessment* of learning and teaching needs in terms of value models, desired competencies for practitioner role perfor-

mance, the student's developmental level of abilities and other characteristics, and resources and requirements for learning and teaching in the field work situation;

3. *planning* an educational program, which involves the formulating of program objectives, beginning with the immediate objectives for teaching and learning activities that will facilitate student functioning in the service role. It also involves the designing of sequential learning experiences and task assignments for the student, the instructor, and others in the teaching situation;

4. *conducting the educational program* with shared responsibility for the implementation of the program plans and the attainment of objectives and tasks;

5. *monitoring and evaluation* of the learning, in a mutual reexamination of the competency standards used and the student's achieved levels of development, along with the taking of corrective action where and when indicated;

6. *termination and disengagement* at the end of the placement, which poses varying degrees of difficulty for the student and instructor depending on the kind of relationship that develops between them.

The specific progression of instructional activity and of the learning process by the student depends largely on a set of three factors:

1. the nature of the content (for example, behavior theory or interactional skills) and the tasks for its learning;

2. the characteristics of the learner (for example, as an intuitive or analytical type);

3. the characteristics of the learning-teaching field situation (e.g., whether it is highly or loosely structured).

There is no preordained, chronological sequence that has to be followed in the teaching and learning of content. The actual cases and service programs within which learning tasks are assigned and accepted by students are largely nonroutine and nonstandardized, and they often have haphazard, chaotic, unpredictable qualities which make a neat, systematic teaching plan unfeasible. It is evident that much student learning is "situational learning" with subject matter brought in and new behaviors acquired as they are required by the service situations. Student abilities and capacities vary tremendously, as do those of field instructors.

The processes and development and learning follow complex cycles and the students' progression of learning in the field may be varied and intermittent. There is little that has to be learned in some precise sequence. We do believe that an ability to establish positive working relationships with applicants for service during intake is a necessary given. A student does need to know and be skilled in certain elementary matters and gain a cumulative mastery, for example, of the functions of the agency and the purposes and eligibility requirements for service. It is very important to recognize that progressive, cumulative, and definite stages and levels of learning have to be surmounted, and specific knowledge and skills have to be mastered within set time periods. However, many things can be learned sooner or later, whether it be computing a budget, developing a working contract with a client or agency, or providing appropriate emotional support. Direct, logical progressions in learning are nice to have; but they often are neither feasible nor essential.

The teaching and learning process is, therefore, a very individualized one. Yet, it does have a certain kind of needed order and structure. As Morris Finder points out about the process of writing:

> The construction of parts that constitute the whole define the tasks and process of writing . . . A process must have a beginning, an order, and an end. The beginning is not necessarily what the writer as a person does first. Rather, the beginning is whenever the first functioning part is constructed. Similarly, the order is not a chronological sequence of human actions but the order of subordination of parts to whole. The process ends whenever the whole is formed and work on the parts is stopped or abandoned.[25]

The field instructor thus provides learning experiences as parts of a whole, a well-functioning student-learner and practitioner-in-the-making. The beginning and the end of the teaching process coincide with the beginning and end of the placement, though the learning process for the student has very different beginnings and endings. The whole is represented by our models of learning objectives for student performance and achievement in a placement period, whether for a quarter, semester, or year. Learning tasks need to have a valid rationale in being based on sound service, teaching, and learning principles. All these give a coherent order to the teaching-learning process.

THE TEACHER-STUDENT RELATIONSHIP

The structure of the teaching-learning process and the achievement of learning tasks depend on the centrality of the instructor-student relationship. The reciprocal role expectations and behaviors and the bonds of understanding, acceptance, and support all provide a medium and stimulus for the student's motivation, commitment, and effort in the learning program. The relationship between the student and the assigned field instructor needs to be positive, collaborative, and complementary. The relational process, however, is characterized by movement from dependence to self-reliance on the part of the student; from a more active, directive position to a less active and more nondirective position on the part of the instructor; and from a rather impersonal to what often becomes a very personal kind of relationship between the two of them.

There is a legitimate dilemma that confronts the teacher in this relationship. Student expectations for help with self-development and personal growth are part of the learning objectives for field work and relate to the development of the professional self. Jessie Taft made this relationship very clear in declaring that the student needs to work on "what it means to experience a change in the very self. . . . To believe in the possibility of growth for the client, one has to have known the release of growth in the self through help consciously sought and professionally controlled."[26] Charlotte Towle emphasized the importance of the "corrective relationship" to be provided for the student by the field instructor.[27] This emphasis continues to be made today in current discussions of field work student learning.

> When students learn about clients, they are learning about human beings
> . . . they are learning about themselves . . . There [is] the growth in self-
> understanding that flowed from confronting and re-working personal con-
> flict. . . . They are working on these "deeply personal things." As Joanie
> said, "Obviously, I'm helping myself."[28]

Along with this view, a traditional distinction has been made by faculty between the helping aspects and the "by-product" therapeutic elements of the field instruction process. It is repeatedly stated that one should avoid "treating" the student. This has meant discussing personal feelings of students only as such discussions can be focused on service and learning requirements, without getting into the sources of internal conflicts and problems. Such a segmental focus is associated with helping the student to develop a "professional," rather than the total, personality. But this traditional distinction is not widely observed by many students and teachers today.

We can accept the validity and desirability of personal relationships between instructor and student in the educational process. An educational relationship is personal in the sense that it is based on a private world of shared experience and understanding, a reciprocal knowledge of each other's authentic selves, of each other's private, self-disclosed experience, some of which can make one vulnerable.[29] Such a personal relationship does not need to be discriminatory for or against a particular student; it can be responsible and impartial and can balance role and genuine human behavior. However, the relationship between instructor and student is not fully reciprocal in that the student is expected to be more self-disclosing than is the instructor. The instructor's authority should be clear and the standards for performance by the student need to be clearly defined and adhered to as impersonal ones. Also, a continuing effort is required directly to face and resolve whatever issue differences may arise between teacher and student.

An educational and personal relationship of this kind enhances the teaching and learning process. Instructor and student each achieve empathic understanding of the other, mutual respect, and trust. For the student there is facilitation of self-awareness, congruence of feelings and actions, and self-acceptance. The student is better able to accept the competent teacher as a model. As Bruner clarifies, the student does this not only to imitate but also to identify with the teacher so that the teacher as model becomes "part of the student's internal dialogue— somebody whose respect he wants, someone whose standards he wants to make his own."[30] And, as Bruner further clarifies, the encouragement of the student's identification and internalization of standards turns over to the student an important degree of control for his own rewards and punishments.

It is out of such considerations about the student-teacher relationship that an instructor can see himself or herself able to develop personal and helping relationships with students, without assuming a therapeutic role, and to maintain needed control of the teaching-learning situation and process. One can emulate Virginia Satir's concern to "keep the process in flow," to check out everything of importance with students, and to be a "strong leader for the process" because the field instructor is the one who knows what the learning process is about.[31] A number of teaching principles, particularly with regard to the assignment of learning tasks and experiences, are presented below.

PROCESS PRINCIPLES

In order to realize this kind of field instruction process and the tasks we have identified, a number of teaching principles appear to be widely used.[32] These principles are generic in nature and apply to the wide gamut of field instruction settings and programs.

1. *The instructor needs to be active with the student or student group in clarifying mutual expectations and role concepts so as to facilitate a complementary, reciprocal, and cooperative relationship.* This is especially true in regard to the beginning-level tasks of engagement and orientation. It means, for example, clarifying the nature of the balance between the supportive and authority

aspects of the instructor's role as well as the student's role in relation to these aspects of instruction.

2. *The instructor needs to provide appropriate learning assignments early in the field experience.* The initial mixture of enthusiasm, over-idealized expectations, resistances, and anxieties on the part of both student and field instructor can be dealt with and utilized directly for work purposes. This can be done by giving the student concrete and appropriate information, materials, and support and by rapidly assigning work tasks for which the instructor is readily available as guide and resource. Experience and research have demonstrated that delay in assignment of case and program responsibilities and tasks increases student anxiety and dissatisfaction and retards learning; whereas, quick assignment of work tasks results in higher levels of learning.[33]

3. *The field instructor needs to provide support and clear expectations for work and learning at high levels of quality and quantity.* Developing a suitable learning climate and positive definition of the teaching situation should mean safety and support for exploration and risk, for errors and failure on the road to change. This kind of climate and situational definition needs to be a collective development in a field placement and service organization, a joint responsibility of the field instructor, co-workers, and administrators.

4. *The field instructor needs to conduct an educational appraisal of the student that holds firmly to a person-situation perspective.* In doing this, the field instructor should individualize student abilities and limitations, identify personality and learning patterns, and do so in relation to both the specific situational job requirements and the school-prescribed models of normative, valued, professional competencies and performance. This means that an educational appraisal is based firmly on a combined personality and situation appraisal and is concerned with the feelings and meanings of the teaching-learning experience on the part of both the student and instructor. Students need to be given credit for their knowledge and life experience. Often these assets may seem lacking because of initial anxieties, transferences, and biases on the part of either the field instructor or student or both.

5. *The teaching program should be planned on the basis of a set of organizing principles which give priority to the process of learning by the student.* Several of these organizing principles for the assignment of learning tasks are as follows:

a. Learning objectives and tasks need to be clarified to indicate the specific theoretical understanding of, feeling about, and instrumental skills that are required for the student's effective helping action. This includes indicating those significant features of the student's own behavior and of the service situation that are controllable and usable through his or her own efforts in the performance and learning of the particular helping action.

b. Learning tasks should be partialized so as to be attainable by the student on a step-by-step basis. This enables the student to analyze the tasks more clearly and to perform them more specifically. It also enables the instructor to have a better focus in the presentation of the learning tasks and in reinforcing the student for the mastery of tasks.

c. Learning tasks should provide for overt performance and repetitive practice of desired behavior, for "learning by doing," and for a variety of experience. These facilitate retention of the learning and generalization so that the new knowledge and skill can be applied in different situations and become habits—particularly if they are satisfying to the student.

d. Each learning task should be structured so as to enable a learning sequence to take place, for preparation, perception, choice, internalization, digestion, and assimilation. The stages of learning may be as suggested by Whitehead: romance (or perception and discovery), precision (in mastering knowledge and analysis), and generalization (or synthesis).[34] Or they may be in accord with the stages suggested by Kurt Lewin: unfreezing, change (exploration and practice), and then refreezing.[35]

e. Learning tasks should be organized, as much as is feasible, in a cumulative sequence in terms of their demands upon the student, in order to develop aggregate abilities. Such a sequence can be attained by advancing from the simpler to the more complex client difficulties, from the narrow to the wider range of responsibility, choice, and action, and from the lesser to the more abstract requirements of knowledge, skill, and effort. Continuity can be obtained by progressive repetition of practice principles and procedures as applied in different situations.[36] The students, therefore, need to be protected from service demands for which they are unready or unskilled, and the field instructor needs to be able to intervene in service situations that become inappropriate for the student.

f. Learning tasks should be provided in terms of a clear conceptual framework (or cognitive organizing structure) to clarify their objectives and purposes and to understand how they fit into the larger picture. Such a framework gives continuity, consistency, and coherence to the program of learning experiences. Emphasis should be given to providing central organizing concepts and integrative propositions and theories upon which behavior and practice principles are based.[37] For example, we emphasize ideas about crisis, internal and external resources, and the relation of feelings of depression to feelings of helplessness.

g. The full participation of the student needs to be gained through the sharing of purposes and procedural tasks, as well as through appropriate negotiations with the student about performance objectives and role responsibilities.

h. The program of rewards should move from the use of external reinforcement by the instructor, such as praise, to the student's use of intrinsic and self-reinforcements, such as the accomplishment of high standards or successful interventions which enhance self-esteem and self-concept.[38]

6. *The field instructor needs to establish balances between student learning and provision of service, freedom and discipline, and autonomy and dependency.* This helps the student attain balance in the learning process.

a. Priority should be given to the student's learning tasks, to facilitating and supporting explorations and service activities, and to balancing this with a concern for meeting the needs of the clients.

b. There also needs to be a balance maintained between what Whitehead discussed as freedom and discipline for the student in accomplishing his or her tasks. Thus the student can be encouraged to use new techniques or develop new types of resources consistent with agency policies and functions. Also, a student can be encouraged to accomplish a set of helping tasks in whatever order seems feasible to him or her within the limits of time and other factors. It is in this regard that the field instructor needs to be in control of the teaching-learning process and situation.

c. Another kind of balance concerns that of the student's autonomy and dependency. Thus, realistic dependency needs should be met wih the expectation that the student will move increasingly toward a self-reliant position. However, the self-reliance should be understood as associated with a continuing need by the student for acceptance of administrative authority, support from fellow profession-

als, and mature consultative and feedback-seeking relationships with more expert social workers.

7. *The field instructor needs to place conscious emphasis on teaching practice principles.* Practice principles (e.g., a situational assessment is best accomplished by the social worker as a partici-
pant observer in the client's life situation) are guides to effective action. They generalize and summarize knowledge, point
to knowledge and skill that apply across many practice situations, enable us to be creative in problem solving with regard
to many different people and problems, and also enable us to
be individualistic in our style of performance. As Towle points
out, "disciplined generalization is the means to the mastery of
knowledge implicit in professional wisdom."[39] The instructor
needs to teach explicit principles and to explain and show their
applicability in varied circumstances.

8. *The field instructor needs to help the student make learning a conscious process by modeling self-awareness and self-monitoring.* This
should directly demonstrate their helpfulness in learning and
skill mastery, yet allow the student to choose and develop his
or her own style. Such effort helps facilitate the operation of
learning mechanisms, expand integrative capacity and expectations of personal efficacy, and enables better self-management
of learning tasks.

9. *The field instructor needs to make the monitoring and evaluation of
student performance a mutual enterprise with the student and school
liaison.* It is the actual changes in the student's behavior that
needs be appraised, and this appraisal should be based on repeated observations by instructor and student.[40] The evaluative criteria needs to be consistent with the staged objectives
and with the content that is consciously taught and learned.
The strengths and weaknesses of the instruction, the developmental level of the student, and the nature of the field work
situation should be included in the appraisal. In the monitoring
of the student's progress, feedback should be provided frequently, both verbally and in written response, to the student's recording so as to provide reinforcement or corrective
action as indicated. The evaluation should involve the school
consultant as standard bearer, mediator, and reality figure.
The written evaluation may not have all of the conclusions
agreed upon by field instructor and student, but it should be
signed by both to signify the mutuality of the effort made.

10. *The field instructor needs to help the student deal with the tasks of
termination.* This includes giving explicit help to the student in

accomplishing the emotional and physical tasks of disengagement and termination with clients, the field instructor, and the field situation. This applies to the work of the successful as well as the unfit and failing student. These tasks also require the field instructor to consciously deal with his or her own feelings about the teaching situation and termination with the student.[41]

EFFECTIVENESS AND OUTCOMES

In following the above principles, the field instructor attains greater assurance of an effective outcome for the teaching and learning process. The field instructor also is better able to account for his or her own efforts as well as those of the student; to maintain the teaching-learning process on a goal-directed course; and to keep the efforts involved efficiently mobilized, focused, and executed so that the desired objectives are achieved.

This process, based on sound knowledge and principles of teaching and learning, is rational in that there is a conscious choice of a teaching program and learning tasks, based on careful assessment, with consideration of valued and differential purposes and of possible consequences. It also is comprehensive in that it is part of a multi-dimensional, system-oriented approach to teaching and learning. It is concerned with achieving the systemic task-functions of an adaptive socialization and educational behavior change for the student, or an integrative teacher-learning situation, and of a goal-achieving resolution of conflicts and crises. In addition, implementation of the process is flexible, to allow for creativity and innovation, unexpected contingencies, and choices of alternative procedures and techniques to be made by the instructor and student.

An ineffective instructional process handicaps, blocks, or frustrates the teaching and learning efforts of the instructor and student. One result is the use of defensive, unhelpful, and objectionable kinds of supervision, as reported by students to Rosenblatt and Mayer who categorize the methods as constrictive, amorphous, unsupportive, and "therapeutic."[42] Also, there is recourse to the maladaptive, depreciating, hostile, and self-defeating games played by both field instructors and students. Several of these are identified by Kadushin and by Hawthorne.[43] The field instructors may play power games of abdication ("They Won't Let Me," "I'm Really a Nice Guy") or demonstration of power ("Remember Who's Boss," "I Wonder Why You Really Said That," "Parents Know Best"). Students may enact countergames to deal with power issues, to control work-demand levels, or to control the relationship ("Be Nice to Me Because I'm Nice to You," "Treat Me, Don't Beat Me," "If You Knew Dostoyevsky Like I Know Dostoyevsky," "I Have a Little List," "It's All So Confusing," "I Did Like You Told Me"). Such game playing may take place along with serious, genuine work on the part of student and instructor. But to counteract such game playing requires much self-awareness by the instructor, as well as frank, honest confrontation and dialogue between instructor and student.

Other outcomes may be unintended or unanticipated. Although field instruction is not intended to help students learn negative behavior, it is evident that some of this does take place. For example, Geoffrey Pearson is sharply critical of the "bad promises" made in the socialization process in social work education.[44] He charges that it trains the student for professional inaction in the face of moral and political ambiguities and injustices and that it distorts student perceptions and motives so as to downgrade the tremendous difficulties of doing a social work job. It also teaches students a "social banditry" in which social workers covertly sabotage and break agency rules or do not enforce them in order to rearrange their jobs and make them workable and to provide real services to clients. Cloward and Piven charge that students are infantalized and indoctrinated to "bureaucratic acquiescence" in order to serve as social control agents for repressive social agency policies and regulations.[45] They declare that student resistance is dangerous for them; students are discouraged by field instructors from serving the real interests of clients; student-teacher conflicts are denied; teachers are more concerned with ingratiating themselves with their superiors than aiding their students in real learning; and student reactions are distorted in the constant psychologizing of psychoanalytic interpretations. A recent study even found that, compared to the general population, personalities of social work graduates are above average in intelligence, warmth, tenderheartedness, trustfulness, and responsiveness but below average in clearheadedness, practicality, and decisiveness of action.[46]

There is, of course, a certain amount of validity to the above criticisms and truth to the educational effects they describe. Both the negative and positive outcomes present certain implications for more effective teaching and more effective learning in social work education, particularly in the field instruction process. Traditional means of preparing, supporting, and complementing field instructors, whether agency or school based, need to be strengthened. There is, for example, a great need for texts and written materials on field instruction to be made available to field instructors and students. Instructional modules are needed that can specify teaching and learning objectives for specific learning content along with indicated methods and techniques of instruction.[47] Such materials could facilitate mastery learning, obviate much close supervision, and help rationally carry out feedback, monitory, and evaluation tasks. The competence of the field instructor can be strengthened by providing such resources. However, many more studies on the field instruction process are needed to develop and expand our limited knowledge of this process. There is also an evident need to find new means for integrating class and field teaching. Suggestions for meeting such needs are offered and examined in other chapters of this book.

CONCLUSION

Having acknowledged our limitations and imperfections, as well as our need to make important changes in the field instruction process, we also should recognize our assets and strengths. The field instruction process that has evolved historically in social work education does appear to be an effective means for helping to educate professional social work practitioners. Students and graduates do perform effective services to clients. Our field instruction and our emphasis on process do express and transmit important humanistic values to which we are deeply committed.

Our students and graduates present many positive outcomes for their educational experiences. They report direct results in professional and personal growth, in an expansion of their professional and personal selves, abilities, and self-understanding. As one student declared:

> The most valuable thing aside from the knowledge and techniques acquired for professional competency that has happened both personally and professionally was the shifting and sliding of old attitudes and ingrained ways of thinking into more mature patterns of reaction. I know that this has made me a happier person, and I feel that this "shake-up" has freed energy which will enable me to be more truly helpful in my work.[48]

Another student reported:

> This experience has been invaluable and will probably take on greater significance as time goes on. Yes, I feel somewhat guilty about leaving. But they, the aged, aren't invisible anymore, and I am a more complete person for having known some of them.[49]

In addition, graduates tell us that much of their learning continues, reverberates, and amplifies after they leave school. They recall meaningful discussions, pieces of advice, and observations by the instructor which take on sudden great meaning or which make insightful connections for them at later points of crisis. Or they report using some pet phrase or technique of the field instructor with their own clients or making the same demands, assigning the same tasks with their own students.

For the field instructor, positive outcomes come largely in the form of intrinsic rewards. We know little about this reward structure and should know more. The field instructor usually is unpaid by the school and is a volunteer whose time is paid for and donated by the employing agency. Field teaching is essentially a gift, a giving of self for the benefit of another. It may be done for altruistic reasons of love or duty and/or for self-interest. One may take on instructional responsibilities as a way of personal advancement in an agency or as a way of moving into a teaching career. One gains vicarious rewards in seeing a student perform well with a client or make some major shift in attitude or behavior that benefits a client or service program. And there are the joys of feeling that one is learning and growing in oneself. Helen Perlman has well described the returns for our efforts:

> All of us, students and teachers alike, strive to be the cause of some "good" effects, the cause of some changes that are held to be desirable. . . . This is what makes us want to lend ourselves to the student and then to support and stimulate him toward his own actualization as a member of our profession. This ideal of ourselves as being a "cause" in the development and change in a new generation, toward its achievement of what we hold to be good, is what drives us to develop and change ourselves, to invest ourselves in study and students toward our own greater competence. This is what sends us back year after year to ponder on teaching and, despite the grind and groaning, to gladly teach.[50]

NOTES

1. For student opinions about the much higher value of field work versus classroom learning, see Margaret Schubert, *Field Instruction in Social Casework* (Chicago: School of Social Service Administration, University of Chicago, 1963), p. 40.
2. Alfred N. Whitehead, *Adventures of Ideas* (New York: New American Library, 1955), p. 275.
3. Bertha Reynolds, *Learning and Teaching in the Practice of Social Work* (New York: Farrar and Rinehart, 1942), pp. 57, 91.
4. This conception of learning is based on the discussion in Ernest R. Hilgard and Gordon H. Bower, *Theories of Learning* (Englewood Cliffs, NJ: Prentice Hall, 1975), pp. 1–27, among other sources.
5. John Dewey, *Experience and Education* (New York: Crowell Collier, 1963), pp. 38–40.
6. This conception of teaching owes much to the discussion by R.S. Peters, "What is an Educational Process," in *The Conception of Education*, ed. R.S. Peters (London: Routledge and Kegan Paul, 1967), pp. 1–23; and to Ralph Tyler, *Basic Principles of Curriculum and Instruction* (Chicago: University of Chicago Press, 1959), pp. 3–28. Also, Hilgard and Bower, *op. cit.*, pp. 606–638; N.L. Gage and David C. Berlinger, *Educational Psychology* (Chicago: Rand McNally, 1975); Mary Louise Sommers, "Contributions of Learning and Teaching Theories to the Explication of the Role of the Teacher in Social Work Education," *Journal of Education for Social Work*, Vol. 5, No. 2 (1969), 61–73.

7. Jessie Taft, "A Conception of the Growth Process Underlying Social Casework Practice," *Social Casework*, Vol. 31 (1950), 311–318.
8. On "type situations," see Reynolds, *op. cit.*, p. 102. On "situational learning," see Eduard C. Lindeman, *The Meaning of Adult Education* (New York: New Republic, 1926), pp. 8–9; and Blanche Geer, et al., "Learning the Ropes: Situational Learning in Four Occupational Training Programs," in *Among the People*, eds. Irwin Duetscher and Elizabeth J. Thompson (New York: Basic Books, 1968), pp. 209–230.
9. Michael Oakeshott, "Learning and Teaching," in Peters, *op. cit.*, pp. 156–176.
10. Alfred Kadushin, *Supervision in Social Work* (New York: Columbia University Press, 1976), p. 196.
11. A more detailed discussion of process is given in Max Siporin, *Introduction to Social Work Practice* (New York: Macmillan, 1975), pp. 47–52, 160–165; and in Saul Hofstein, "The Nature of Process: The Implications for Social Work," *Journal of Social Work Process*, Vol. 14 (1964), 13–53.
12. Charlotte Towle, *The Learner in Education for the Professions* (Chicago: University of Chicago Press, 1954), pp. 27–53 and 94–106. Also John E. Mayer and Aaron Rosenblatt, "Sources of Stress Among Student Practitioners in Social Work," *Journal of Education for Social Work*, Vol. 10, No. 3 (1974), 56–66.
13. Towle, *op. cit.*, p. 33.
14. *Ibid.*, pp. 132–133.
15. *Ibid.*, pp. 15–16. On the distinction between "task" and "process" objectives in the helping process, see Jack Rothman, "An Analysis of Goals and Roles in Community Organization Practice," *Social Work*, Vol. 9, No. 2 (1964), 24–31. In Neil Gilbert and Harry Specht, "Process Versus Task in Social Planning," *Social Work*, Vol. 22 (1977), 178–183, the authors believe that process objectives are more applicable to the beginning than to the later stages of the helping process. A different position is taken here and in Siporin, *op. cit.*, p. 264. For a discussion of process helping and process parenting see Bunny Duhl, "Changing Sex Roles—Information Without Process," *Social Casework*, Vol. 57 (1976), 80–86. On process teaching see David E. Hunt and Edmund V. Sullivan, *Between Psychology and Education* (New York: Dryden, 1974). On a process approach to therapy and life in general, see Carl R. Rogers, *On Personal Power* (New York: Delacorte, 1977).
16. Peters, *op. cit.*, p. 8.
17. Geer, et. al., *op. cit.*
18. Benjamin DeMott, "Hot Air Meeting," *Harper's Magazine*, July, 1975.
19. Among such efforts to describe the field instruction and learning process see Annette Garrett, "Learning through Supervision," *Smith College Studies in Social Work*, Vol. 24, No. 2 (1953), 3–109; Rosemary Reynolds, *Evaluating the Field Work of Students* (New York: Family Service Association of America, 1946); Silvia Astro, et. al., *Guide to the Content of Second-Year Field Teaching in Casework* (Chicago: School of Social Service Administration, The University of Chicago, 1961); Bessie Kent, *Social Work Supervision in Practice* (Oxford: Pergamon Press, 1969); and Dorothy E. Pettes, *Supervision in Social Work* (London: George Allen and Unwin, 1967).

20. Bertha Reynolds, *op. cit.*, pp. 75–84, suggested most of the stages given in quotes.

21. On the use of developmental and structure-function system models, see Siporin, *op. cit.*, pp. 106–109.

22. Robert M. Gagné, *The Conditions of Learning* (New York: Holt, Rinehart, and Winston, 1965).

23. Jerome Bruner, *Toward a Theory of Instruction* (Cambridge: Belknap Press of Harvard University, 1966), pp. 40–41.

24. Malcolm S. Knowles, "Innovations in Teaching Styles and Approaches Based upon Adult Learning," *Journal of Education for Social Work*, Vol. 8, No. 2 (1972), 32–39.

25. Morris Finder, *Reason and Art in Teaching Secondary School English* (Philadelphia: Temple University Press, 1976), p. 102.

26 Virginia P. Robinson, ed., *Jessie Taft: Therapist and Social Work Educator* (Philadelphia: University of Pennsylvania Press, 1962), pp. 246, 329.

27. Towle, *op. cit.*, p. 173.

28. Kloh-Ann Amacher, "Explorations into the Dynamics of Learning in Field Work," *Smith College Studies in Social Work*, Vol. 46 (1976), 163–217.

29. In P.H. Hirst and R.S. Peters, *The Logic of Education* (London: Routledge and Kegan Paul, 1970), pp. 88–105, the authors present these characteristics of an educational and personal relationship and make suggestions for their implementation.

30. Bruner, *op. cit.*, pp. 122–124.

31. Virginia Satir, "When I Meet a Person," in *Tidings of Comfort and Joy*, ed. Robert S. Spitzer (Palo Alto, CA; Science and Behavior Books, 1975), pp. 111–127.

32. Many of the principles that follow are adapted from those identified by Towle, *op. cit.*, and Tyler, *op. cit.*

33. Schubert, *op. cit*, pp. 123–124. Strong support for the early and high frequency of assignments of service responsibilities to students is reported from the study by John Korbelik and Laura Epstein, "Evaluating Time and Achievement in a Social Work Pacticum," in *Teaching for Competence in the Delivery of Direct Services* (New York: Council on Social Work Education, 1976), pp. 51–59.

34. Alfred N. Whitehead, *The Aims of Education* (New York: Harper and Row, 1951), pp. 28–31.

35. Kurt Lewin, *Field Theory in Social Science* (New York: Harper and Row, 1951), pp. 188–237.

36. Towle, *op. cit.*, pp. 168–169. See also Bernece Simon, "Design of Learning Experiences in Field Instruction," *Social Service Review*, Vol. 40 (1966), 397–409.

37. Leonard M. Bloksberg and Louis Lowy make these suggestions in their paper, "Toward Integrative Learning and Teaching in Social Work," *Journal of Education for Social Work*, Vol. 13, No. 2 (1977), 3–10.

38. Bruner, *op. cit.*, pp. 41–42.

39. Towle, *op. cit.*, p. 171. This emphasis on the teaching of principles was stated by John Dewey in 1904; see "The Relation of Theory to Practice in Education," in *John Dewey on Education*, ed. R.D. Archambault (Chicago: University of Chicago Press, 1974), pp. 313–338.

40. Tyler, *op. cit.*, p. 69. See also the discussions by several authors of the criteria and issues about student evaluation in Morton L., Arkava and E. Clifford Brennen, eds., *Competency-Based Education for Social Work* (New York: Council on Social Work Education, 1976).

41. Dorothy Large, "Four Processes of Field Instruction in Casework," *Social Service Review*, Vol. 37 (1963), 263–273.

42. This general view by students is reported by Aaron Rosenblatt and John E. Mayer, "Objectionable Supervisory Styles: Student Views," *Social Work*, Vol. 20 (1975), 184–189. A similar student view, but with some show of opposition to the supervisor's authority, is given by Richard A. Cloward and Frances Fox Piven, "Notes toward a Radical Social Work," in *Radical Social Work*, eds. Roy Bailey and Mike Brake (New York: Pantheon, 1976), pp. vii–xlviii.

43. Kadushin, *op. cit.*, pp. 239–253. Lillian Hawthorne, "Games Supervisors Play," *Social Work*, Vol. 20 (1975), 179–183.

44. Geoffrey Pearson, "Making Social Workers: Bad Promises and Good Omens," in Bailey and Brake, *op. cit.*, pp. 13–45; and Geoffrey Pearson, "The Politics of Uncertainty: A Study in the Socialization of the Social Worker," in *Toward a New Social Work*, ed. Howard Jones (London: Routledge and Kegan Paul, 1975), pp. 45–68.

45. Cloward and Piven *op. cit.* More recently in Phyllida Parslow, "How Training May Unfit People," *Social Work Today*, Vol. 9, No. 4 (September 20, 1977), 15–18, the author, an English social work educator, declares that social work training may "unfit" students for their later jobs—to work within a bureaucratic organization, to contend with actual workloads and pressures, to help clients with financial problems, to work with groups of colleagues and clients.

46. David Rutherford, "Personality in Social Work Students," *Social Work Today*, Vol. 8, No. 20 (February 22, 1977), 9–10.

47. Kay L. Dea, describes such modules in his book, *The Instructional Module* (New York: Council on Social Work Education, 1971).

48. Garrett, *op. cit.*, p. 101.

49. Quoted in Ruth Cohen, "Student Training in a Geriatric Center," in *Issues in Human Services*, ed. Florence W. Kaslow, et. al. (San Francisco: Jossey-Bass, 1972), pp. 168–184.

50. Helen H. Perlman, "And Gladly Teach," *Journal of Education for Social Work*, Vol. 3, No. 1 (1967), 41–51.

12

Structuring Field Learning Experiences*

Helen Cassidy

The object of all professional education is to prepare aspirants to fill the role expectations of that profession as interpreted by contemporary society. Social work educators strive to attain this goal by designing a curriculum that supplies the necessary knowledge base plus an experiential exposure that allows use of the total self in learning professional practice. To achieve within a limited time a relative balance of knowledge base and beginning skill components is the challenge. To help the intelligent beginning student with a solid undergraduate background and a modicum of interest and idealism to move into the role of a beginning practitioner ready to offer professional social services is the educational task.

The concept of role as used here refers to "goal-oriented ideas, emotions, and patterns of behavior developed in response to an external context and internalized by the learner."[1] This definition seeks to put the concept of role in appropriate perspective and to distinguish it from the loose and careless manner in which the term *role* is frequently employed, often emerging as a facade for action rather than describing a capacity to assume real and authentic responsibility. Professional

* I wish to acknowledge with gratitude the consultation given by Dr. Walter I. Kindelsperger, dean emeritus of the Tulane School of Social Work, respected colleague and collaborator whose scholarly interest, research, and vision have contributed significantly to the advancement of the theoretical aspects of field instruction.

roles entail knowledge, judgment, and decision making. The development and integration of one's role concept is ongoing throughout life.

In social work education the transition from aspiring student to beginning social worker is achieved by the realization of an educational plan made up of the dual dimensions of class and field practicum, each reinforcing and complementing the other as do two sides of a coin. The classroom introduces the concepts while the field experience or practicum provides the laboratory in which the concepts are tested, additional experiences provided for trying oneself in professional practice, and supplemental opportunities afforded for exposure to content and unique learning dimensions that are not realized otherwise in the curriculum. This classroom–field practicum interplay meets the ideal of the perfect circle. The class presents the concepts and provides for discussion of them. Through the practicum, the student tests out these concepts with the full range of sense data that builds into the role from the beginning. The additional dimensions supplied by this practice then afford new feedback at the conceptual level for classroom review, speculation, and discovery.

As an important dimension in helping individuals become practitioners, the field component has been a part of the transition from layman to social worker from the early days. Social workers were aware that practice could only be learned by doing it. The experience of "doing" the service transformed the uninitiated into the practitioner.[2] The social agency, with its services to troubled human beings, served as the setting for learning practice, and experienced social workers were the practice teachers. Even when social work education moved into the university, the field practice component continued as an apprenticeship, running parallel with the classroom experience. However, this distinctive contribution to the professional formation process was something of a mixed blessing because the awareness of the significance of the practice component was not matched by the know-how to convert it into a vehicle that could match the classroom curriculum and meet the demands of a rigorous university graduate program. Universities and colleges, always suspicious of any program related to apprenticeship, had serious questions about according academic credit to this part of the social work curriculum. Despite the uneasy tolerance that existed for nearly fifty years, after social work education became university based, it was scarcely two decades ago that a concerted effort was made to tailor field experiences to curriculum goals and structure.

In addressing the topic of structuring field learning experiences, each school must raise a series of basic questions about its approach. First of all, it must address field instruction itself: What does field instruction really represent? What is its status in the curriculum? Is it a curriculum component that possesses its own raison d'être? Is it a laboratory vehicle by means of which classroom content finds a practice expression? Or is field instruction all of these and more—a course with its own integrity that serves as a laboratory, that translates cognitive material into practice, and, most of all, that represents the unique medium in which the student discovers self and, through the struggles that bridge the gap between intellectual knowledge and its practice expression, accomplishes his or her emergence as a professional?

When we speak of structuring experiences, are we talking about structuring the total practicum learning experience or the individual learning tasks that comprise the total experience or both? When we refer to structuring, we gain the impression that it shapes what the student will, shall, or can learn from successful completion of the structured experience. What the student learns is only tangentially related to the curriculum of the school and to its field design. Certainly these are both important factors. A poor design or poorly conceived curriculum content will stymie the gifted, motivated student and preclude optimal achievement. On the other hand, the most powerful format cannot guarantee excellent results because of the basic complexity of the interface between the learner and the structure which is goal-directed to professional social work practice.

FORMULATIONS FROM LEARNING THEORY

What the student learns actually depends on other factors which are influenced only partially by the decision of the school or the actions of the field instructor. Influences include all the living and learning experiences of the student throughout his or her life cycle, both formal (all classroom experiences) and informal (family, home life, social interaction with peers). An impressive list of theorists in the fields of child development and educational psychology have provided an abundance of information on the conditioning that the student brings into professional study.

Arnold Gesell, in his studies of child development during the 1940s and 1950s, brought new insights about the individualized ways in which people learn, live, and deal with the responsibilities of life. His research on developments during infancy and early childhood emphasized particular styles of learning that manifest themselves from birth and may exercise a major influence on the student's mind throughout his or her career.[3]

Jean Piaget, in his rigorous observations of the developing infant and child, offered valuable inputs that must be reckoned with, whatever the educational level.[4] In his view, human beings advance their intellectual potential by the manner in which they respond to the environment. He described how children develop a scheme of action derived from their experience and apply it to each new object and situation. This process he called *assimilation*. When the environment is not responsive to the child's experientially based cognitive schemata, Piaget observed that the child seeks new modes of behavior in order to adapt successfully to unknown environmental demands. This behavior is known as *accommodation*. Except in very young infants, this process is manifested in behaviors such as exploration, questioning, trial and error, experimentation, and, finally, reflection. Memory symbols and imagination as intellectual operations in the adolescent gradually replace the concrete, overt actions of the younger child. This process results in *adaptation* to the environmental demands. Simultaneous with adaptation is the process of *internalization* wherein symbols, imagination, and representation take over in the older child and adolescent.[5] "Thinking, including its memory aspects, grows gradually through the internalization action."[6] What we gain from Piaget's theoretical frame is the importance of each person's activities and the ability to organize them in relation to opportunities afforded within the environment.

The educational theorist Jerome Brunner offered still another set of formulations that warrant thoughtful consideration. His contributions notably apply to the instructional side rather than directly to the learner. The interrelationship between the formulations and the individuals for whom they are designed is very clear. Bruner's theory of instruction has four mandates:

1. A theory of instruction should specify the experiences which most effectively implant in the individual a predisposition toward learning.

2. A theory of instruction must specify the ways in which a body of knowledge should be structured so that it can be most readily grasped by the learner. "Optimal structure" refers to a set of propositions from which a larger body of knowledge can be generated. Structure must always be related to the status and gifts of the learner.

3. A theory of instruction should specify the most effective sequences in which to present the materials to be learned.

4. A theory of instruction should specify the nature and pacing of rewards and punishments in the process of learning and teaching. The movement is toward the intrinsic rewards inherent in solving a complex problem for oneself.[7]

Bruner emphasized that students should be given an understanding of the fundamental structure of what they are to learn. "To learn structure, in short, is to learn how things are related."[8] The teaching and learning of structure, rather than simply the mastery of facts and techniques, is the center of the classic problem of transfer.[9] He then advances his thesis that mastery of the structure provides the ability to transfer principles. Hence, it is the initial learning of a general idea rather than a skill that provides the possibility for recognizing subsequent problems to which the idea can be applied.[10]

Ralph Tyler, whose work in curriculum building is well known, is still another educational theorist who has supported the notion of structure as a significant consideration for those who engineer and build educational plans. In his design he advocated the trinity of continuity, sequence, and integration as essential features.[11]

To conclude this summarized theoretical review of the context in which learning takes place, we turn at last to the work of Sir Charles Sherrington, the renowned British neurophysiologist. He specified three levels of human activity which may be translated to specify levels of reality as experienced in the social processes: the *cognitive*, the *verbal*, the *human act*.[12] The human act is considered the most objective; the cognitive the least objective. This framework places the field experience at the third level of reality because it involves the human act, signifies experiencing and involvement, and affords presence learning which requires response behavior.

SOCIAL WORK EDUCATORS AND STRUCTURE IN FIELD LEARNING

Social work educators have emphasized the need for building structure into field instruction. They favor a graduated sequence of learning demands commensurate with the student's knowledge base. While promoting focused learning objectives for field as well as class, they ordinarily eschew the acquisition of skill as a serious goal of social work educational programs.

> The potential solutions to the problem of vestigial apprenticeship training in field instruction lie not only in the design of learning experiences but also in the teaching methods by which the learning experiences are proffered.[13]

Margaret Schubert warns that exclusive concern with skill could cause regression to apprenticeship. She makes a sharp distinction between the apprenticeship emphasis on procedures and the educational emphasis on the principles underlying the procedures.[14] Stressing conceptual learning as a characteristic of professional field instruction, Finestone cited as a precondition for conceptual teaching that "... the field instructor is clear about selected concepts and generalizations that are to be taught and [that] these concepts and generalizations are related to those which underlie class content."[15]

Still another social work educator, Sidney Berengarten, identified different patterns in normal learners in the field experience.[16] His classification system identified: (1) the "doer" who learns primarily from repetitive experiences rather than from reflection; (2) the "intellectual-empathic" learner whose style is reflective, imaginative, and self-aware and whose performance shows a repertoire of helping capacities; and (3) the "experiential-empathic" learner who moves from initial stress and anxiety to evidence of intuitiveness and reflectiveness as he or she becomes responsive to given client situations.

At any rate, whatever framework serves us in studying this aspect of the curriculum, field instruction places the student in the immediate presence of the phenomena under consideration, or the sense data. It thereby provides the basic elements of thinking and doing in a framework with constant feedback, one to the other, the flow moving in both directions. "Such a state would utilize the power of generalizations built on sense data and regularly corrected in the milieu of sense data."[17]

In exploring the topic of structure, the time structure of block versus concurrent field instruction will be reviewed; then some of the major field instruction structures currently being used, including developments of the last two decades will be briefly presented. Among the new ventures, the training center as an environment for field learning will be presented in detail because of my familiarity and personal experience with this format. The presentation will indicate that the decision to change the basic structure of field instruction is a serious one when undertaken and acted on. Conviction by the school that its mission in social work education can best be fulfilled in this manner is essential. The rationale for change, and clarity about how this idea can be developed within a curriculum context, must precede implementation of the plan. The objective is a structure that is operative and productive. The odyssey of one school will in some way symbolize what any school experiences in moving into the new and unknown. However, it should be noted that behind such an evolutionary process is the studied consideration of the various factors that influence a school's choice of a structured plan for field instruction. Major factors include: (1) the school's conception of the graduate it wishes to produce; (2) the school's philosophy of professional social work education and its conception of the educational task that will implement that philosophy; (3) educational assumptions about the learning process; (4) the educational focus of field learning as it relates to responsible entry into the profession; and (5) manpower, community agency, and financial resources available to mount the desired structure.

BLOCK VERSUS CONCURRENT FIELD INSTRUCTION

The controversy regarding the relative virtues and potential drawbacks of block versus concurrent plans of field instruction has been present since the early days of social work education. For the most part the argument has remained at the discussion level, with advocates ready to advance support on either side. The adoption of one plan instead of the other is often a question of expediency due to geographical accident rather than consideration of the merits of the chosen plan.

Eleven of thirteen block-plan graduate schools that responded to a survey conducted as part of a doctoral dissertation indicated the lack of adequate or appropriate field placements in the vicinity of the school as a major factor in its adoption of the block plan.[18] The temptation may be to impose "order and logic on activities in retrospect" and hence rationalize the scheme. Whatever the basis, there is an absence of definitive studies to evaluate the relative efficacy of the two major time-structured arrangements for field instruction. Writings remain at a descriptive level. Proponents of each type are avid advocates of their respective plans. The field instruction plan adopted by schools may be one of the sacred cows of our profession not to be tampered with lest we be judged iconoclasts. The fact that both schemes have produced effective social workers is proof that there is not "one way." Newer explorations may focus on the relative advantages of one plan as contrasted with the other in terms of particular goals, student background and level, and similar variables. At present, social work educators who have done serious thinking and study on field instruction have furnished useful and convincing materials that support one or the other of the plans. Their conclusions are usually derived from their individual experiences with a particular plan and provide evidence of its value.

Margaret Schutz Gordon considers that concurrent field instruction affords the greatest advantage in providing "learning experience in the field far closer in time to cognitive learning of the elements of knowledge."[19] She cites "partializing" as another sound learning principle that is furthered by this plan. This concept enables the student to gain a firm grasp of knowledge in pieces as he or she moves along, provided that the parts are seen in the context of the whole; thus, the student is given many available pieces for use in a live situation that requires field service responsibility.[20]

She points out as additional advantages reinforcement in a relatively short period of time following original learning, opportunity for application of knowledge in a variety of situations, and opportunities for immediate evaluation of the extent of learning and for applying correctives where needed. Also, the opportunity afforded for feedback allows for a revelation of knowledge that has not been fully grasped and for the introduction of new experiences by the field instructor so that learning of a given concept can be strengthened.[21]

Supporting the effectiveness of block placements, Alice Selyan considers that the dominant theme distinguishing the block plan is the concept of gestalt. "The student in the block plan is involved in a total way in a total environment and becomes, for a predetermined and specific period of time, a fully interacting part of that environment."[22]

Selyan then balances the benefits with the hazards of total immersion into the agency culture and responsibilities and warns against the pull toward apprenticeship which exists in this milieu. She sees the safe-guarding of the student's experience and the reinforcement of his or her role as learner as of paramount importance in the field instructor's role. Thus, she emphasizes the conceptual approach to the processes of treatment and cautions the field instructor against taking on the "guise" of a worker whose primary task is the management of a caseload.[23] Further supporting the virtues of the block plan, Selyan deems as a positive the opportunity to integrate classroom content in one concentrated period so that the student is equipped with a body of knowledge and a beginning sense of professional identity prior to entry into the field experience.

Somewhere between these two widely separated concepts of field instruction falls the "delayed entry" plan.[24] This plan provides for substantial classroom content before the student undertakes client responsibility. Some plans of this type are not completely devoid of practice experiences but provide for the application of partialized aspects of learning in the beginning before the student formally undertakes a full field instruction assignment. The companion field experience in these instances is just as likely to be the concurrent placement since field instruction format per se is not the target of the preparation; the goal sought is the attainment of an initial body of knowledge before beginning practice.

AGENCY-CENTERED PLACEMENTS

The institution most renowned over the years for providing the setting in which social work practice is learned has been the community social agency. Before social work education became university based, it was in the social agency that the aspirant, as an intern, learned social work practice. The internship was one of trial and error, of observation of the professional at work. These agency professionals continue to be the backbone of field instruction through their traditional roles as teachers of students either on a one-to-one basis or in groups.

Whatever new designs of field instruction are inaugurated, most schools retain the pattern of assigning one or two students to agency staff members who are usually provided teaching time in their work-load. They assume this additional responsibility because of a special interest in teaching and a wish to participate in the time-honored obligation of all professions to educate and induct younger members into its practice.

Given the choice, most schools prefer that a minimum of two students, instead of one, be assigned to an agency placement because of the advantages for both student and field instructor. The student benefits by having a peer who is a companion learner and who opens up informal learning dimensions for both; the agency instructor has the stimulation of two students whose different learning styles and special rhythms and flairs in performance afford leverage and comparison in carrying out the teaching role.

The intimacy of the agency placement for one or two students presents both advantages and disadvantages. On the plus side, this format allows individualized attention to students and the nurturing of their special capacities. Also, the social worker–teacher who is on home ground in the agency provides a model of professional practice. On the minus side, the dangers of apprenticeship are strong. Furthermore, the staff worker must constantly straddle the two worlds of education and practice, with a primary commitment to practice. To educators, this field instructor is the perennial protagonist in the recurring theme of "how best to integrate class and field."

The introduction of student units into social agencies during recent years has added positive dimensions to agency-based learning. These units are taught by field instructors whose primary role is that of educator. These teachers may be agency sponsored and paid or school-assigned faculty members. It is certain that learning opportunities increase in the presence of six to eight learners with a common educational goal. To supplement the traditional individual conference as the primary learning vehicle for the student, additional pedagogical devices come into play, including activities such as the weekly seminar, planned consultations, and didactic sessions that offer relevant content. The assigned instructor is primarily an educator, but within the agency setting he or she has the opportunity to do clinical practice if interested.

The student group is task oriented and productive at any level of learning, either in the first and second years of graduate study or in undergraduate programs. Because of the history of greater utilization of groups at the first-year graduate level, evidence of group effectiveness has been most impressive for this particular year. An acquisition of knowledge and values, an introduction to social problems and human need in its various expressions, and an intellectual grasp of organization, methodology, and interventive strategies are common learning needs of all beginning social work students. The student group under a professional educator emerges as an excellent medium for teaching and learning social work practice.

A SAMPLING OF SOME NEWER FORMS
OF FIELD STRUCTURE

Each experimental form of field teaching is the practice expression of a curriculum focus. That is why each structure has unique aspects and is an integral piece of the total curriculum. A new field structure cannot be introduced in isolation and apart from adaptations and changes in classroom courses. (New wine is not to be put in old casks.)

Cited here in brief are several examples of major innovative thrusts in field learning. In the *service-center concept* teaching-learning, demonstration, and research functions are coordinated with services to a community. The service center, under the control of a school of social work, became the first facility of its kind that was analogous to the teaching hospital or the laboratory school.[25] The social-problem-area concept, as a second-year model, is a one-agency placement with some utilization of an organized group of selected agencies (called a teaching-learning complex in the social problem area) with the school assuming responsibility for educational control of quality. Total class and field curricula are organized around agreed upon perspectives of social work practice. Knowledge and utilization of effective interventive strategies is an integral part of this plan.[26] The social-problem-area concept, as a first-year, school-based model, has educational control in the form of school faculty members as field instructors, curriculum design, and formulated objectives, content, and learning goals. The student in this setting utilizes the problem area primarily as an incidence of need in the community where the existing coping mechanisms are brought into play and the relevant professional social work role is called upon. Although developed and implemented at the first-year graduate level, this format would have much to offer the undergraduate student group.[27] The *autonomous social worker* is conceived of as an "end product" of a graduate social work curriculum. Accordingly, a field structure that engages the student in a learning situation that tests initiative, resourcefulness, and decision-making capacities becomes the environment for learning professional practice.[28]

THE TRAINING CENTER AS A LEARNING ENVIRONMENT

When serious research in field instruction was undertaken at Tulane University,[29] a core group of faculty members was convinced that structure and sequencing could be introduced so that a student's engagement in practice could be articulated with classroom learning. Hence, following a long period of inaction and dissatisfaction with the field program and its ill-fitting place in the graduate school curriculum as described earlier in this chapter, there emerged a new experimental framework that was not dominated by the agency focus.[30] This is to say that, instead of assigning students directly to social agencies to gain their practice experience, the school assumed responsibility for setting up a learning structure in which learning experiences were specifically designed to implement curriculum goals. Community agencies collaborated in this endeavor through careful planning with school faculty members. This coordination made it possible to incorporate into the student's learning services to clients which were appropriate to the function of the respective agencies involved. This was a major breakthrough which meant that the same rigorous appraisal regularly given to classroom courses could be applied in the field.

Within this format of field instruction the focus shifted from the agency and its dimensions as the parameters of practice to a broadened view that incorporated new perceptions concerning the ways in which adults learn.[31] Structured learning experiences fell more into line with the educational demands of the classroom. Apprenticeship learning, which characterized many agency-centered experiences, had often forced the student to cope with demands that surpassed his or her knowledge base and readiness. The student's survival method too frequently was to depend upon a supervisor or field instructor for necessary knowledge and wisdom.[32]

Fundamental to the changes at Tulane were their tenets about field instruction:

1. Field instruction is an integral part of the curriculum.
2. Field instruction is a sequence in its own right, with a body of material to be taught.
3. Field instruction is that section of the curriculum where the availability of sense data supplies the appropriate environment for testing theoretical formulations.
4. Field instruction supplies that mode of learning essential to any professional school—making knowledge available for use.
5. Field instruction serves as a crossroads where new ideas and theoretical formulations about practice can be tested for their efficacy in relation to contemporary and future social work jobs.[33]

An examination of the first-year field instruction sequence pinpointed specific objectives that could be enumerated and standardized. Although this plan was devised for beginning graduate students, the majority of whom had not had work experience, it possessed structural elements that would equally well serve students in undergraduate curricula. The following are the objectives for beginning field instruction in this plan.

1. to standardize content, learning experiences, and instructions so that all students have the opportunity to achieve the minimum basic core of learning;
2. to structure objectives, content, and learning experiences for sequence, continuity, and integration;
3. to teach major concepts of all curriculum areas in the field instruction context;

4. to integrate the content taught in class and field;
5. to achieve effective progression of the student's assumption of professional responsibility;
6. to maintain and develop student initiative, creativity, and independence;
7. to integrate and balance the intellectual and relationship components of the professional role;
8. to teach the concept of "agency" under conditions that minimize individual agency apprenticeship influences.[34]

A companion objective not enunciated in the specific points outlined above was an overall goal of preparing students for job demands of current and future social work practice. At the same time, this plan would equip them with the capability of practicing within at least two of the instrumental technologies (casework, group work, community social work, etc.) at·a major and minor level of beginning competence and provide them with a familiarity with the other phases of practice.[35]

Insight deriving from the concept of class and field as dual modes of learning, the growing body of information about how adults learn, and general concern about preparing social work students for a profession of the future all led to the question, How can the field experience serve these new exigencies?

The formulation of dual modes of learning would conclude that class and field complement and enrich each other and in unison provide for an exponential development in the professional growth of the student. The underlying assumption here is that "the modes are firmly connected on an interdependent scale and that in large part they are controlled by the same dynamics of learning."[36] This plan presumes a unified curriculum for the school—a set of basic concepts to be taught, each to be exploited according to the limits of the most appropriate mode for conveying the content.[37]

Learning theory and social process components include: linkage of the student's present professional education to his or her past living experience so as to maximize the past and harness its positive forces in order to enhance present learning tasks; the importance of self-discovery in expressing the self and finding one's metier among myriad learning opportunities; peer learning and peer validation as significant forces in adult learning; and socialization processes carried on with minimum loss of satisfactory ego functioning.[38]

The mandate from the Council on Social Work Education, "to gain new knowledge and understanding in all content areas of the curriculum," and "diversity and breadth . . . in social work practice," raised some practical issues about field instruction settings.[39] Fundamental questions asked for clarity about what schools are trying to accomplish in field instruction, what is the product being sought in the professional social worker, and what goals will engage the student after completion of the course. The mission of the profession, the philosophy of the school, and the conceptual organization of teaching are focal points in evaluating how field settings serve professional education.[40]

As an alternative to providing student field learning in the traditional agency, which offers a service to specified clientele or deals with specific social problems, Tulane University chose to experiment with the training center, sometimes known as a teaching center. As implemented, the center provided: (1) an enriched learning environment with a corps of teachers; (2) a range of agencies from which selected, appropriate learning opportunities could be drawn; (3) the possibility for students to relate themselves closely to a total neighborhood environment; and (4) a vantage point for defining social problems, identifying differentially the interventive strategy appropriate to problem amelioration, and for teaching beginning practice skills appropriate for intervention.[41]

In this format, student learning opportunities are expanded by a conceptual design of agencies and services into a social service system, organized at the neighborhood level (generic centers, usually at the first-year level) or around specialized types of service giving at the advanced level (such as meeting health service needs in a medical center complex or centered on other community institutions such as the law, the public health system, etc.). Community agencies and services are viewed as individual units with their own integrity but fused into a service system. It is simple enough to identify features of their activities that synchronize with educational objectives of the school. The training center provides a suitable vehicle for teaching the entire curriculum at the level of object presence. There is opportunity for diversity. The burden shifts to the selection and delineation of learning experiences designed to achieve predetermined goals and the learning mode most appropriate to goal attainment. This plan calls for clear development of educational objectives around which to cluster various learning experiences.[42]

This approach makes the educational offerings of specific agencies subordinate to the curriculum of the school, yet it respects and makes maximal use of the agency's integrity and its program. Agencies gain the spotlight on the educational scene because of their contribution to the total picture. Different agencies pursuing their own service commitments contribute in definitive ways to the curriculum mosaic.

The end product calls for curriculum content that links and integrates class and field into a unified whole. Faculty members share common concerns and assume joint responsibilities for utilizing and maximizing the interrelationship of these two learning modes. The class no longer appropriates sole right to set the pace for content presentation with the onus on the practicum to make sure that students "are getting it." The field with a new sense of the clarity and purpose of its mission can identify flaws in timing of classroom presentation of material and bring about changes. A new sense of collaboration of the two dimensions of the curriculum is effected. Interchange of teaching responsibilities to a certain extent by faculty members within the class-practicum rounds out the process of planning, exchange, mutual decision making, and integration.

Once committed to a practicum that is subjected to the same discipline as the class, faculty members relate to the rigors of "planning the sequence, implementing educational objectives, devising learning experiences to reach designated objectives, making decisions about pedagogical devices appropriate to the plans. The continuing work of timing experiences, testing their validity, identifying core concepts to be taught differentially via the experiences available in the different centers, and measuring student progress is omnipresent."[43]

The student may enter the training-center system at many points, to offer services and gain from the educational experiences, according to readiness as measured by his or her knowledge base and the comfort he or she experiences in engaging self. Opportunities exist for the researcher, the advanced student, and those with various educational needs for whom learning experiences can be individually tailored. The range of opportunities afforded in such a teaching center are limited only by the ingenuity and creativity of its teaching personnel.[44]

SUMMARY

The review of structure presented here only grazes the surface of field practicum learning-teaching issues. Exploration of this subject is exciting and challenging because it experiments with the live dimension. Various elements that enter into structure are identified in research and speculation. The issue of practice, or learning by doing, opens up basic questions in education for all of the human-service professions. What is the definition of practice and how are the skills of practice taught? It means attacking the problem in the clinical area and rationalizing certain identified issues so that they become part of the knowledge.

Medicine is a companion profession so often compared with social work in relation to the practice dimensions of its educational scheme. Enormous developments in science, burgeoning knowledge about disease, and the growing body of technological advances to enhance the treatment of disease together pose the basic question of preparation for responsible practice: What is a rational sampling process? How does the clinical know-how become converted into expertise in the young professional ready to carry on the medical tradition? Groping for answers, the medical profession has on several occasions turned its research lens on itself to study its methods of furthering the educational process. The most recent study is the Millis Report on *The Graduate Education of Physicians*.[45]

The social work scene presents similarities. The range and variety of advances in clinical practice are reminiscent of the unfolding practice arena of the 1920s, as a cursory review of current social work journals will show. For example, there is an enormous production of literature about children. How will social work students be introduced to this large practice area so that they can reduce it to their own and choose the aspects for which they have a flair and which fit their competency? What is the sampling process and how can it be taught? What does it mean to pull it all together? The discrete practice act has yet to be rationalized into knowledge.

The study of structure in field practice inevitably introduces the dual dimension of class and field as interlocking components of the total graduate social work curriculum. As issues such as class and field find resolution, new questions and problems arise that call for novel solutions. The basic educational-practice question very likely is not about the class-field dichotomy or axis, depending on how this combination is regarded. Instead, it is the question of content that must be mastered in preparation for successful and responsible practice and how the individual student will integrate this body of content into his or her practice. This may be the most complicated and demanding of the learning issues and one that must be addressed in the future.

NOTES

1. Walter L. Kindelsperger, "In-Service Staff Education," in *Staff Development in Mental Health Service*, eds. George W. Magner and Thomas L. Briggs (New York: National Association of Social Workers, 1966), p. 29.
2. *See* Chapter 2 of this volume by Gordon and Gordon for a review of the frame of reference. It suggests how students learn and covers the three kinds of learning required for knowledge-guided practice, including the third level—learning to "do."
3. Arnold Gesell and Frances L. Ilg, *Infant and Child in the Culture of Today* (New York: Harper and Brothers, 1943), pp. 43–46.
4. Ruth Beard, *An Outline of Piaget's Developmental Psychology* (New York: Basic Books, 1969), Chapter 1, "The Development of Intelligence," pp. 1–17.
5. *Ibid.*, p. 5.
6. *Ibid.*, p. 7.
7. Jerome Bruner, *Toward a Theory of Instruction* (Cambridge, Belknap Press of Harvard University, 1966), pp. 40–53.
8. Jerome Bruner, *The Process of Education* (Cambridge; Harvard University Press, 1965), p. 7.
9. *Ibid.*, p. 41.

10. *Ibid.*, pp. 17–18. Also, *see* Chapter 4 of this volume for a full discussion on curriculum development presented by Ann Pilcher.

11. Ralph Tyler, *Building the Social Work Curriculum*, Report of the National Curriculum Workshop (New York: Council on Social Work Education, 1961).

12. Walter L. Kindelsperger, "Modes of Formal Adult Learning in Preparation for the Service Professions," in *Field Learning and Teaching: Explorations in Graduate Social Work Education* (New York: Council on Social Work Education, 1968).

13. Bernece K. Simon, "Design for Learning Experiences in Field Instruction," *Social Service Review*, Vol. 40, No. 4 (December, 1966), 402.

14. Margaret Schubert, "Curriculum Policy Dilemmas in Field Instruction," *Journal of Education for Social Work*, Vol. 1, No. 2 (Fall, 1965), 39.

15. Samuel Finestone, "Selected Features of Professional Field Instruction," *Journal of Education for Social Work*, Vol. 3, No. 2 (Fall, 1967), 14.

16. Sidney Berengarten, "Identifying Learning Patterns of Individual Students," *Social Service Review*, Vol. 31, No. 4 (December, 1957), 407–417.

17. "Abstract concepts not originated and validated by an individual are less his property than those he has transferred from sense data" (Kindelsperger, "Modes of Formal Adult Learning," p. 41).

18. Alice A. Selyan, "Learning Theories and Patterns in Block and Concurrent Field Instruction," in *Current Patterns in Field Instruction in Graduate Social Work Education*, ed. Betty Lacy Jones (New York: Council on Social Work Education, 1969), p. 88. Selyan is quoting from a chapter dealing with the block field plan from a doctoral dissertation by Ruth Gilpin, "Learning Theories and Patterns in Block and Concurrent Field Instruction," (University of Pennsylvania, 1959).

19. Margaret L. Schutz, "The Potential of Concurrent Field Instruction for Learning," in Jones, *op. cit.*, p. 105.

20. *Ibid.*

21. *Ibid.*

22. Selyan, *op. cit.*

23. *Ibid.*, pp. 88–89.

24. As described in Schutz, *op. cit.*

25. Donald Brieland, "A Social Services Center for a Multi-Problem Community," in Jones, *op. cit.*, pp. 61–64.

26. Mildred Sikkema, "Analysis of Explorations Reported by Schools in the Working Party," in *Field Learning and Teaching*, p. 20.

27. *Ibid.*

28. Unpublished paper and personal communication.

29. A few other schools were making their own changes and carrying out their own experimentation about the same time. These were developments of the late fifties and sixties.

30. Mary Lewis, Dorothy Howerton, and Walter L. Kindelsperger, "An Experimental Design for First Year Field Instruction," *Tulane Studies in Social Welfare*, Vol. 6 (New Orleans: The School of Social Work, Tulane University, 1962), 4.

31. *Ibid.*

32. Helen Cassidy, "Maximizing the Use of Traditional and Atypical Field

Placements" (Unpublished paper presented at the Annual Program Meeting of the Council on Social Work Education, Cleveland, Ohio, January, 1969), p. 148.

33. Helen Cassidy, "The Role and Function of the Coordinator of Field Instruction," in Jones, *op. cit.*, p. 148.
34. Lewis, Howerton, and Kindelsperger, *op. cit.*, pp. 7–8.
35. Cassidy, "Role and Function of Coordinator" p. 149.
36. Kindelsperger, "Modes of Formal Adult Learning," p. 31.
37. *Ibid.*, p. 42.
38. Walter L. Kindelsperger and Helen Cassidy, *Social Work Training Centers: Tentative Analysis of the Structure and Learning Environment* (New Orleans: School of Social Work, Tulane University, 1966), pp. 22–23.
39. *Manual of Accrediting Standards* (New York: Council on Social Work Education, 1965), Appendix I, p. 58.
40. Cassidy, "Maximizing Use of Traditional Placements," pp. 15–16.
41. See Kindelsperger and Cassidy, *op. cit.* Also, Cassidy, "Role and Function of Coordinator," p. 151.
42. Kindelsperger and Cassidy, *op. cit.*
43. As summarized in Cassidy, "Role and Function of Coordinator," p. 154.
44. Kindelsperger and Cassidy, *op. cit.*; Cassidy, "Maximizing Use of Traditional Placements," pp. 19–20.
45. "Medical knowledge has been growing so rapidly that no practitioner can safely rely on what he has learned as a student or consider his own resources as adequate for optimal patient care. It is now widely recognized that for a physician to remain highly competent his education must not terminate at the end of a formal residency but must continue as long as he practices" (*The Graduate Education of Physicians*, Report of the Citizens' Commission on Graduate Medical Education [Chicago: Council on Medical Education of the American Medical Association, 1966]).

13

The Methods of Field Instruction

Carl M. Shafer

Educational research clearly indicates that curriculum organization, course content, and instructional methodology must be closely related to a definition of the professional competence these things are designed to produce.[1] Social work educators, perhaps more than is common in other professions, have been able to identify the knowledge, attitudes, and skills they expect their students to have at the completion of the course of study. Yet, they are aware that the achievement of professional competence frequently has not been realized. In fact, when these educational endeavors have been subjected to scrutiny, the findings suggest that instruction is aimed mainly at the transmission of basic knowledge without adequate connection to skill development.[2] Because the task of integrating knowledge, attitudes, and skills learning falls upon the field experience, it is essential that the educational objectives and the methods of evaluation are clear in order to give coherence to the selection of methodology.

Field instruction should provide the opportunity to apply, validate, and integrate what the student knows and values. Through selected and organized opportunities to practice, the student becomes engaged in an experiential learning process which helps to integrate knowledge and understanding with professional attitudes and skills. These skills include collecting, processing, and interpreting information; using a variety of resources (including consultation); ordering priorities and

215

making decisions; intervening with a situation in order to alter it; and monitoring consequences of interventions to respond appropriately to the altered situation. Hence, knowledge about social welfare programs and issues, the dynamics of human behavior, social work research, and the methods by which services are offered need to be related to field experiences.

Content, learning experiences, and instructional methods in field work should impart basic core learning appropriate to the student's educational level. The interrelationship among the psychological, biological, and social systems, and the social work values that derive from ethical and philosophical assumptions can be highlighted in early assignments. Subsequently, through sequential ordering of learning experiences to ensure continuity of learning, the student is exposed to increasingly complex cognitive and applied tasks which draw upon learning from other parts of the curriculum. It is through this process that cognitive and affective components of classroom and field learning are integrated into practice behavior.

PLANNING FOR FIELD TEACHING

Several elements confront a school in its planning of the structure of a field teaching program and the teaching methods to be employed. Depending upon the view one takes, they may be enabling forces or they may be constraints that limit educational decisions. Nonetheless, they do operate to influence the patterns of arrangements under which field instruction is offered. Perhaps the most obvious influence is the approach a school takes to its mission as an educational institution for the profession. The academic goals it selects, its philosophy and values, and its relationship to the community in which it exists are components that determine the general direction of its curriculum and influence the plan for field instruction. The environmental conditions that exist in the region of the school are another set of factors that operate to influence a field program. Social, economic, and cultural realities present opportunities or constraints to curriculum planning and teaching and determine the direction, focus, and type of field experiences available to students. As identified in Chapter 1, these factors are expressed in a school's program objectives.

A generalist approach to curriculum, for example, would require a structuring of field teaching to advance the interpretation of this practice concept through experiential learning oriented to identification and development of basic direct-practice skills and methods of community intervention. The ability to implement such a program is in turn a function of the range of field-setting choices available to a school. Ways in which either a scarcity or abundance of resources may affect the structure of a field-work program readily come to mind and need no elaboration. It is sufficient to note that program objectives and resources are important determinants in the process of planning and decision making regarding the field course.[3]

The wide range of settings in which students are placed for field instruction includes agencies that differ in auspices, program objectives, flexibility, degree of autonomy, role of the social worker within the agency, and the professional group carrying major responsibility. However, the educational content, objectives for student learning, and standards of instruction and student performance should be appropriate to the expectations of the competence to be achieved for a particular setting.

Finally, the criteria for selection of agencies and field instructors are an important influence on the possible directions of the field-work program. The criteria and the process through which they are developed may vary among schools, resulting in differences in field instruction format, types of agencies utilized, and patterns of field instruction.[4]

PATTERNS OF FIELD INSTRUCTION

Because of the influence of these variables upon educational planning, no two patterns of field instruction are expected to be identical. In some instances, more than one approach to field teaching may exist within a single school's program. However, there are several patterns of field instruction with sufficient conceptual differences to distinguish them from one another in their structure, rationale, and learning objectives.

The teaching objectives in field instruction generally are to assist the student to achieve affective and cognitive learning through a series of sequentially ordered experiences and to achieve the integration of theoretical knowledge with practice. The specific elements contained in this broad objective include: (1) ability to apply knowledge to the processes of problem analysis, planning, and provision of social work services; (2) achievement of a level of skill adequate for responsible entry into professional practice; and (3) development of an attitude of inquiry that can be applied to testing, modifying, and extending professional services and contributing to solutions of social problems. Put another way, the student is expected to demonstrate basic social work skills in assessment, planning, and delivery of service as well as knowledge, comprehension, and attitudes appropriate to professional social work practice.

Patterns of field instruction have been identified using a variety of conceptual models to distinguish the characteristics of each. However, the specific methods of field instruction discussed below represent the major categories found in the literature.[5]

The Apprenticeship Method

This approach utilizes the field instructor as a model for the student. By observing the field instructor and other staff in the agency, the student is presumed to be able to acquire and incorporate the skills and style of the experienced practitioners being observed. The student may be present during an interview conducted by the instructor, be seated behind a one-way mirror, or view a videotape of the instructor's work. The tape offers the added possibility of stopping the action at any point for discussion and review. Usually the episodes of observation are followed by critiques that enable the student to identify the practice principles and theoretical issues associated with the observed interventions. This teaching method frequently is used in combination with other methods. To the extent that it provides the student with direct exposure to skilled practitioners as role models, it aids in the development of an identification with practice competence and contributes to the learning of practice skills. However, if the aim of field instruction is to develop the best capacities of the student and to avoid the destruction of initiative and curiosity, exclusive reliance upon the apprenticeship method would seem to have marked limitations.[6]

Ultimately students advance beyond passive observation to co-therapist status and work directly with clients of their own. Peer observation often becomes a part of the learning and teaching experience in settings that utilize the apprenticeship method.

The Tutorial Method

What might be termed the tutorial method is based upon a close one-to-one relationship between teacher and learner with the field instructor taking a facilitating and enabling approach. Using the individual conference with the student, this method has been a traditional model for field instruction. It offers the student an opportunity to share learning concerns and to evaluate progress with the field instructor. For the instructor, such conferences are useful to discuss theoretical material and assignments and to clarify expectations. The tutorial method also provides an opportunity to deal directly with student attitudes that impair effective work with clients. Helping the student develop insight into the social work relationship contributes to his or her professional growth to the extent that it enhances self-awareness in the student which, in turn, increases the student's use of self.

While the field instructor carries the chief responsibility for teaching, opportunities for interaction with other staff within the field agency or in other professional settings gives the student exposure to other professions and staff with varied perspectives. In this way the student is able to participate in and evaluate with the field instructor various models of intervention. Such exposure assists the student to develop an understanding of the unique contribution of social work among the helping professions, helps the student develop appreciation of the roles other professions play, and prepares the student to work cooperatively and in collaboration with others.

Within this model of field teaching, a range of teaching materials and methods may be introduced. Selected case assignments are discussed in individual conferences based upon recordings or other materials presented by the student. Case presentation in staff or student group meetings for discussion and consultation often is used to supplement individual conferences.

In the tutorial method, direct service experiences are most frequently used in preparing students for practice. Work with individuals, families, and small groups have tended to be the most common learning experiences in field work. Field instruction in community organization and in social work administration usually is limited to the few students having strong or special interests in these areas of learning. The field experience helps these students develop analytic, interactional, and technical skills; in addition, administration students are preparing for roles in supervision, staff development and training, program development and analysis, and program management. The community-oriented field experience offers the student opportunity to identify community needs outside professionally defined services, exposure to a variety of interventions in a community setting, and experience in assisting an agency to examine the relevance of its service to some community problem.

Some experiences for which there may not be situations available that are timely for student learning require laboratory or simulation experiences as a substitute. In a simulated experience, the student is placed in a situation that is analogous to some aspect of reality with a problem designed to draw upon the student's knowledge in initiating and carrying through a series of inquiries, decisions, and actions. Although the problem can be presented in a standard form to each student, it should be designed to evolve in a variety of ways dependent on the unique interventions made by each participant.[7]

Generally some form of recording is used by the student as a basis for discussion of his or her work as well as to assist in developing objectives with clients, to assess problems presented by clients, and for purposes of evaluation. The student's application of learning to practice, the interactions between the student and clients, and the development of professional attitudes may be revealed in the recording. Process, summary, and audio and video recordings are some of the usual ways in which the work of the student may be presented for discussion with the field instructor. Some instructors prefer verbal presentations by the student as a more efficient and constructive use of supervisory time. The method selected is perhaps best left to the individual preferences of student and instructor since there are no established criteria for determining the most effective way of conveying what occurred in a professional encounter. Audio-visual recording, while it records actual behaviors of the participants, does not reveal what the student might have been thinking or feeling. In combination with written or oral commentary from the student, however, it can be a powerful teaching-learning tool.

The following example illustrates the process of instruction by the tutorial method.

> Mr. R. was a first-year student who had had no experience in social work prior to coming into graduate school. He displayed unusual sensitivity to clients' feelings and at times revealed startling insight into the meaning of the behavior of others. However, he was oblivious to the way in which his insecurities, which stemmed from his status as a beginner, created impediments in his work.
>
> He brought to the conference hour a question regarding the way he should have responded to a client's inquiry about his personal life. He had recorded an interview in which the client had asked him whether he was religious. He had responded by asking the client why this mattered to her. She had stated that she could not accept anyone's imposing strong religious views upon her. The student had then directed her through questions to explore the source of her feelings about religion but had evaded a direct answer to her question.
>
> The instructor asked the student to talk about his views regarding revealing himself to others. The student referred to the literature dealing with the professional role and the importance of objectivity but finally said it made him uncomfortable to not be able to give direct answers. The instructor agreed, pointing out the difficulty for clients to respond to someone who is unemotional, aloof, and unrevealing of himself. This gave the instructor the opportunity to enunciate the principle that one should not use the hour for gratification of personal needs, but responding to a client's direct inquiry does not abrogate the professional role. In fact, in every encounter with clients something is revealed about the social worker. Hence, the social worker should answer the question or give the reasons for not answering.

In this illustration, the problem brought by the student was related to his beginning insecurity in a new professional role and to his effort to integrate learning with doing. His personal discomfort was utilized to help him move to some resolution of what appeared to be conflict. The instructor clarified the underlying principle and confirmed the student's own decision to be open.

The Clinical Treatment Method

An approach significantly different from the tutorial method deserves separate mention. Because it goes beyond teaching and undertakes the task of producing change in the student, an appropriate term for it might be the clinical treatment method. This approach grew out of a concern "not only with the knowledge imparted to students but also with their personality growth."[8] Since most models of treatment are conceptualized in a nonjudgmental framework, it is difficult to imagine a situation in which education, an evaluative process in part, can be combined with therapy. An example serves to identify the area in which instruction ends and treatment (preferably by someone other than the field instructor) should begin.

> A second-year graduate student described in detail her work with a middle-aged woman. The field instructor noticed that the student had difficulty recalling what had occurred in interviews without frequent reference to her notes and that her comments to the client seemed to be uncharacteristically curt. The student had become concerned about the client's increasing resistance, lack of progress, and thinly disguised hostility toward the student. The field instructor noted a similar attitude on the part of the student toward the client. The student responded immediately with a torrent of words describing how irritating she found this client who reminded her of an older sister with whom she had a strained relationship. In the discussion on her feelings, the student recognized the unresolved conflict with which she would need help. The field instructor tactfully supported the idea.

Pointing out that the student's dislike for the client placed her in a conflicting rather than helping relationship with the client was instructional. Dealing with the reasons behind the student's reactions and behavior were matters to be taken up in a separate treatment situation. Because there can be close overlap of the two roles at times, it is important that field instructors be able to identify when the needs of the student are outside what is appropriate for the educational aims of field instruction.

Group Field Instruction

This teaching method permits broadening the scope of the learning experience to include consideration of the learning dynamic of the student group itself. Seeing the student unit as a group enables the students to analyze their own group in terms of its development and process. There also may be opportunities for learning enrichment through sharing with peers. This method should be confined to small groups of students, perhaps no more than six, in order to give each the opportunity for full participation. As students become more experienced and advanced in their practice, the possibility of peer supervision may develop within the group.

  The advantage of this method is the richness provided by peer learning. The presentation of case material to the group by each student multiplies the experience for all. The group may become a source of support for each student as well as an arena for testing ideas. Often used in combination with individual conferences, the group method offers the benefits of both intensive individual examination of the student's work and more generalized group discussion.

For undergraduate students, group supervision is useful because of the opportunity to expand the individual experiences of the beginning student by exposure to the experiences of others. It also provides group support that may be helpful. The instructor may wish to utilize the group to help students integrate their practice experiences with knowledge from other courses. Both affective and cognitive learning are combined in the group experience.

Graduate students' learning needs would seem to require individualized instruction that the group method cannot provide, particularly for students with advanced, specialized interests. Frequently, both the tutorial and group methods are used in combination. The individualized learning gained through the tutorial method is supplemented by opportunities to share with peers and reinforce learning.

An example which illustrates the combination of both methods is a report of a group meeting in which four students and their field instructor discussed the problems of termination.

The field instructor presented several criteria for recognizing that a client may be deciding to terminate service. Prior to the meeting, one of the four students had dealt with this issue in his individual conference, in relation to a client who had begun raising questions about continuing service. In the group meeting, the student revealed his personal feeling of satisfaction in the progress the client had made but also brought up his feelings about ending. The other students readily joined in this discussion, sharing similar feelings they were experiencing. Eventually, the group discussion picked up on the factual (cognitive) material the instructor had introduced, and the group members were able to apply it to some of their own clients.

The field instructor had seen in the individual conference with the first student an opportunity to bring the subject of termination to the group. In the group, the student felt free to share his feelings which brought the discussion to an affective level before the factual material could be discussed in a meaningful way.

Team Teaching

Team teaching, another method of field instruction, may take several forms. In some instances, one field instructor takes major responsibility for the student's learning experiences while one or more other staff members supervise the student in specific or specialized practice areas, such as work with children, family therapy, or work with groups. In complex settings such as hospitals, students may have a preceptor to whom he or she is assigned on a ward for supervision. However, selected client situations are discussed with the field instructor on a regular basis.

Another approach utilizes two or more field instructors with equal responsibilities for the student. An example is the instruction of a student placed in one agency giving direct services and in another agency requiring work in the community. Equally shared teaching also may occur when the student works in two distinctly different departments within the same agency such as the inpatient and outpatient departments of a community mental health center.

Team teaching approaches usually require coordination between the instructors to assure that the student is able to integrate the separate experiences. Frequently a regularly scheduled group meeting with students and field instructors serves to support the team teaching method. As with any method, the team approach requires prior planning in order to ensure a learning experience that will have coherence and will meet the student's learning objectives.

SELECTION OF STRUCTURE AND METHODOLOGY

In organizing the field work course itself, a framework for structuring such a course has been suggested based upon three general dimensions.[9] First, Schubert identifies the level of responsibility, ranging from observation to supervision itself, as the first of these structural categories.

The second dimension is the level of intervention such as individual, family, small group, community group, and larger organizations. Specific attributes of the individuals at each of these levels might be considered variables. Age, ethnicity, socioeconomic status, and type of problem are examples of the subcategories for each level of intervention.

Finally, the level of performance expected might be a guideline for assignment selection, timing of exposure to specific experiences, and measurement of progress. The assessment process should be continual and goal oriented throughout the course and should always include the student as a participant. Since the students' learning requires that they develop and improve their assessment skills with themselves as well as their clients, evaluation should be based upon standards considered minimal for competent practice. The areas that may appropriately be designated for evaluation include a student's: (1) use of learning opportunities; (2) adjustment and management in the agency; (3) integration of professional functioning; and (4) skills.

The student's use of learning opportunities should lead to the development of ability to identify, conceptualize, and integrate knowledge of principles, theories, and methodology appropriate to his or her level of learning. In addition, the student should demonstrate the capacity and motivation for independent study and action. Central to this learning is the field instructor who carries responsibility for designing a sequence of learning experiences with which the student may integrate his or her developing knowledge base with skill development. The method selected for teaching should be consistent with these objectives.

The guides to curriculum design for field instruction help to define what the student is going to be doing, the client size with which he or she will be working, the demographic and problem focus of specific assignments, the setting in which the work will take place, and the progression of skill development that may be expected. However, crucial to the design of a field work curriculum is the way in which integration of classroom and field learning is brought together into an articulated learning experience.

Integration of classroom and field teaching requires effective communication between campus faculty and field instructors. Creative use of joint assignments, visits to agencies by classroom faculty, and similar procedures that allow for interaction lead to improved coordination of the student's learning. Experiences with campus-based faculty who teach practice courses in field work agencies have been encouraging and support the idea of an instructional center to promote integration of class and field learning. Advantages of such a facility include opportunities for enrichment of instruction and shared responsibilities through team teaching.

CONCLUSION

In field instruction the learning from other sequences comes together in the experience of offering direct services. Cognitive and affective learning is combined with skill in the analysis of specific service needs, the selection of interventive strategies, and the application of appropriate techniques. Field instruction, therefore, provides the student with an opportunity to practice those skills to which the entire curriculum contributes.

This chapter has reviewed a variety of methodologies of field teaching. It has advocated a systematic approach to the planning and implementation of the field-work course that requires a clear delineation of specific learning objectives and demonstrable skills. These then determine the content and the logical sequence of learning episodes and the selection of setting and teaching method. Modeling, individual tutorial instruction, group discussion, team teaching, and laboratory simulation are methods that may be used and matched with a variety of agency and learning-center settings. Through measurement of progress, the evaluation of the field learning experience may then be determined by the degree to which the student can demonstrate that he or she can do what he or she was expected to be able to do. It should be noted, however, that while a systematic approach to curriculum planning in the field yields obvious benefits, difficulties can be expected when courses depend upon precise definitions of learning objectives. Such planning requires considerable time and some adjustment for teachers accustomed to conventional instructional roles. However, once teachers develop an appreciation for educational principles, they will find it worth the effort to make explicit statements of learning objectives and to plan their courses using these objectives as guides to selection of content, structure, setting, and methodology.

NOTES

1. Benjamin S. Bloom, ed., *Taxonomy of Educational Objectives: The Educational Goals, Handbook I* (New York: David McKay, 1956), pp. 29ff; and George E. Miller, "Educational Objectives," in *Development of Educational Programmes for the Health Professions*, Public Health Papers, No. 52 (Geneva: World Health Organization, 1973), p. 26.
2. Miller, *Idem* , p. 31.
3. Elmer T. Tropman, "Aging Constraints Affecting Links between Practice and Education," *Journal of Education for Social Work*, Vol. 13, No. 1 (1977), 8–14.
4. Eileen Blackey, "Summary: Observations and Questions About Structure," in *Field Learning and Teaching: Exploration in Graduate Social Work Education* (New York: Council on Social Work Education, 1968), p. 62.
5. See Mavin H. Wijnbey and Mary C. Schwartz, "Models of Student Supervision: The Apprentice, Growth, and Role Systems Models," *Journal of Education for Social Work*, Vol. 13, No. 3 (Fall, 1977), 107–113.
6. Rudolf Ekstein and Robert Wallerstein, *The Teaching and Learning of Psychotherapy* (New York: International Universities Press, 1972).
7. Christine H. McGuire and Frederick H. Wezeman, "Simulation in Instruction and Evaluation in Medicine," in *Educational Strategies for the Health Professions*, Public Health Papers, No. 61 (Geneva: World Health Organization, 1974), p. 19.
8. Wijnbey and Schwartz, *op. cit.*, p. 108.
9. Margaret Schubert's three levels for structuring a field course were presented in her paper, "Structured Environment for Learning," at the 1968 Tulane University symposium, Working Party on Field Learning and Teaching, and reported in "Response to the Symposium Discussion on Evaluation" in *Field Learning and Teaching*, p. 55.

14

Integration of Learning in Field Instruction

Donald E. Chambers
Richard Spano

Field learning offers unique opportunities to pursue integration of all the learning occurring in a professional curriculum. The idea sets learned as abstractions elsewhere in the curriculum are required to be reified (acted upon) in field practice. Thus, reification is central to the integration process. The abstractions become ideas about which the learner develops personalized definitions. In this way, the ideas become embedded as part of the learner's world view and, to that extent, the learner's self-identity. According to the Gordon-Gordon learning paradigm described in Chapter 2, unless positive reification occurs it is unlikely that there will be much integration.

ASSUMPTIONS OF THE LEARNING PARADIGM

It is important to recognize that there are strong assumptions and biases underlying this learning approach. One of the more important assumptions is that of a strong rational component in the conduct of social work practice. In the learning paradigm, integration must speak to both the affective (emotional) and cognitive (thinking) levels. Thus, the way the integration problem is discussed here and the solutions proposed are not likely to be compatible with an approach to practice that relies totally on affective concepts, such as "warm personal regard" and "being," as main interventive mechanisms. However, no case is being made here that the affective approaches, as concepts or means to practice ends, are not useful notions.

Another major bias is that the learning process is viewed as learning for doing. The learning-for-doing notion prescribes a step in which the practitioner self-consciously chooses a set of ideas and then examines its utility for grappling with the empirical world. Such a view is not opposed to, but rather subsumes, the learning-by-doing model. It is important to mark this distinction because the learning-by-doing notion historically has been preferred in professional discussion of field instruction problems. This assertion is believed to be well within the spirit of John Dewey's principles; his belief is that learning does *not* simply spring forth fully formed out of the doing.[1] As Gitterman notes, Dewey "urges enabling students to involve themselves in problem solving and personally experiencing the living character of the abstractions. . . ."[2] Learning for doing entails both a theoretical and empirical strategy. The learning-for-doing strategy is considered superior because it avoids the assumption that a practitioner can approach a practice situation without influential stereotypes from prior experience. Since *a priori* cannot be avoided, it is best controlled by keeping it prominently displayed where it can be watched for mischief.

ASSISTING THE LEARNER

How can the field instructor assist the learner at the direct instructional level? The main context for helping students do the integration task lies in helping them through the reification process. Thus, the question becomes how does one go about helping the student reify, that is, self-consciously apply ideas to real situations? It is an odd question, in fact, since students are often told *not* to reify their own beliefs in helping encounters. That advice, in its most direct sense, will not be contradicted here. Certainly, it is a mistake for new learners (or any practitioner for that matter) to assume that their own life experience, beliefs, and conclusions about human behavior are applicable in any and all circumstances. To reify in this sense is naive and wrong-headed, if not destructive. It is simply another version of the notion that "What is good for General Motors is good for the country!"

Unfortunately, the problem is not solved by the simple nostrum ". . . don't reify." That advice is like saying to a drowning person, "Just don't breathe under water." In both cases it is impossible. Professional helping requires actions based on cognitive and affective beliefs, self-consciously selected and reified. The issue for those learning to be helpers is not *whether* but *what* to reify. The view taken here is that the selection of a particular set of ideas, generalizations, or explanations is a crucial practice act and one of the initial steps in conducting a professional helping encounter. It is crucial to the integration of learning because it is here that the learner first begins to extrapolate from "knowings" to "understandings" (and, eventually, to action). This selection problem is ripe with possibilities for integration because so many ideas from the total curriculum package intersect at this point.

For example, the problem of selecting which of several competing idea sets to use to help a client must involve a consideration of the relationship between the client's and the helper's view of the problem. Getting the client's view of the problem requires that the learner act on the ideas learned in a practice class about "listening," about "openness" to others, and so on. It also requires explicitly acting on the view that there are multiple and competing versions of reality, a view that students should have become acquainted with in both the research course material on the issues of theory construction and epistemology and the human behavior course material considering the problem of equifinality or multiple causation. The learner should also have become familiar with the idea that "thinking" and "feeling" are complementary but different means of understanding the world and that clients, like all humans, can be expected to present their view of the world in either or both modes. Practice in listening and openness skills, explicit acting to elicit the client's own unique version of the reality that is identified as the problem, actively listening for the difference between an emotional and an intellectual interpretation of the reality presented by a client, and assessment of a single practice instance using two theories are all examples of extrapolating from knowing learned to behaviors understood in an actual human context. They all require the reification process. They can all be expected to provide experiential feedback that will both personalize the abstraction for future ease in reification as well as sharpen a learner's cognition about it.

The field instructor aids the learner in accomplishing the reification task by several means. First, the instructor helps the learner identify, understand, and focus on the selection task (*what* ideas to reify) as a distinct practice problem. The instructor also helps the student relate the selection task to the problem of "getting the client's view" and helps the student realize that this step is not just a simple utility but is related to a whole complex helping process. It is reasonable to expect that learners will have more problems wrestling with these ideas as a basis for action than wrestling with them at a strictly cognitive classroom level. Field instructors are in the premier position for helping learners accomplish the integration task. Providing a context for that "wrestle" and helping a learner identify the issues and adopt a personal stance toward them is an important way of helping students deal with integration.

The task of selecting knowledge for practice also makes clear the intersection of professional values and the use of knowledge. Client self-determination, for example, is a fundamental social work value. If a practitioner subscribes to that value, it implies that there ought to be strong compatibility between the basic personal values and biases of the client and the biases embedded in the idea sets selected by the practitioner for use in the helping encounter. The view here is that all idea sets describing the human condition have value biases that are relatively arbitrary. If that is so, then it implies that clients have a right to and a role in the choice of the idea sets that will play an important part in shaping their lives. At the least, clients have a right not to be led into encounters calculated to change their personal lives based on value biases *contrary* to those they hold dear. This issue lies at the heart of the intersection of professional values, professional practice decisions, and the use of knowledge in dealing with the human condition. Field instructors can use this issue as a constant and not-so-subtle practice problem for purposes of furthering the integration of all the learning possessed by a student. In this context the student must come to some decision not only in regard to which theory or generalization about human behavior to reify in a particular instance but also about what implications it has for the professional value of client self-determination. For example, a student may be dealing with the problem of a family trying to cope with the deterioration of an aged grandparent living in the household. While the student may find a behaviorist model a perfectly acceptable basis for directing intervention here, this choice must involve a decision as to whose goals the student is working toward. The grandparent may not wish this behavior to be modified. At whose expense shall the social work value of client self-determination be exercised—the aged grandparent, his or her children, the grandchildren?

DEVELOPING COGNITIVE SELF-CONSCIOUSNESS

It is important to note that such reification decisions have a potential for integration that is actualized only when the interrelationships between the idea sets, values, and the concrete situation are self-consciously identified and thought out. Integration implies synthesis, but unless a learner is conscious of interrelating these elements, it is difficult to see how any synthesis can occur. Helping a student develop cognitive self-consciousness is an important item for the field instruction agenda. Learners need training in how to use a reflective rather than a reflex approach to practice. Thus, to the extent learners are helped to achieve a cognitive self-consciousness in the course of the field experience, they are enabled to carry responsibility for the integration on their own shoulders.

In some fundamental way, it is likely that all methods of helping students develop a cognitive self-consciousness reduce to a matter of helping them increase their own cognitive complexity. Indeed, cogni-

tive complexity is a reasonably well verified social-psychological concept, and there is some initial suggestion that it accounts for variability
in the effectiveness of personal helpers.[3] One of the important aspects
of cognitive complexity is the range of possible explanations for a given
phenomenon. This suggests that one of the most obvious methods of
helping students increase their cognitive complexity, and thus their
cognitive self-consciousness, is to help them identify a range of cognitions that could be brought to bear on the problem with which they
are dealing.

The first step in that process is to set out the ideas that are brought
to the helping encounter by the participants without much effort on
anyone's part. It is obvious that both the client and the helper will do
some cognitive processing of material about the situation and the initial
helping encounter. The instructor can help the student develop a
cognitive self-consciousness by constructing a dialogue focusing on the
range of ideas that are being brought spontaneously to the problem, its
human participants, and the helping encounter itself. For example, in
relation to a child's school problems, the appropriate opening questions to the student are: What assumptions are *you* making about
whether the problem lies with the child, the teacher, or the family?
What assumptions is the child or his or her parents making or what
assumptions is the teacher making about the same matters?

The second step is to focus the student-instructor dialogue on
alternative idea sets or assumptions, those which are not spontaneous
but deliberately sought by way of enriching the range of possibilities.
For example, if the student is assuming that the problem is the child's
behavior, then the appropriate guiding questions are, for example:
What factor is it in the child's behavior that produces this particular
response by the teacher? How would a behaviorist explain the relationship? How would a Rogerian explain that relationship?

The first step helps develop cognitive self-consciousness by increasing the student's awareness of the cognitive assumptions that
frame, constrain, and give meaning to the actual responses the student
(and others) is making to the client and the situation. It also increases
processing and that of the client; that is, the impact and potential importance of the way the student actually thinks about the client and the
problem. Helping students understand the consequences of their
cognitive processing is one way of developing their cognitive self-
consciousness.

The second step increases cognitive self-consciousness by actively
engaging students in an important part of the cognitive "work" of
practice. Indeed, they may not be fully aware of the possibility of
approaching social problems from a variety of viewpoints.

A third step in this method is to engage students in the process
of sorting the rival and competing approaches to the helping situation

for appropriateness to social work intervention, client's personal values, client's preferred outcomes, and potential utility with regard to those specific outcomes.

The criteria for selecting a particular idea to guide a helping encounter are many, but for beginning students two should be given priority. The first criteria, selecting idea sets appropriate to social work intervention, entails viewing the phenomenon in particular ways. For example, social work perspective demands viewing the person-in-situation (i.e., the "simultaneous dual focus" on the person, the situation, and the interaction between the two). Idea sets, cognitions with which to approach the particular practice instance, that view only the person, only the situation, and/or only the interaction can certainly be constructed. Such idea sets would not be appropriate for social work intervention, although they would be appropriate for other disciplines or professions. For example, there is nothing intrinsically wrong, from the neurologist's view, of looking at the person as a brain or a spine. The view here is that any idea set that would not allow the simultaneous dual-focus perspective is not appropriate for a social worker.

The second criteria for selection is the fit of the basic assumptions and ideology of the idea set with the client's personal values. It is a reasonably straightforward issue. For example, an approach which involves a fundamentalist Christian in an educational sexual experience with a sex therapist is not likely to be successful, nor is it ethical from the view that social work has a strong commitment to client self-determination and thus a right to have personal values left alone. If a client chooses to ask for help in reorienting personal values and sees that as a basic problem (not an unlikely or even rare problem), it is, of course, a different matter. This criterion is not only a matter of choosing not to use certain kinds of idea sets. A client's personal values may also represent certain kinds of opportunities for use of cognitive sets that, for other clients, would be neither appropriate nor useful. One could usefully assume that theological issues and concepts are important features of some clients' personal value systems. Accordingly, an idea set containing theological elements will help such clients deal with the problems presented in the helping situation.

The central function of the instructor is to engage the student in a dialogue that helps clarify the range of cognitive approaches that are possible and in a subsequent sorting of idea sets according to the above criteria. The final choices are largely up to the student since only the practitioner actually works according to the cognitive set that is ultimately chosen. Obviously there are a number of approaches with which the student practitioner cannot be comfortable. They may not be cognitively mastered, they may not be ideologically compatible, they may simply not be preferred, and so on. Perhaps one of the most interesting student-teacher interchanges comes at the point where such considerations are being discussed, since the professional obligation extends beyond using ideas and techniques that are most comfortable. It also extends beyond using only those ideas and techniques that are known and come readily to hand. Kaplan's discussion of the "Law of the Instrument" is appropriate here. Succinctly put, this law says, "Give a small boy a hammer and he will beat to death everything in sight." Students need to come quickly to the realization that knowing an idea or a technique is not sufficient justification for using it and that this principle applies equally to all ideas and all techniques.

This topic shouldn't be left without observing how frequently phrases such as "the work of practice" and "responsibility" have been used in this chapter. All these earnest phrases obscure the fact that the integration task and its cognitive elements have a joyful, playful aspect as well. The task of selecting an idea set for use in a practice situation is a matter of sorting rival and competing approaches for appropriateness to such considerations as the social work frame of reference, the client's personal value scheme, the client's preferred outcomes, and the helper's attitudes, abilities, and preferences in those same regards. Trivial, capricious, and even ridiculous explanations and idea sets can and should be constructed and included in the array of all that might be useful. Time ought to be made for mental playfulness. Social work practice is better from a joyful perspective. Apart from the fact that they reinforce further effort and relieve tension, playfulness and humor involve the imaginative juxtaposition of elements—putting things next to each other that are not ordinarily thought of as belonging together. A good many experts on the subject believe that juxtaposition is an important element in creativity. Both the act of social work practice and thinking about social work practice usually suffer from humorlessness and lack of playfulness.

The integration we have discussed is related not to children but to adult learners. On that account it seems worthwhile to consider some principles about helping adults learn. Knowles has developed some principles of adult learning for which he uses the term *andragogy*.[4] The principles of andragogy seem entirely consistent with the Gordon-Gordon learning paradigm (knowing-understanding-doing). These principles rest on certain assumptions that emphasize the need for interaction between the student and his or her educational experience. The andragogy notion assumes that as a person matures: (1) the conception one has of one's self changes from dependence to that of a self-directing autonomous person; (2) there is an accumulating reservoir of experience that is increasingly useful as a resource for learning; (3) one's readiness to learn becomes increasingly more oriented to how to perform tasks of social roles; and (4) one expects to be able to use what is learned for problem solving rather than for accumulating knowledge for its own sake.[5]

Andragogy has some direct relevance for students dealing with the integration problem. It suggests that adult learners will come to the field with more *a priori* stereotypes than younger learners and are more ready to rely on them as idea sets by which to guide action. The notion here is not that this fund of experience will always be inappropriate; quite the contrary, it may be extremely valuable to both learner and client. But the instructor will probably find it important (and probably difficult) to engage the student in a process of selecting ideas to guide practice which identifies a large variety of possible choices.

Andragogy also suggests that for adult learners integration will probably be more likely to occur as they experience uncomfortable problems in practice than in preplanned, subject-centered interactions with the field instructor. Another implication of the andragogy idea is concerned with the relationship between the student and field instructor. We have already discussed the notion that the development of certain kinds of skills is important in order for learners to be ready to assume responsibility for the integration tasks they will face in independent practice. Andragogy anticipates that the adult learner moves towards greater independence as a part of the learning process. Eduard Lindeman suggests a new function for the teacher:

> He is no longer an oracle who speaks from the platforms of authority but rather the guide, the pointer-out, who also participates in learning in proportion to the vitality and relevance of his facts and experiences.[6]

CONCLUSION

1. The Gordon-Gordon learning paradigm (knowing-understanding-doing) is useful in investigating the problem of integrating field learning within the total learning experience. It suggests that the reification process is a central context for helping students with the integration task.

2. The reification process itself promotes integration of field learning with the total learning experience for several reasons: (a) it reinforces tentative affective commitment to the idea sets used to guide the action required in field learning; (b) it yields strong feedback experiences which reshape the learner's original way of thinking about the abstractions used as guides to action; and (c) because of the unique experiences in actually using a concept to guide action, the learner comes to create a personalized definition of the abstraction which tends to

make the idea the learner's own personal property through increased personal identification with it.
3. Field instructors can aid a learner in accomplishing the reification task by identifying the major cognitive decisions in practice. Among these are: (a) the selection problem—deciding
which among the many available idea sets to reify in a given
practice instance; (b) decisions concerning the fit between the
client's (or client system's) value and knowledge biases and
those inherent in the idea sets proposed for use; (c) decisions
concerning the links between professional ideology and the
ideology underlying the idea sets proposed for use in particular instances; (d) decisions concerning criteria to be used (bench-
marks) to decide whether outcomes preferred by a client (or
system) have, in fact, been reached and whether, in fact, those
effects can be attributed to the use of the idea sets guiding the
action of the helper.
4. A basic task in field instruction relating to integration is to help
learners develop a cognitive consciousness, a tool necessary
for practitioners if they are to take continuing responsibility for
their future integration needs.

NOTES

1. As quoted by Alex G. Gitterman in "Comparison of Educational Models,"
   in *Issues in Human Services*, ed. Florence Kaslow (San Francisco: Jossey-
   Bass, 1972), p. 27.
2. *Ibid.*
3. James Bieri, et al., *Clinical and Social Judgment* (New York: Wiley and Sons,
   1966), pp. 185–186.
4. Malcolm Knowles, "Andragogy: An Emerging Technology," in *The Modern
   Practice Education* (New York: Wiley and Sons, 1966), p. 38.
5. *Ibid.*, p. 39.
6. *Ibid.*, quoting Lindemann, p. 52.

Part V

SELECTION AND DEVELOPMENT OF LEARNING TASKS

The final part of this book is made up of a single chapter by Dea, Grist, and Myli. This material becomes highly specific, pointing to ways the instructor can help a student identify and select learning experiences from the opportunities which present themselves in social work practice. It is in this part that the book completes its progress from the broad overview of field instruction presented in Chapter 1, through progressively more concrete material in the succeeding chapters, to this final chapter on the actual selection of learning experiences.

Dea, Grist, and Myli recognize that the development, selection, and management of learning tasks require the recognition of the school's learning objectives and support system for field instruction while, at the same time, drawing on the resources of the agency and the strengths of the individual student. The integration of these elements is a difficult task which requires careful planning. These authors helpfully identify some of the questions which the field instructor might consider and point to the implications of different responses to those questions.

Without attempting to develop an all-purpose master list of learning tasks, the authors use a problem-solving framework to organize examples of the practice tasks, educational content, and student learning tasks at each stage of the problem-solving process (i.e., engagement, assessment and planning, intervention, evaluation, and termination). An interesting piece of case material is introduced which serves as a vehicle for demonstrating how an instructor might clearly relate learning objectives to learning tasks in helping the student carry out the practice responsibilities required of the case situation. In a statement that captures the theme of this book, the authors conclude:

The opportunity to shape the professional growth of students is an opportunity to reaffirm one's own professionalism. It is an opportunity to affirm the student's skill in service to others and to reckon with the possibility of what might be. Let us hope that field instructors will pursue excellence with a fervor that ignites creativity in the minds of those we serve.

15

Learning Tasks for Practice Competence

Kay L. Dea
Marah Grist
Ruth Myli

THE DEVELOPMENT, SELECTION, AND MANAGEMENT OF LEARNING TASKS

The development, selection, and management of learning tasks in field instruction are complex activities that require joint consideration of a school's educational objectives, the teaching resources available within the practicum agency, and the unique strengths, limitations, and needs of each student. Although it is possible to define meaningful learning tasks solely across any one of these variables, the ultimate success of field education is dependent upon the creative convergence of all three. The educational objectives of the school define the primary knowledge, skills, and values students must achieve in preparation for practice. Agency policies, structure, and services determine the parameters within which field learning occurs, including the variety of different professional assignments available to facilitate student growth. Finally, the unique needs and career objectives of each student determine the appropriate use and packaging of learning tasks to facilitate personal goal achievement.

In considering each of these three areas, field instructors must recognize that integration does not come easily or automatically. Although logic suggests a natural convergence of curriculum objectives, student needs, and agency resources in support of field learning, the independent forces which act upon student, school, and agency sometimes combine to create conflicting and competitive demands upon students. It is the responsibility of the field instructor to minimize conflict in the packaging of learning tasks and to assist students to mediate between the complex forces that shape field learning.

The following questions should be considered in identifying, creating, packaging, and managing student learning tasks.

Questions Related to the School

What assumptions does the school make about social work practice? How does the school define practice? What models are used to integrate practice? What are the specific knowledge, skills, and values emphasized by the school in student preparation for practice?

Answers to these questions should influence both the content and the structure of field-work learning tasks. For example, a school might define differential levels of social work practice and assume that baccalaureate practitioners generally are employed under MSW supervision, within formal bureaucratic institutions, for the delivery of basic services to individuals and groups. In that case, the learning tasks appropriate to prepare baccalaureate students for practice necessarily would emphasize content related to service delivery, the use of supervision, and the functional use of bureaucratic structures. Since the structure of learning tasks, whenever possible, should provide opportunities for students to learn within the actual roles for which they are preparing, the practice assignments for this example would require that baccalaureate students be given service assignments with individuals and groups within a supervisory framework. MSW students, on the other hand, would be assigned major learning tasks related to the supervisory responsibilities they would be expected to assume upon graduation. In the event that a school defined practice differently and/or made other assumptions about practice, it would be necessary, of course, to modify both the content and structure of field-work assignments to support a different curriculum. The curriculum objectives of the school, then, are of primary importance in determining student learning tasks.

Questions Related to the Agency

Two sets of questions must be considered in relation to agency concerns in the specification of learning tasks. The first set relates to the service objectives of the agency and the responsibilities of students to contribute to the fulfillment of these objectives. The second relates to agency resources available to support student learning.

Questions Related to Agency Objectives. The primary objectives of field instruction are educational, but field instruction agencies must be concerned with the quality of services students provide to consumer groups. Consequently, in defining learning tasks, it is necessary for field instructors to consider the following questions: For what purpose does the agency exist? What are the primary services provided by the agency? To whom is the agency accountable? How do agency structure and policies impinge upon consumer groups, professional staff, and students? In what way can students support the fulfillment of agency objectives?

Consideration of these questions should assure that student learning tasks are compatible with and in support of agency objectives. In addition, this consideration should assure that attention is given to the development of student skills in the functional use of institutional and bureaucratic structures. Since social work is practiced in institutional contexts for the purpose of improving, supporting, and enhancing relationships between people and environment, it is imperative that students learn to use institutional structures in support of consumer needs and to resolve dysfunctional relationships between institutional systems and consumer groups. These objectives can be accomplished only if students learn to work within institutional systems. Thus, it is crucial that field instructors consider agency goals, structure, and policies in defining student learning tasks.

Questions Related to Agency Resources. The second set of questions related to field agencies in the development of learning tasks focuses upon agency resources available to support student learning. How broadly does an agency define and sanction services to consumer groups? What are the specific services to which students have access? How flexible are agency structures to accommodate the special learning needs of individual students? To what extent are special restrictions imposed upon the use of selected agency resources? What physical facilities, clerical services, and other concrete resources are available to support student activities?

Answers to these questions are needed to plan for the efficient and effective use of learning opportunities in a field instruction agency. In considering the resources available to support students, however, caution should be given to assure that resources do not dictate learning objectives. It is easy to fall into the trap of assuming that an agency can provide learning experiences only within the context of existing service structures and resources when in fact a creative field instructor may utilize existing resources in unique combinations to form new patterns of service delivery. Also, field instructors may negotiate for modifications in agency policies and structure to facilitate special educational programming and to stimulate the creation of new agency resources. Finally, supplementary experiences may be developed outside the formal structure of an agency to assure that student educational objectives are achieved.

In the use of social work cases as a resource for learning, the specific case to which a student is assigned usually is not as important to student learning as is the specification of learning tasks to be addressed within the context of case management and intervention. Every social work case provides opportunities for a variety of learning experiences. It is the responsibility of the field instructor to help students package those experiences in a manner that assures maximum growth in the student and appropriate service to agency consumers. This requires that the field instructor be cognizant of curriculum objectives and student needs in helping the student plan potential interventive strategies for agency consumers. More importantly, it requires the ability to help students link theory to practice—to apply theoretical concepts in actual service situations. Success in each of these areas requires an objective consideration of agency goals, services, policies, and structure in the development and management of student learning tasks.

Questions Related to the Student

Perhaps the most important variable to be considered in the development of learning tasks is the student to whom the tasks will be assigned. What are the unique strengths, limitations, and needs of the student? In what way do the student's life experiences and professional goals shape learning expectations? How does the student respond to field instruction? To what extent is the student ready to assume new responsibilities? What kinds of support does the student need to maintain growth?

Answers to these questions facilitate an "educational diagnosis" of student learning patterns and accomplishments necessary to create and organize individualized learning programs. These "student assessments" enable the field instructor to develop and assign learning tasks selectively in response to each student's needs and readiness for growth. In addition, these assessments enable the field instructor to protect the mutual interests of student, agency, and consumer by sequencing student learning experiences in relation to emerging student competencies and existing support systems. It is evident that the student is at the center of field work education. Consequently, the central concern in developing learning tasks must be that of assessing student motivation, capacity, and opportunity for learning.

ILLUSTRATIVE LEARNING TASKS

As indicated previously, the learning tasks to be incorporated into a social work field practicum should be determined by the specific curriculum objectives defined by the school, the structure and service objectives of the agency, and the individual strengths and limitations of the student.

Given the diversity and uniqueness of educational institutions, agencies, and students, it is impossible to develop a master list of learning tasks appropriate for all social work educational programs. In fact, it is difficult to specify mandatory field learning tasks for all students enrolled in any single educational program since field instructors must tailor assignments to capitalize on the strengths of individual students and agencies.

The learning tasks developed in this section have been specified in relation to a problem-solving framework for social work practice. They are designed to illustrate potential educational assignments that field instructors may use to support student learning across various stages of problem solving. For the purpose of this chapter, these stages have been defined as engagement, assessment and planning, intervention, and evaluation and termination. While these stages are analyzed separately, it is recognized that they overlap and interact dynamically in practice.

The format adopted to analyze each of these stages (Figure 15–1) emphasizes a conceptual definition of each, the identification of practice tasks students must master to work effectively within each stage, and identification of illustrative learning tasks that might be selected to aid students in mastery of knowledge, skills, and values associated with practice tasks. The learning tasks may be selected singly or in combination to teach both the practice tasks and the educational content.

APPLICATION OF LEARNING TASKS
TO PRACTICUM ASSIGNMENTS

Reference has been made to the fact that the specific social work cases to which a student is assigned are not as important to student learning as the particular learning tasks identified and developed within each case. Also, it has been noted that field instructors must select from each case those learning tasks appropriate for the unique needs and level of readiness demonstrated by the individual student to whom the case has been assigned. The case material which follows has been selected to illustrate the way in which learning tasks may be packaged to facilitate student learning.

FIGURE 15–1
A Planned Change Approach to Student Learning Tasks

1. *Engagement*

Engagement is the beginning phase in the problem solving process during which the primary attention of both student and client system is directed toward exploring needs and eligibility for service.

Practice Tasks (professional competencies related to the educational objectives of social work education)	*Educational Content* (knowledge, skills, and values to be mastered by students in preparation for practice tasks)	*Typical Student Learning Tasks Related to Engagement* (activities assigned to students to facilitate mastery of educational content)
The professional worker must be able to respond to different types of referral systems with empathic communication and knowledge of agency resources.	The student must develop knowledge of voluntary and involuntary referral systems and the impact of each on consumer groups. Knowledge of agency purpose, target populations, policies, and service structures are necessary to determine consumer eligibility for service. Empathic communication is needed to engage client systems in exploring service requests.	Attendance at individual and group orientation sessions to review agency goals, structure, and services Attendance at agency staff meetings to observe agency structure and process Selected review of agency service manuals, records, and other reports for the purpose of assessing the application of eligibility requirements to consumer requests
The worker must be able to establish a benign environment for professional intervention.	Knowledge of and skill in using the relationship principles of confidentiality, non-judgmental attitude, acceptance, and self-determination are necessary to establish a benign environment. Students must recognize, value, and respect individual differences in consumers.	Observation and analysis of intake interviews conducted by regular staff Role playing for the purpose of developing therapeutic communication Case assignments involving client-system initial contacts with the agency

The worker must be able to explore service requests through responsive listening and relevant questioning designed to collect data related to client system needs.	Responsive listening and relevant questioning require skill in maintaining a focus on the needs and problems of client systems. Students must understand and have skill in using the principles of individualization, purposeful expression of feelings, and controlled emotional involvement.	Attendance at individual and group conferences with field instructor for the purpose of reviewing principles of individuality, acceptance, and self-determination with analysis of application to own case assignments
The worker must be able to clarify and interpret agency resources and services.	The student must be able to assess agency resources available to meet specific client system needs.	Completion of process records and/or use of audio and video tapes to facilitate study of self in interaction with client system
The worker must be able to mobilize referral and other resources.	The student must have knowledge of community resources and social policies. Skills in preparing client systems for referral, in making referrals, and in following up referrals are needed to assure effective use of community resources.	Review of professional codes of ethics and agency policies concerning confidentiality Use of individual conferences with field instructor to identify the way in which personal values, expectations, and attitudes interact with those of client systems

2. Assessment and Planning

Assessment consists of analyzing the client situation to determine the nature of services needed. Planning entails the specification of interventive goals to be achieved and the social work methods to be used in this goal achievement.

Practice Tasks	*Educational Content*	*Typical Student Learning Tasks Related to Assessment and Planning*
The professional worker must be able to organize and evaluate data from different sources in relation to service requests of client systems.	The student must understand sources of data available to assess needs of client systems, and develop techniques for obtaining data from these sources. The student must develop skills in organizing data in relation to problems, needs, and service requests of client systems.	Review of intake and other data across own case assignments for the purpose of identifying service requests, problems, and needs of client systems, noting additional information needed for case assessment and planning, and for the purpose of identifying potential resources available to support different interventive strategies
The worker must be able to assist client system to specify and prioritize needs and goals to be achieved.	The student must be capable of recognizing and responding to verbal and non-verbal messages of client system needs. A knowledge of and skill in using the principles of "purposeful expression of feelings" and "acceptance" are needed to assist client systems to express both negative and positive aspects of a problem situation. In order to assess and to prioritize needs and goals, the student must have knowledge of the way in which various systems impact upon problems, including institutional structures, social welfare policies, and the behavior of individuals and groups.	Completion of social studies requiring the collection, analysis, and recording of data in support of interventive plans Negotiation of interventive contracts with client systems in which objectives, services, and role responsibilities are specified across an appropriate framework of time Use of process recordings, video tapes, and audio tapes to assess own skills in facilitating involvement of client system in planning intervention. Use of consultation and collaboration to assist in planning for case managements

The worker must be able to identify the personal and environmental resources of client systems available to meet needs and objectives.	The student must have knowledge about functional and dysfunctional behavior and be able to apply the principle of "individualization" in identifying strengths and limitations of client systems. The student must have an understanding of bio-psycho-social factors related to different client systems and an ability to identify their impact on motivation, capacity, and opportunity for service.	Use of individual and group instruction for the purpose of testing out proposed intervention strategy Assists client to identify those areas that need modification and to identify strengths which promote social functioning
The worker must be able to develop alternate strategies for professional intervention by reviewing viable options with client system and matching service needs with available resources.	The student must have knowledge of agency services and community resources available to meet client-system needs. Skills to be developed include the ability to involve client system in planning and implementing action for problem resolution (self-determination) and the ability to package resources in unique combinations in support of client system needs (individualization).	
The worker must be able to select interventive strategies and specify measurable outcomes to evaluate progress in goal achievement.	The student must develop the ability to recognize capacity of self and client systems to implement different interventive strategies. The ability to work within a variety of different interventive approaches is needed to	

assure that planning is primarily in response to client-system needs rather than student skills. The student must have an openness to evaluation, a commitment to research inquiry, and basic skills in data analysis to facilitate ongoing assessments of client progress and interventive methods.

3. *Intervention*

Intervention is the process of managing worker and client system activities to support functional behavior and institutional structures and to modify dysfunctional behavior and structures toward the achievement of specified goals.

Practice Tasks

The professional worker must be able to intervene with individuals, groups, and communities in the delivery of service to client system.

Educational Content

The student must be able to assess the appropriateness of different social work strategies and methods in working with individuals, groups, and communities. Knowledge of and skill in using different interventive models must be developed to facilitate flexibility in responding to client system needs and service requests.

Typical Student Learning Tasks Related to Intervention

Works in continuing case assignments involving individuals, groups, and communities

Demonstrates use of communication skills in interaction with client system for the purpose of supporting and reinforcing functional behavior. Includes use of supportive techniques such as sympathetic listening, reassurance, and encouragement

The professional worker must be able to reinforce client system use of self and environmental resources for goal achievement.	The student must understand the apprehension and uncertainty which accompany change and their effect upon efforts to modify personal and environmental systems. Skills must be developed in identifying, developing, and reinforcing support networks.	Uses process recordings, video tapes, audio tapes, and other forms of recording to demonstrate ability to promote or discourage particular behavior patterns in client systems; to use skills in advocacy; to facilitate therapeutic catharsis; and to promote client system understanding of its behavior and its consequences
The worker must assist client system to recognize and modify dysfunctional behaviors.	The student must develop techniques for clarification and confrontation based on theoretical understanding of dysfunctional behaviors in client and environment.	
The worker must fulfill professional responsibilities to client systems as outlined in interventive plan.	The student must understand the use of self in completing contractual tasks and be prepared to handle relationship elements such as resistance, transference, and counter-transference.	Participation in individual and group conferences with field instructor to identify own feelings about client systems and elements of transference and counter-transference which effect the intervention process
The worker must be able to clarify and reassess the continuing, emerging, and changing needs and resources of client systems for the purpose of redirecting and/or reinforcing interventive strategies.	The student must be committed to an ongoing assessment of forces acting upon client systems. Skills must be developed to identify, assess, and control biases in sources of data used to revise interventive plans.	Writes treatment and diagnostic summaries for use in field instruction conferences and for inclusion in agency records

4. Evaluation and Termination

Evaluation is the ongoing, orderly review of client system progress toward goal achievement. Termination is the process of planned conclusion related to this goal achievement.

Practice Tasks	*Educational Content*	*Typical Student Learning Tasks Related to Evaluation*
The professional worker must be able to assist client system to assess levels of goal attainment and the effectiveness of worker/agency intervention.	The student must be committed to the value of involving the client system in assessing goal attainment, worker performance, and agency effectiveness. The student must have ability to create a climate in which client system is willing to share positive and negative opinions of services received.	Critiques the agency evaluation forms used for feedback from client systems in assessing services received Use of individual and group conferences with field instructor to review evaluation processes utilized by agency, consumer, and students in assessing effectiveness of service and one's own performance
The worker must assess effectiveness of self and agency in meeting client needs and assist agency to use this evaluative data in building and strengthening programs.	The student must acknowledge professional accountability to client system and agency for appropriate delivery of services. The student must understand different kinds of data that may be used to assess self performance and agency effectiveness in meeting needs of client systems. Skill in channeling these data through agency structure is needed to facilitate change.	Explores the meaning of separation with client system in order to individualize termination process Prepares closing summaries for case records Uses various forms of recording to identify and analyze recurring patterns of behavior related to the separations

The worker must understand the significance of separation, a phenomenon in all termination experiences and develop appropriate procedures to assist clients to manage separation.

The worker must be able to assist client systems to anticipate future needs and to identify potentially helping resources. This may include "leaving the door open" to return for additional services by client system. Recognition of goal achievement must be given in support of independent functioning.

The student must have knowledge about the multi-faceted implications of separation including its impact on the vulnerability of different groups and its relationship to past separation experiences and to separations of a recurring and unexpected nature. The student needs to develop an awareness of the level of own resolution to separation experiences.

The student must understand ambivalence as a dynamic of termination. The student must be able to demonstrate expressions of confidence in client system to meet own needs and promote client-system actions, feelings, and attitudes in support of independent functioning. The student must be able to identify and link appropriately community and other resources in support of anticipated needs.

Uses field instruction for purpose of examining own and/or client system's ambivalence during termination process

Assists client system to identify sources of self and environment support

Uses process recording to assess own practice

249

Case Situation

Betty, the eldest of five children, was a pretty and intelligent sixteen-year-old high school junior at the time she was referred to a state child welfare agency for placement in a foster home. In a sense, she was self-referred. She had run away from home following a violent quarrel with her father. She had traveled to the home of a friend "with only the clothes on her back," and it was her friend who had helped her get to the state agency.

At the time, Betty's parents knew where she was, but agreed not to contact her. Also, they agreed voluntarily to release her to a foster home for an indefinite, but hopefully short, period of time. Since Betty was extremely fearful and vocal in her opposition to the thought of seeing her father, the parents agreed that they would not see her until such time as she could tolerate contact with them. They refused to provide financial assistance, but they sent clothes to her friend's home.

Initial contacts with the family revealed that Betty's parents were in their mid-thirties and that they owned their own home in a small community bordering a large city. The family was experiencing some economic pressure, but not of a critical nature. The major family problems centered in parent-child conflicts. Relationships with other children were also strained. Three months prior to Betty's placement, a fourteen-year-old sister had run away from home. No direct messages had been received from her, although a girl friend had reported a telephone call indicating that she was all right. Family efforts to locate the sister had failed, and the parents expressed resignation about her absence. It was the family's decision not to involve the police, recognizing their elimination of one potential source of help.

Betty's departure from the home, however, reopened the anxiety and guilt associated with her sister's running away. The parents were shaken considerably by having two daughters leave home. They were upset that their girls had expressed wishes never to see them again, and they were afraid that their case might end in a court referral. Consequently, they expressed interest in receiving counseling.

As is true in most foster-home placements, Betty was given a medical examination. She was also referred for a psychiatric evaluation to determine the extent to which her family conflicts had caused emotional problems. The medical examination revealed adequate general health and confirmed a story of severe beatings by her father. There were extensive bruises and lacerations over her back. Betty had reported, also, that her father had sexually abused her, but not to the point of intercourse. The medical examination confirmed the accuracy of this story.

In reporting on the psychiatric interview, the psychiatrist described Betty as a frightened, severely depressed girl who found it difficult to distinguish between her own responsibility and her parents' responsibility for the conflicts at home. She was suspicious of people, trusting no one. She frequently fantasized solutions to her problems, and she expressed intense guilt over her family's situation. The psychiatrist cautioned that she was potentially suicidal.

The agency worker, in consultation with the psychiatrist, concluded that Betty needed to be placed in a protected and supportive foster home and that both Betty and her parents should receive counseling.

In early interviews with Betty, the agency worker found that she had strong feelings against leaving the high school in which she was enrolled. Betty said that she liked some of her teachers, that she was getting good grades, and that she had friends at the school. At the same time, she did not want to return home. She was afraid of her father and angry with her mother. She stated that she had run away because she couldn't tolerate them any longer. She pleaded for a foster home in the same school district. In exploring alternatives with her, Betty's eyes lit up at the idea of living with a young couple who had expressed interest in her. She wondered, however, if they would be able to accept her. It was agreed that the home would be given a trial. In taking this action the worker recognized that Betty needed to be involved in making the decision and that she needed to remain in a school setting where she could feel the support and acceptance of a known peer group. Her foster parents were encouraged to involve her in decision making appropriate to her age, such as selection of friends, curfew, and household chores. Casework appointments were scheduled to help her work out her feelings of rejection and personal inadequacies and resolve conflicts with her natural parents as well as to facilitate her adjustment in foster care.

The family with whom she was placed consisted of a twenty-five-year-old father and a twenty-four-year-old mother with two small sons, ages one and three. Although there was concern about the ages of the parents, the home was felt to be the best available choice. The mother was an active leader in a local teenage organization, and the caseworker hoped she would be able to help Betty become acquainted with other teenagers. The father was an easygoing, likable, relaxed person who related well to teenagers. Both parents expressed a desire to help Betty.

Although the original plan was to provide regular counseling to Betty and her family, during the initial weeks of placement little supervision was actually given to them. Some evidence was noted that the foster mother tended to be a perfectionist, demanding much from Betty, but the caseworker was unable to spend time in resolving potential conflicts in this area. It was at this time that consideration was given to assigning Betty to a social work student.

Role of the Field Instructor

In determining the appropriateness of assigning Betty's case to a student it was necessary for the field instructor to assess the following areas:

1. the potential learning experiences that could be packaged in providing services to Betty;
2. the needs of Betty and her two families;
3. the educational needs of the student to be assigned to the case and the student's ability to meet Betty's service needs.

In addition, the following educational objectives, defined by the school, had to be considered in reviewing potential learning assignments:

1. to assist the student to understand agency programs, policies, procedures, and resources as well as limitations in meeting client needs;
2. to help the student accept clients whose lifestyles, values, and ethnic backgrounds are different;
3. to assist the student to define his or her own role and responsibility while clarifying and identifying the respective roles and responsibilities of other individuals within the client system;
4. to assist the student in involving the client in a working relationship and in maintaining client involvement for an optimal time;
5. to help the student develop interventive skills;
6. to enable the student to identify the significance of the Code of Ethics in work with clients.

It was concluded that Betty's case was appropriate for assignment to a student. The field instructor noticed, particularly, that Betty had responded positively to prior agency contacts. Consequently, it was felt that she would be able to provide a student with a positive experience in relationship building. It was noted, also, that the case could provide a student with the opportunity to work with two sets of parents and to work collaboratively with school personnel and other agency staff members. The variety of ages represented by different persons associated with the case, the stages of growth and development represented by Betty, and the dynamics of separation and family conflict were all viewed as rich resources for student learning.

The Student

The student selected to work with Betty was a young, single woman with no previous social work experience. It was felt, however, that she had a natural ability to relate to adolescent girls and that she would be able to work effectively with the parents providing she received good field instruction. Her own stable background was viewed as a strength for potential role modeling.

When the field instructor explored the possibility of assigning Betty to this woman, the student expressed anxiety at being assigned to a case in which "relationships to natural parents were severely strained." She was disturbed with the physical and sexual abuse inherent in the situation and expressed fears that she could never really accept Betty's father.

The field instructor recognized that the student's anxiety was normal for someone who had no prior exposure to the problems displayed by Betty and her natural parents. Her initial contacts with the student were designed to provide her with information concerning the factors commonly associated with family violence and to assure the student that initial contacts with Betty could focus on areas that she was ready to handle. The student was prepared for engaging the client by identifying a variety of concrete services that she could provide to assist Betty in adjusting to her foster home.

Engagement. Given the nature of Betty's problems and the amount of anxiety expressed by the student, the initial learning tasks needed to be focused on engagement activities that could reduce the student's anxiety while developing and affirming feelings of self-worth in Betty. These engagement activities had to prepare the student for extended work with both sets of parents.

Learning Objectives

To develop skills in gathering and assessing information concerning previous services given to client and the nature of client strengths and problems.

Learning Tasks

Review the agency record for pertinent information concerning Betty's present situation with particular emphasis upon prior arrangements between the agency and client system and upon the strengths of Betty and her family (this task should assist the student to increase her respect for the family members—seeing them as persons and not problems).

To develop collaborative skills that can be used to assess client response to termination, transfer, and separation.

Meet with Betty's prior worker to determine the nature of the previous relationship and the potential effects it may have on a new relationship.

To develop knowledge of agency services and how they are selected to meet specific needs.

Gather information about agency services in the area of foster care.

To develop skills in preparing for initial client contacts in a planned and coherent manner.

Meet with the field instructor to plan a strategy for first contact with the client; outline what is known about Betty, what information is needed, what service requests may be of priority, and what can be done to facilitate engagement.

The first interview was conducted with the following learning objectives and tasks in mind:

Learning Objectives
To develop knowledge of the different ways in which separation, termination, and transfer impact on various client systems; to assist the student to understand the social work principle of "beginning where the client is," acknowledging that a client's description of feelings and facts is a dynamic phenomenon.

Learning Tasks
Assist Betty to express her feelings about a transfer to a new worker; help her describe her current situation and identify problems or concerns for continued services.

To develop skills in establishing a benign environment.

Provide a climate of trust and support in which Betty can feel accepted, appreciated, and valued.

To develop a commitment to professional accountability in terms of the student's own behavior, including the acceptance of responsibility to keep promises to clients and to assess the outcome of self-behavior.

Record the process of interventive contacts with Betty, especially noting those areas in which follow-up activities have been promised or have been implied; include both verbal and nonverbal exchange between the student and client system; develop a plan for follow-up activities.

To develop skills in relationship building and a commitment to professional ethics such as confidentiality.

Establish empathic communication leading to a sense of trust between the student and Betty by keeping appointments on time, listening to Betty, and showing respect for her ideas.

The assessment of these engagement learning tasks was a continuous process between the student and field instructor. Regular conferences provided opportunities to review the student's progress in developing professional relationships with Betty, both sets of parents, and other significant persons and institutions in Betty's life. Since the beginning student was somewhat overwhelmed by a situation in which more needs emerged than she was prepared to initially meet, the field instructor consistently assisted her to anticipate "next steps" and to recognize that some problems do not need immediate attention. This was accomplished by helping the student give priority to areas of emphasis during the engagement process.

Assessment and Planning Learning Tasks. Like engagement, assessment and planning are ongoing processes that must take into account the dynamic nature of change in client systems. Students must be given learning tasks that enable them to assess the varied facets of client and environment as they impact on problem resolution. In the case of Betty, it was necessary to assure that student learning tasks allowed for ongoing assessment and planning in relation to her needs and to those of her foster parents and her natural parents. Consideration had to be given, also, to peer groups and other institutional structures of significance in her life.

The following learning tasks were designed to support student mastery of methods associated with assessment and planning:

Learning Objectives

To develop respect for the client's capacity to achieve change including an understanding of the way in which individual differences and capacities relate to client value systems and life experiences. To develop understanding of the principle of self-determination and the ability to apply this principle in practice.

Learning Tasks

Assess the individual strengths and capacities that Betty demonstrates in managing her affairs. Indicate approaches that may be used in reinforcing these strengths and affirming her self-worth. Examples include: a) her ability to remove herself from a fearful situation with her father; b) her judgment in seeking help from friends rather than heedless running; c) her acceptance of the foster home; d) her use of the agency to resolve problems within foster placement and her ability to relate to agency personnel.

To develop diagnostic skills related to client use of defense mechanisms including the ability to differentiate between those causing dysfunctional behavior and those that provide support for psychosocial functioning.

Identify areas of dysfunctioning in Betty's situation. Assess the way in which Betty's behavior contributes to this dysfunctioning. Indicate approaches that may be used to help Betty to modify this behavior. Examples include: a) low opinion of self as evidenced in lack of personal grooming and frequent use of cutting comments; b) depression; c) unreasonable guilt feelings; d) poor communication skills.

Learning Objectives

Learning Tasks

Make a similar assessment to identify behavior that helps Betty function in interpersonal relationships. Identify approaches that may be used to reinforce that behavior.

To develop skills in understanding that every situation has its own dynamics and is in constant change, necessitating continuous involvement in assessment and planning from the first interaction through the termination phase.

Review Betty's present situation in contrast to conditions that existed at the time she fled home. Assess changes that have occurred in her life and their implication for future activities.

To develop an understanding of and commitment to protecting the rights and responsibilities of the natural parents in the delivery of foster care services.

Review goals with Betty and her foster parents to determine if they are mutually understood and accepted. Inform Betty of the worker's need to visit her natural parents. Reassure her of the confidentiality in the worker's contacts. Use the visit with her parents to identify their concerns for Betty and to understand current family relationships.

To enhance skills in assessing the impact of client values, life-styles, culture, and problems upon the professional relationship and the ability to demonstrate acceptance as a social work principle.

Describe the way in which Betty acts during service contacts. Evaluate Betty's own reaction to her behavior. Assess the extent to which the client and worker share similar or different life-styles, values, and culture. Indicate the way in which differences may have influenced the professional relationship including Betty's acceptance of the student.

To enhance skills in assessing and understanding the impact of the student's own values, life-styles, and personal behavior upon the client system.

Review with the field instructor the student's own attitudes, feelings, and anxiety concerning Betty and her natural parents; use this review to identify similarities in the student's background with the life-style, culture, and values of Betty's family in order to reduce the student's anxiety about working with Betty and her parents.

Learning Tasks in Intervention. Interventive learning tasks must assure that the student has the opportunity to utilize social work knowledge and skills in a planned and coordinated fashion to meet client needs. This requires the ability to direct activities of self and client system toward goal fulfillment. In the case of services to Betty, opportunities were available for the student to work with individuals, groups, and communities in the resolution of personal, family, and community problems. Much of the work had to be directed toward helping each of these different systems to recognize and to capitalize on their innate strengths. A crucial factor in programming for student learning was the need to assure that intervention encompassed services to these multiple systems in support of the school's objectives to prepare students for general social work practice. The learning tasks below were developed to provide these broad experiences. Learning tasks associated with individuals and families are:

Learning Objectives
To develop skills in providing supportive services to clients. (In this situation, Betty's need for nurturance and the natural parents' need for clarification related to family roles.)

Learning Tasks
Provide Betty with a nurturing relationship characterized by responsive caring to compensate for earlier parental deprivation. Assist her foster parents to recognize and respond to her needs for love and acceptance without jeopardizing the normal emancipation processes of adolescent development.

Assist foster mother to reduce unrealistic expectations on Betty's behavior. Help foster parents to recognize opportunities to reinforce positive behavior related to such areas as school adjustment, grades, curfew, personal grooming, household chores, and babysitting.

To develop skills in setting limits on client behavior, in placing expectations for client performance within the professional relationships, and in utilizing techniques of direct influence.

Assist Betty to set limits on her own behavior and to accept outside limits imposed by the agency and foster parents.

Assist natural parents to express their own anxiety and concerns regarding the family situation, supporting their earlier interest in receiving counseling services. Prepare her natural parents for referral to a counseling agency with services appropriate to their needs.

Learning Objectives	*Learning Tasks*
	Involve natural parents in planning for Betty's continued care, including clarification of their parental responsibilities for emotional and financial support.
To develop skills in the use of consultation.	Consult with the agency psychiatrist to identify approaches to help Betty minimize her use of withdrawal and fantasy to cope with family problems.

Learning tasks associated with social work practice with groups:

Learning Objectives	*Learning Tasks*
To develop skills in utilizing indigenous groups to support client functioning and resolution of problems.	Assist Betty to explore group activities that may be available to help her develop additional friendships. Help her to express feelings of ambivalence and anxiety which may be present in her efforts to form group relationships.
	Identify group resources available in the agency and the community to promote self-enhancement and self-esteem.
To develop referral skills in using formal group programs within the community and direct skills in providing group services.	Initiate referral to appropriate group resources, collaborating with the group leader regarding Betty's preparation for participation in a group. If possible, arrange for an opportunity to serve as a co-leader or a participant observer in a similar group.
To develop diagnostic skills related to the assessment of group behavior.	Use knowledge of small group dynamics to assess Betty's interaction with her family.

Learning tasks associated with social work practice with communities:

Learning Objectives	*Learning Tasks*
To develop knowledge of the impact of social systems on the individual including the ability to assess potential roles for advocacy or social change.	Compile data from other community agencies to determine the extent of community problems related to child abuse and runaway youth. Determine community resources available to service those areas.

| To develop skills in organizing and presenting data for the purpose of community planning. | Summarize data compiled from other agencies for submission to agency administrators and community planning agencies in assessing the need for new services. |

The total packaging of learning tasks in intervention, of course, must be related to the readiness of the student to assume responsibilities in each service area. Had the student in this case demonstrated a limited ability to work beyond the specific needs expressed by Betty, arrangements could have been made to have regular staff members assume responsibility for the extended work that was accomplished with the community and the natural family. At the same time, had the student exhibited more experience and professional maturity, increased responsibility could have been given to her to provide the natural parents with direct counseling, to develop and lead adolescent therapy groups, and to coordinate community activities in support of developing facilities to care for runaway youth. The learning tasks assigned to the student could have been packaged in a variety of ways with various educational support systems, depending upon the needs of client, student, agency, and school.

Learning Tasks in Evaluation and Termination. During the extended period in which the student worked with Betty to resolve the conflicts which had led to her leaving home and to enhance her ability to cope with new situations, several accomplishments were noted. Betty became more confident in herself and less fearful of her natural father. She reestablished a relationship with her mother, devoting several afternoons to special activities with her. She learned to express both positive and negative feelings in socially acceptable ways.

As Betty became more comfortable with negotiation, she raised questions about the number of her household chores with her foster mother and was able to resolve some differences through discussion. With her parents' initiation, Betty talked with her family about plans for a trip to California, expressing ambivalence—something she had not been able to do before. She improved her personal appearance and grooming, made additional friends at school, and began dating. These improvements were noted by the student social worker and reinforced in personal contacts with Betty. At the time of termination, however, they were not viewed as sufficient to close Betty's case without additional services.

Ideally, termination is planned in relation to client achievement of predetermined goals. In Betty's case, termination with the student worker resulted from the student's completion of school and concurrent withdrawal from field work. Consequently, the student had to assume responsibility for introducing Betty to the impending separation and for preparing her for termination. The following learning tasks were designed to facilitate and reinforce student understanding of termination and evaluation:

Learning Objectives	*Learning Tasks*
To develop skills in the application of techniques used to evaluate goal attainment, recognizing the mutuality of evaluation with the client systems.	Assess the degree of goal achievement perceived by Betty, her foster parents, and her natural parents. Indicate approaches that may be used to reinforce these achievements as strengths to be used in meeting future needs.
	Review the way in which Betty has coped with past separations. Identify areas in which she may feel vulnerable at the time of termination. Assess the implications of these factors for planning termination.
To develop a commitment to the professional responsibility of assessing the student's own performance in the delivery of services and skills in self-evaluation.	Review the way in which the student's own activities have assisted the client to goal achievement.
To develop skills in assisting client systems to cope with impact of termination, recognizing the pervasive nature of separation anxieties.	Introduce Betty and her two families to the impending termination with the student worker. Help them to express their feelings about this development. Involve them in planning for a transfer to another worker and/or in the development of other plans for future support and supervision. Provide Betty with information concerning community and other resources available to assist her with continuing needs.
To develop understanding of the student's own reactions to client termination.	Explore with the field instructor the meaning of termination to the student.
To develop understanding that termination is part of the treatment process, and that it can be utilized to facilitate growth in client.	Assess the way in which time-limited structures motivate and/or impede client progress; assess the way in which termination may reinforce accomplishments of client systems.

To develop a commitment to the necessity of keeping adequate records and using supervision and research to enhance service delivery.	Use conferences with the field instructor to review the dynamics of separation and to identify appropriate procedures to assist Betty in managing separation.
	Prepare a transfer summary for the agency record.

As in the case of practice-focused learning experiences associated with other phases of the problem-solving process, the student performance across these learning tasks was evaluated primarily through the use of supervisory conferences, process recordings, and student reports. This ongoing assessment was helpful in providing the data needed to assess the overall success in this case.

CONCLUSION

It must be emphasized that all field learning should be developed on a "need-to-know" basis which allows students to partialize the problem-solving process into the specific activities of immediate concern in service delivery. Students vary in their capacity to respond to specific situations, yet each is confronted with the responsibility to meet the evolving and changing needs of client systems with appropriate intervention action. The paramount questions which field instructors must answer, then, are: 'What does this student need to know in order to provide meaningful service? and How can this knowledge be developed in support of educational objectives?

In answering these questions it has been stressed that consideration must be given to the educational objectives of the school, to the service objectives of the agency, to the specific needs of client systems, and to the unique strengths of each social work student. Factors to be considered in relation to each of these variables have been discussed. As one considers these factors the packaging of learning tasks in field work becomes one of the most challenging and difficult tasks in social work education. It may be, however, that this task is the most rewarding of all activities in social work. The opportunity to shape the professional growth of students is an opportunity to reaffirm one's own professionalism. It is an opportunity to affirm the student's skill in service to others and to reckon with the possibility of what might be. Let us hope that field instructors will pursue excellence with a fervor that ignites creativity in the minds of those we serve.

Annotated Bibliography

Richard G. Mimiaga

A substantial, extensive, and diverse body of literature specific to field instruction has developed over the past two decades. A few comprehensive collections have been published by the Council on Social Work Education and several schools of social work during the last decade. This annotated review of the literature is intended to provide the reader with an overview of the field instruction literature and an introduction to specific and specialized content relative to field instruction. The categories and annotations included reflect the diversity in perspective and attitude toward field instruction. A common theme of "learning through doing" exists and is heavily promoted as an essential ingredient for social work education. The preparation of social work practitioners for knowledge-value-guided practice requires a considerable and interrelated effort on the part of schools, students, agencies, and the profession; and it is this—these often conflicting efforts—that contributes to the uniqueness of social work.

The annotations contained here were selected from a thousand-item bibliography on field instruction developed through 1980. The bibliography was developed using CSWE publications on field instruction, *Social Work Research and Abstracts*, and Hong-Chon Li's bibliography on social work education. Doctoral dissertations contain considerable research related to field instruction but were not used in this review due to their limited access.

A classification scheme was developed to aid field administrators, educators (faculty and practitioners), and students to find subject matter of interest. The annotations were selected on the basis of representativeness and resourcefulness. Additional criteria for selection are presented in introductory comments to each section. The annotations are numbered and cross-referenced when applicable to more than one category and are designed to introduce the reader to the literature.

This selection of references was severely limited by space, availability, and to some extent my own biases. Limited attention was given to publications prior to 1970. Gaps are present in the field instruction literature particularly within specialized fields of practice and in regard to research. Too much of the literature is descriptive with little attempt to generalize for the benefit of the reader. Comprehensive literature has also been sparse. More recent literature is becoming increasingly critical of the present field instruction structure within schools of social work with increasing conceptualization around issues of competency and evaluation.

262

ADMINISTRATION OF FIELD INSTRUCTION PROGRAMS

The administration of field instruction programs is a difficult and time-consuming endeavor which must balance the requirements of the school with the sometimes contradictory learning needs of the student practitioner and the service needs of the agencies. The selection of field settings; the coordination of field instructor, consultant, and agency administrator in their interrelationships; and the orientation and ongoing support of field instructors are addressed in these annotations. Certainly there are other administrative concerns, many of which are addressed elsewhere.

Cassidy, Helen. "Role and Function of a Coordinator or Director of Field Instruction." In *Current Patterns in Field Instruction in Graduate Social Work Education*, ed. Betty Lacy Jones. New York: Council on Social Work Education, 1969, pp. 147–156.

> *An experiment at Tulane University in the mid-sixties is described. The author attempts to show that the field instruction administrator role derives from the curriculum. Convictions about curriculum led to the use of faculty-appointed field instructors for the first year of graduate school and an increased use of faculty field instructors for second-year students. Training centers were developed as ideal learning environments. The public relations and coordination functions of a field instruction administrator are emphasized.*

Irving, Howard H. "A Social Science Approach to a Problem in Field Instruction: The Analysis of a Three-Part Role Set." *Journal of Education for Social Work* 5 (1969): 49–56.

> *The roles of the agency-employed field instructor, agency administrator, and school-based field consultant are examined in their interrelationships from a systems perspective. Contradictory role expectations of the administrator and field consultant are described as a dilemma for the field instructor. The difficulty of obtaining primacy of student learning over agency service with agency-based field instruction is elaborated upon with considerable conceptualization using role theory.*

Krop, Lois P. *Developing and Evaluating A Training Manual for Social Work Field Instructors Using Elements of the Behavioristic System of Learning*. Arlington, Va.: ERIC Document Reproduction Service, 1975.

> *This self-instructional guide for field instructors facilitates the selection of course content, behavioral objectives, learning activities, and means for assessing student learning.*

Towle, Charlotte. *The Learner in Education for the Profession as Seen in Education for Social Work*. Chicago: University of Chicago Press, 1954.

> *A classic presentation on social work education from a psychoanalytic perspective. See listing under "Significant Publications" for annotation.*

Werner, Ruth. "The Director of Fieldwork—Administrator and Educator." In *Current Patterns in Field Instruction in Graduate Social Work Education*, ed. Betty Lacy Jones. New York: Council on Social Work Education, 1969, pp. 157–164.

> *A "new" department of field work at the School of Applied Social Sciences, Case Western Reserve University, is described. Emphasis is on the primary responsibility of a field work administrator as educator and not problem-solver. Elaborates on the educational functions of orientation and education for field instructors and on the area of experimentation that will enhance student learning.*

AGENCY-SCHOOL RELATIONS

The relationship of school and agency in carrying out a shared responsibility for the education and training of practitioners has been the subject of numerous articles over the last three decades. Two central themes of forty-five articles reviewed are partnership and communication. A few critical articles question the mutuality and suggest that the agencies are being used by the schools to assist in training student practitioners with little or no benefit to the agency. This myth of mutuality and partnership is described by Michael Frumkin as "the professional commitment fallacy." Elmer Tropman is much more positive on the potential for linkage while recognizing the serious agency constraints. Margaret Schutz and William Gordon suggest that the school's function is to prepare students for practice and that the agencies' function is to teach field students to practice, requiring a major shift in responsibility between agencies and schools. Kay Dea and Harriet Bartlett provide a more historical and traditional perspective on the issue of agency-school relations. Some of the more recent articles contain considerable references to other sources.

Bartlett, Harriet M. "Responsibilities of Social Work Practitioners and Educators toward Building a Strong Profession." *Social Service Review* 34 (1960): 379–381.
  Professional responsibilities of social work practitioners and social work educators are discussed in comparative terms. The roles and contributions of each are identified as well as their joint responsibilities. A section particularly relevant to field instruction describes some problems of communications between educators and practitioners such as differences in goals, language, and thinking.

Dea, Kay. "The Collaborative Process in Undergraduate Field Instruction." In *Undergraduate Field Instruction Programs: Current Issues and Predictions*, ed. Kristen Wenzel. New York: Council on Social Work Education, 1972, pp. 50–62.
  Traditional field instruction patterns of university, agency, and mutually directed programs are reviewed from a historical perspective. Collaborative relationships based on a transactional model of field instruction are strongly encouraged by the author for more effective field instruction. Fiscal, academic, philosophical, role, political, and community restraints to the development of collaborative relationships between schools of social work and the agencies are presented.

Frumkin, Michael L. "Social Work Education and the Professional Commitment Fallacy: A Practical Guide to Field-School Relations." *Journal of Education for Social Work* 16 (1980): 91–99.
  On the basis of a review of field instruction literature, agencies and schools are viewed from an interorganizational perspective, and an analytical framework is suggested for facilitating field-school relations. The existing literature with few exceptions is characterized as descriptive, piecemeal, and based on a fallacy of agency commitment to student training. Suggestions and criteria are proposed for facilitating improved field-school relations.

Hill, William G. "The Impact of Undergraduate Field Instruction Programs on Manpower Development." In *Undergraduate Field Instruction Programs: Current Issues and Predictions*, ed. Kristen Wenzel. New York: Council on Social Work Education, 1972, pp. 80–92.
  Schools of social work and social agencies are encouraged to jointly enhance educational opportunities for students, to develop a differential manpower system, and to develop a career ladder for practitioners. This encouragement is provided from a background discussion of the problems of employing agencies, employment opportunities, and the cost-benefit ratio of field instruction to the agency.

Schutz, Margaret L., and Gordon, William E. "Reallocation of Educational Responsibility among Schools, Agencies, Students, and NASW." *Journal of Education for Social Work* 13 (1977): 99–106.
  The credential-giving or gatekeeping function of schools, agencies, students, and the professional association are reviewed and critiqued in terms of their impact on school-agency relations. The authors propose a major shift of the gatekeeping function away from schools and students. They

propose that schools prepare students for practice and that the agencies teach field students to practice, with final competence certification by a public-based licensure board.

Tropman, Elmer. "Agency Constraints Affecting Links between Practice and Education." *Journal of Education for Social Work* 13 (1977): 8–14.

Field Work is described as one linkage between educational institutions and community agencies. Constraints inherent to the agency are delineated as they affect the potential harmonious and complementary relationship between education and practice. Included are constraints related to agency history and tradition, agency responsibility for providing service, affluent Anglo boards, issues of confidentiality, and superiority conception.

FIELD INSTRUCTION CURRICULUM DEVELOPMENT

Approximately seventy articles related to the development of curriculum for field instruction were reviewed. Many, if not most, are descriptive of an individual school's experience with curriculum building. Responsibility for generalization to other schools is left to the reader, reflecting the difficulty that exists in developing curricula useful for others. The rationale and justification for the Council on Social Work Education's accreditation requirement that field instruction be an integral part of the total curriculum is often written about in council publications and journal articles with general agreement that the field instruction component of any social work curriculum should be reflective of the practice, human behavior and social environment, social policy, and research components of the curriculum. The literature on the practice component is almost exclusively approached from a casework or "micro" perspective, except for those articles that deal with a specialized methodology. This micro perspective is even evident in the articles that purport to present a generalist frame of reference for field instruction.

Kettner, Peter M. "A Conceptual Framework for Developing Learning Modules for Field Instruction." *Journal of Education for Social Work* 15 (1979): 51–58.

A comparative analysis of field education manuals and field evaluation instruments from thirty-five graduate schools of social work provides a 1976 look at the state of the art in relation to field objectives, content, and the design of monitoring and evaluation systems. A conceptual framework for modularizing field instruction is suggested along with a discussion of problems and possibilities.

Krop, Lois P. *Evaluating the Effectiveness of a Modern Systems Approach to Field Instruction in Graduate Social Work Education: Curriculum Development Module.* Arlington, VA: ERIC Document Reproduction Service, 1973.

A self-instructional unit designed for the teaching and learning of Biestek's principles of relationships was developed, tested, and evaluated for use in field instruction. The rationale, procedures, results, and recommendations are described with attention given to problems of class-field integration, equal learning opportunities for all students, and independence in learning. The self-instruction unit and form for module evaluation are included in the appendix.

Matson, Margaret B. "Field Experience for the Undergraduate Social Welfare Student," in *Undergraduate Social Work Education for Practice: A Report on Curriculum Content and Issues,* ed. Lester J. Glick. Washington, D.C.: U.S. Government Printing Office, 1972, pp. 80–92.

Written shortly after the CSWE's and the NASW's recognition of the social work bachelor's degree as the first practice degree. This chapter describes the relationship of field education/instruction to curriculum and to practice. The organization and operation of field instruction is described with an emphasis on knowledge-value-guided practice.

Mehta, Vera D. "Integrated Methods Approach—A Challenge Possibility in Field Work Instruction." *Indian Journal of Social Work* 35 (1975): 335–344.

The author recognizes a serious imbalance in U.S. social work curriculum which favors casework over group work and community organization. She contends that the Indian social worker is more a generalist than the social worker trained in the United States. Even in India, however, field work training is weighted in favor of casework. An argument is made for field instruction that teaches social work practice through three fundamental units of society—family, social group, and community. Several case illustrations describing social work processes from a generalist perspective are provided. Agency resistances to generalist practice are noted and considerable responsibility is placed on the schools to promote an integrated methods approach.

Schubert, Margaret. "Making the Best Use of Traditional and Atypical Field Placements." In *Current Patterns in Field Instruction in Graduate Social Work Education*, ed. Betty Lacy Jones. New York: Council on Social Work Education, 1969, pp. 3–12.

A strong argument is made for the central role of the field instructor in identifying and arranging learning experiences, in assisting students to analyze these experiences, and in joint evaluation of educational goals. An outline for inventories of levels of responsibility and potential experiences is presented. Preoccupation with form and structure is presented as a reaction against apprenticeship. Criteria for development of educational objectives for the field are also presented and discussed.

Taber, Merlin. "Curriculum Development on the Urbana Campus, University of Illinois." In *Modes of Professional Education: Functions of Field Instruction in the Curriculum*, Tulane Studies in Social Welfare, edited by Helen Cassidy, vol. 11. New Orleans: Tulane University, School of Social Work, 1969, pp. 5–21.

The background, faculty actions, articulation of field and class, and consequences of developing curriculum over a five-year period are described. Their experience suggested: that field work had been made a scapegoat for the intellectual poverty of students; greater attention should be paid to structural changes (which affect function) than to comprehensive curriculum planning (which restricts openness). The author speculates on a curriculum structure labeled an "intern program" where field instruction occurs after graduation and greater responsibility for beginning practice competency is turned over to the field.

Wenzel, Kristen, ed. *Curriculum Guides for Undergraduate Field Instruction Programs*. New York: Council on Social Work Education, 1972.

Four curriculum guides contain practical and illustrative materials to assist undergraduate programs develop their own field instruction models. The first chapter provides an analysis, comparison, and suggested application of the curriculum guides from four different undergraduate social work programs. A companion volume by the same editor is Undergraduate Field Instruction Programs: Current Issues and Predictions. *Both were developed by an undergraduate field experience demonstration project co-sponsored by the Council on Social Work Education and the Veterans' Administration.*

Zalba, Serapio. "The Pros and Cons of Using a Curriculum in Undergraduate Field Instruction." In *Undergraduate Field Instruction Programs: Current Issues and Predictions*, edited by Kristen Wenzel. New York: Council on Social Work Education, 1972, pp. 29–49.

The author concludes with a definition of curriculum that suggests field instruction should be ". . . a personal trip with a knowledgeable native available for guidance." Goals, objectives, and tasks involved with teaching and learning in the field are presented from a bias in favor of inductive and experiential learning.

INSTRUCTIONAL PROCESSES AND TECHNIQUES

The use of supervision to facilitate student learning varies according to the knowledge, values, and practice styles of every field instructor and student.

The diversity of materials on this subject also varies and overlaps considerably with articles annotated elsewhere in this bibliography. These annotations were selected on the basis of their recency, availability, and review of related literature. The selected annotations on techniques, field seminars, and recordings are included for the assistance they provide field instructors and students in the process of integrating knowledge with practice. The integration of field practice with theoretical and practical knowledge learned in the classroom is addressed throughout the literature on field instruction, at least indirectly. The relationship between knowing, understanding, and doing is directly related to the problem of class-field integration. This problem is reviewed by Mildred Sikkema through four historical periods between 1898 and 1964.

General

Amacher, Kloh-Ann. "Explorations into the Dynamics of Learning in Field Work." *Smith College Studies in Social Work* 46 (1976): 163–217.
Ideas about students in field instruction, the learning process, and the art of supervision are shared with considerable quotes excerpted from numerous tape-recorded interviews of four first-year students (all female) and their supervisors. A summary comments on the relationship between maturation and the development of professional identity in field instruction.

Dawson, Bettie Guthrie. "Supervising the Undergraduate in a Psychiatric Setting." In *The Dynamics of Field Instruction.* New York: Council on Social Work Education, 1975, pp. 10–19.
The learning sequence of a "typical" undergraduate student in field instruction at a large psychiatric hospital is described in three phases—beginning, intermediate, and termination. Students are expected to complete the third phase after two semesters of field instruction. The role of the field instructor (supervisor) is to guide the student, using either a "case" or "task" approach, through a three phase continuum of growth—self-centered, problem-centered, and client-centered. Supervisory tools of readings, role playing, written outlines, observation, and conferences are suggested.

Finestone, Samuel. "Selected Features of Professional Field Instruction." *Journal of Education for Social Work* 3 (1967): 14–26/Also in *Current Patterns in Field Instruction in Graduate Social Work Education,* ed. Betty Lacy Jones. New York: Council on Social Work Education, 1969, pp. 71–86.
Conceptual teaching is defined as the art of stimulating generalized and generalizable learning. Concepts are distinguished from propositions, principles, and theory. A method of conceptual teaching in the field is presented which stresses the importance of social-policy and social-service content, describes the impact of organizational features on practice, and discusses the role of scientific inquiry. An orientation to change and reverse feedback of knowledge from field to class is emphasized as a criterion for professional practice.

Knappe, Mildred E. "The Training Center Concept: Educating Social Workers for a Changing World." In *The Dynamics of Field Instruction.* New York: Council on Social Work Education, 1975, pp. 50–59.
Experience with the Cedar Rapids Social Work Training Center is shared with considerable attention paid to an andrological teaching-learning perspective derived from Malcolm Knowles and Carl Rogers.

Manis, Francis. *Openness in Social Work Field Instruction: Stance and Form Guidelines.* Goleta, Ca.: Kimberly Press, 1979.
The author expands his previously published concern with student responsibility for learning. See listing under "Significant Publications" for annotation.

Matorin, Susan. "Dimensions of Student Supervision: A Point of View." *Social Casework* 60 (1979): 150–156.

An experienced practitioner-administrator heavily involved with field instruction examines the transition a social worker must make from practitioner to field instructor. Practitioner self-doubt, empathy, use of authority, and ability to cope with dependency needs are discussed as aspects of student supervision. The responsibility of a student supervisor to update practice skills is stressed. The author makes excellent use of the literature on student supervision.

Nelson, Judith C. "Relationship Communication in Early Fieldwork Conferences." *Social Casework* 55 (1974): 237–243.

Tape recordings of early conferences between nineteen field instructor-student pairs were studied in relation to content of discussion, teaching techniques used, student responses to the teaching techniques, and relationship messages implying equality or authority. Inferences relative to issues of authority and equality in supervisory relationships are presented.

Rosenblatt, Aaron, and Mayer, John. "Objectionable Supervisory Styles: Students' Views." *Social Work* 20 (1975): 184–189.

Constrictive, amorphous, unsupportive, and therapeutic supervision are identified as objectionable supervisory styles based on an analysis of approximately fifty autobiographical, descriptive accounts by field students of "offensive supervision." Coping efforts by students are described and often involve compliance and concealment. Suggestions are made to reduce the inherent strain between supervisors and students.

St. John, David. "Goal-Directed Supervision of Social Work Students in Field Placement." *Journal of Education for Social Work* 11 (1975): 89–94.

A goal-directed paradigm for student supervision is presented which includes five phases of placement: screening, minimum orientation, goal worksheet, body of placement, and evaluation and termination. A goal worksheet is illustrated for a field student with a Veterans' Administration drug-abuse program, with four major goals on a horizontal axis and four graduated levels of achievement on the vertical axis. Supervision facilitates the development and achievement of goals consistent with the agency program, school requirements, and individual needs.

Sikkema, Mildred. "A Proposal for an Innovation in Field Learning and Teaching." In *Field Instruction in Graduate Social Work Education: Old Problems and New Proposals.* New York: Council on Social Work Education, 1966, pp. 1–22.

An innovative approach to first-year learning and teaching in the field (field instruction) is presented in an effort to facilitate the learning of basics and independence in learning. The problem of integrating class and field work is reviewed in four periods of historical perspective from 1898 through 1964.

Smith, Philip L., and Skelding, Alexis H. "Issues in Field Instruction." In *The Field Consortium: Manpower Development and Training in Social Welfare and Corrections,* edited by Michael J. Austin. Collaborative Planning in Higher Education for the Professions, Monograph Series #3. Florida: Florida State University System, 1972, pp. 18–34.

Issues in field instruction from the perspectives of the student, school, and agencies are reviewed. Traditional and innovative models are presented as a process for putting knowledge into practice by facilitating student self-awareness and socialization toward the profession. A major issue presented is the lack of conceptualization on the building of competency. The ability to do or to perform is described as the essential payoff for the agency. A field consortium model is proposed as a way of combining the best of the traditional and newer models—field instruction with greater attention paid to the building of competency. A bibliography on field instruction contains forty-nine items.

Towle, Charlotte. *The Learner in Education for the Professions as Seen in Education for Social Work.* Chicago: University of Chicago Press, 1954.

See listing under "Significant Publications" for annotation.

Field Seminars

Williams, J.K. Mark. "The Practice Seminar in Social Work Education." In *The Dynamics of Field Instruction*. New York: Council on Social Work Education, 1975, pp. 94–101.

Key concepts of small group theory a la Gordon Hearn are related to the use of the practice seminar as distinguished from the academic seminar. Experience with a 30-hour "integration" seminar for practitioners is reported on as one model of a practice seminar.

Techniques

Ames, Lois. "Use of a Daily Journal in Supervision of Undergraduate Students' Field Work." *Social Casework* 55 (1974): 442–444.

The advantages and hazards connected with the use of a daily journal as a supervisory device are presented and discussed. Advantages include time-savings, record of supervision, introduction to process recordings, opportunity for self-analysis, and ego support for students. Hazards include manipulation of journal by students and problems of intimacy and confidentiality.

Kadushin, Alfred. "Interview Observation as a Teaching Device." *Social Casework* 37 (1956): 334–341.

Reports on the use of direct interview observation as a training resource based on a questionnaire sent to 54 faculty, 51 staff development specialists, and 57 family agency executives. Findings indicated limited use of interview observation based on considerations derived from casework theory, educational theory, and ethical observations to clients. Sympathetic points of view are also presented.

Larsen, Jo Ann. "Competency-Based and Task-Centered Practicum Instruction." *Journal of Education for Social Work* 16 (1980): 87–94.

Competency-based education is described as an emerging and promising form of instruction for the teaching and learning of specific social work skills. Eight interpersonal skills are identified and clearly defined along with task-centered instructional techniques for facilitating student mastery of these skills.

Paonessa, John J. "A New Learning Experience in Undergraduate Field Observation." *Social Work Education Reporter* 18 (1970): 59–60, 64–65.

In response to student concerns about either underinvolvement or overinvolvement, the author suggests a new approach to field observation to precede traditional placement: assign the student a closed case which he or she would follow chronologically, interviewing administrators and service workers. Examples of social work principles in action would be written. A twelve-step outline which includes seminars and five papers is proposed.

Schur, Edith L. "The Use of the Co-worker Approach as a Teaching Model in Graduate Student Field Education." *Journal of Education for Social Work* 15 (1979): 72–79.

The author's experience with the use of two-student partnerships working with individuals, families, and small groups is described as facilitative of practice and learning goals. Co-worker conferences with the field instructor permit expanded and effective use of role playing of client sessions promoting learning of analytical and interactional skills and self-awareness. Advantages are discussed along with several descriptive examples.

Wells, Richard A. "The Use of Joint Field Instructor–Student Participation as a Teaching Method in Casework Treatment." *Social Work Education Reporter* 19 (1971): 58–62.

The author reports on teaching experience in which field instructor and students work with clients jointly as a therapeutic team. Advantages and disadvantages are presented along with a historical background of co-therapy.

Recording

Holden, W. "Process Recording." *Social Work Education Reporter* 20 (1972): 67–69.

The author, a field instructor, advocates the continued use of process recording as a learning tool. He provides a response and suggestions for three basic types of recording (complete process, structured, and summary) as well as for three additional kinds of reporting to support process recording. The lack of timely response to student recordings is cited as the core of student morale problems in process recording.

Urdang, E. "In Defense of Process Recording." *Smith College Studies in Social Work* 50 (1979): 1–15.

In response to criticism and the increased use of audio-visual recording, an ardent defense is made of progress recording as a learning tool for field students. Analysis and examination of recall based on process procedures is illustrated in five skill areas for professional practice.

Wilson, Suanna. *Recording: Guidelines for Social Workers.* New York: The Free Press, 1980.

In a self-instructional format, an extensive review of recording based on the author's experience, designed for students, practitioners, supervisors, field instructors, and classroom faculty. The purpose and varieties of recording are described with numerous examples and self-instructional exercises. Issues of confidentiality are reviewed. A bibliography of selected readings contains fifteen categories related to recording. Of particular interest is the section on process recording as a tool for student education.

PERFORMANCE AND EVALUATION

Accountability, competency, performance, evaluation, grading, examinations, and judgment are all concepts very much in vogue. The evaluation and grading of student performance in field instruction remains very much an art; it is, however, an issue in most field instruction programs with no standardized evaluative tools. The experiences of the authors annotated here, from Margaret Schubert in 1958 to Peter Kettner in 1979, should benefit field students, instructors, consultants, and administrators. The sections on curriculum development and the teaching-learning process should also be reviewed for a better understanding of the issues of accountability and evaluation.

Arkava, Morton, and Brennen, E. Clifford, eds. *Competency-Based Education for Social Work: Evaluation and Curriculum Issue.* New York: Council on Social Work Education, 1976.

In a response to the need for accountability in social work education, the authors review assessment efforts including knowledge and value inventories, skill assessment scales, and simulation models. Three separate attempts to appraise student competence are reviewed. The University of Montana's experience in assessing practice skills of its baccalaureate social work students in practicum settings is thoroughly reviewed and evaluated. A working definition of social work practice skills was developed as a competency criteria base for the assessment effort. Written and oral exams related to practicum assignments are presented in the text. Evaluation issues, examination results, and limitations of the assessment procedure are discussed. The curriculum developmment process and related issues at the University of Montana are explicated with attention paid to the impact of the exam to class and field. A general outline of their revised curriculum is presented with reference to competency areas and accreditation standards.

Green, Solomon H. "Educational Assessments of Student Learning through Practice in Field Instruction." *Social Work Education Reporter* 20 (1972): 48–54.

Based on the author's unpublished doctoral dissertation on the bases for judgment of field performance, this essay provides a brief historical review of the place of field instruction in the social work curriculum along with a discussion of problems inherent in judging student performance. Selected studies are reviewed as the nature of competence and the evaluation process are examined with a concluding plea that field instruction be viewed as a learning process in itself, not as a test of classroom knowledge.

Johnson, Gladys. "Advanced Standing in Practicum I by Examination: One School's Experience." *Journal of Education for Social Work* 12 (1976): 59–64.

Enrolled students with practicum prerequisites completed and with social work practice experience under the supervision of a person holding an MSW degree were permitted to place out of the first of three practicums through a series of written, oral, and skill examinations. The evaluation and report of this experience is positive with a conclusion that it is educationally sound to recognize previous experience for advanced standing in practicums.

Kelly, Nancy; Perlmutter, Morton; and Visweswaran, G. "Assessment of Student Performance in the Field Course." In *Current Patterns in Field Instruction in Graduate Social Work Education*, edited by Betty Lacy Jones. New York: Council on Social Work Education, 1969, pp. 125–134.

The development of one school's approach to field teaching is traced. An attempt is made to identify the commonalities of concept and theory basic to all social work practice. Using Lippit's model of planned change, four groups of skills are presented as relevant to planned change for all sizes of client systems. They are communication, data-collection, decision-making, and intervention skills. Progressive and sequential levels of expectation are presented through four semesters along with a five-point scale for evaluating student performance.

Kettner, Peter M. "A Conceptual Framework for Developing Learning Modules for Field Instruction." *Journal of Education for Social Work* 15 (1979): 51–58.

See entry under "Field Instruction Curriculum Development" for annotation.

Schubert, Margaret. "Field Work Performance: Achievement Levels of First-Year Students in Selected Aspects of Casework Service." *Social Service Review* 32 (1958): 120–137; and "Field Work Performance: Repetitions of a Study of First-Year Casework Performance." *Social Service Review* 34 (1960): 286–293.

These two articles report on the results of a study designed to assess student achievement in field work through the evaluation of the student process recordings by independent experts using a schedule as an evaluative instrument. The schedule which is included in the Appendix is based on field-work objectives, Charlotte Towle's material on teaching and learning, and on Perlman's problem solving process. Descriptions of student performance in three categories—attitudes, perceptions, and diagnostic and treatment actions—are presented. The use of a schedule to assess process recordings was found to be an effective and economical method for evaluating student performance.

Schubert, Margaret. "Field Work Performance: Suggested Criteria for Grading." *Social Service Review* 32 (1958): 247–257.

On the basis of experience with assessing student performance using independent evaluations of student process recordings, criteria are suggested for ratings of superior, good, barely passing, and failing. Grade inflation was found to be characteristic in the good and barely passing categories. A scoring system for performance in nine areas weighted by case complexity is presented. Consistency in performance and the relationship between performance scores and field grades are explored.

RESEARCH ON FIELD EDUCATION

Research on the quality, sophistication, and impact of field instruction varies considerably. These few annotations represent to some extent the historical and continuing interest in gaining a better understanding of the field instruction component of social work education curricula. The difficulty of identifying, objectifying, and controlling variables affecting field learning is apparent as research articles are reviewed. The necessity of focusing for research purposes often obscures and makes it difficult to comprehend the whole of a teaching-learning process. Margaret Schubert's research on the evaluation of field-work performance and its relationship to grading is an essential departure point for those interested in research on field education.

Gitterman, Alex. "The Faculty Field Instructor in Social Work Education." In *The Dynamics of Field Instruction: Learning through Doing.* New York: Council on Social Work Education, 1975, pp. 31–39.

   Role strain of agency-based and faculty-based field instructors is differentially associated and examined. Data were collected from 131 agencies and 27 faculty field instructors.

Gordon, William E. and Schutz, Margaret. *FIRP: Final Report of the Field Instruction Research Project.* Saint Louis: George Warren Brown School of Social Work, Washington University, 1969.

   An extensive narrative which considers the fundamental nature of social work and the role of field instruction within social work education in preparing practitioners overshadows the findings of this research report. The narrative contains considerable theoretical and practical material related to the knowing-understanding-doing continuum so essential for knowledge-value-guided practice. The authors build on empirically supported conclusions based on experimental control-group research which compares the outcomes for two different kinds of field instruction. The difficulties of measuring and comparing educational outcomes, the authors suggest, are not adequate instruction and design but lack of clarity on expected outcomes. They conclude with a strong recommendation that field instruction be removed from school auspices and be transferred to an "instrumentality of the practicing profession."

Kolevon, Michael. "Notes for Practice: Evaluating the Supervisory Relationship in Field Placements." *Social Work* 24 (1979): 241–244.

   Methodology, results, and implications of research directed at understanding the nature of the supervisory relationship are presented. Data were collected from 17 percent (N=42) of all full-time graduate students in a graduate school of social work using a relationship scale, an adjustive activity scale, and a field evaluation form. The study found that students who were more critical of their supervisory relationship were more likely to engage in gamesmanship and that gamesmanship was not effective in securing better evaluations. A presentation of significant situational variables (race, first year, individual supervision, female supervisor) leads to some interesting implications for field instruction administration. The major finding was that faculty field instructors experience significantly greater role strain than agency-based instructors which negatively affects field instruction performance, job satisfaction, and job stability. Use of agency-based adjunct clinical professors and school-administered service systems are suggested structural alterations for more effective field instruction.

Nelson, Judith C. "Teaching Content of Early Fieldwork Conferences." *Social Casework* 55 (1974): 147–153.

   Sixty-eight tape recordings or early supervisor-student conferences (eleven field instructors and nineteen students) were coded and studied in relation to supervisors' use of teaching, student responses, and content of discussion. All three variables were found to be related and influenced by particular settings. Settings included family service, child welfare, public assistance, and medical and psychiatric agencies.

Rose, Sheldon D.; Lowenstein, Jane; and Fellin, Phillip. "Measuring Student Perception in Field Instruction." In *Current Patterns in Field Instruction in Graduate Social Work Education,* edited by Betty Lacy Jones. New York: Council on Social Work Education, 1969, pp. 135–144.

   A relationship scale developed by Sheldon Rose for a research study in the Netherlands is used to measure student perception of field instruction. There was a lack of support for the proposition that criticism of the field instructor's behavior decreases with advanced levels of learning. For casework students, criticism in fact increased. Other data examine the relationship of student perception of field instruction to methods, type of instruction, sex of student and of instructor, and grade.

Schubert, Margaret. "Field Work Performance: Achievement Levels of First-Year Students in Selected Aspects of Casework Service." *Social Service Review* 32 (1958): 120–137; "Field Work Performance: Repetitions of a Study of First-Year Casework Performance." *Social Service Review* 34 (1960): 286–293; and "Field Work Performance: Suggested Criteria for Grading." *Social Service Review* 32 (1958): 247–257.
  See entries under "Performance and Evaluation" for annotations.

Wedel, K.R., and Press, A.N. "Expectations for Field Learning: An Initial Assessment." *Journal of Social Welfare* 4 (1977): 5–14.
  The ranking of seven expectations for field instruction and the relative extent of their achievement by 160 pairs of field students and their instructors are analyzed. The findings reported general agreement between students and field instructors on the ranking and on the extent to which expectations are met. However, there was a lack of agreement between individual students and their own field instructor on their priority of expectations and assessment of performance. Implications of these findings on performance ratings are discussed. Skill development, integration of theory in practice, and professional self-awareness were ranked the top three. Expectations and exposure to ethnic and cultural diversity was ranked last.

SIGNIFICANT PUBLICATIONS

The ten publications annotated in this section were selected for their comprehensiveness and historical value. Early and continuing concern for practicum education or field instruction is evidenced by the writings of Edith Abbott and Charlotte Towle and by numerous collections published by the Council on Social Work Education and its predecessors. The latter reflect the state of the art in the 1960s and 1970s and, to facilitate the reader's access to the material, articles annotated elsewhere are cross-referenced. The bibliography by Hong-Chon Li is a valuable source for references on social work education in general and field instruction in particular, while the two texts by Francis Manis are unique in their single authorship and concentration on the responsibility of the field student as learner. The school or individual wanting to develop a basic field instruction library would be well advised to include these publications.

Abbott, Edith. "Education for Social Work." In *U.S. Bureau of Education Report.* Superintendent of Documents No.I 16 1/1: 1915, pp. 345–349.
  Reviews the first eleven years of professional education and training beginning with a 1898 summer training class organized by the New York Charity Organization Society. A history of the organization of five professional schools of philanthropy is given with training or field work as an essential component equal to classroom instruction. Field work is defined as a system of social apprenticeship.

Abbott, Edith. *Social Welfare and Professional Education.* Chicago: University of Chicago Press, 1931, pp. 44–80.
  Edith Abbott wrote in 1928 that "the provision of adequate field work and its educational organization is the most difficult and most unique side of our work and should be carried out at the same time as the academic courses so that one may serve to strengthen the other." After outlining six essential fields of study in education for social welfare, she devotes considerable discussion to the importance of a balance between class and field education. She uses the term field work instructor, compares the development of field work within social work education with the law and medical professions, critiques the "farming out" of students to social agencies and the limitations of single field experiences, calls for paid field instructors, and emphasizes the importance of a social science background for professional social workers.

Cassidy, Helen, ed. *Modes of Professional Education: Functions of Field Instruction in the Curriculum*, Tulane Studies in Social Welfare, vol. 11. New Orleans: School of Social Work, Tulane University, 1969.

Twelve scholarly papers, under four major headings, from a variety of faculty and agency personnel critically consider implications of change in field instruction content and structure. The teaching center is emphasized throughout for its unique learning and teaching capabilities.

Council on Social Work Education. *The Dynamics of Field Instruction*. New York: Council on Social Work Education, 1975.

Eleven articles on undergraduate and graduate field instruction covering rural, research, generic, community, psychiatric, and administrative field settings. Issues and concerns discussed in the articles include: generalist vs. specialist; field supervision; urban vs. rural models; agency vs. faculty-based field instruction; and practice and interdisciplinary seminars.

Jones, Betty Lacy, ed. *Current Patterns in Field Instruction in Graduate Social Work Education*. New York: Council on Social Work Education, 1969.

The "state of the art" for field instruction is reviewed with seventeen articles under five headings. Many of the articles were written by faculty responsible for the administration of field instruction programs.

Li, Hong-Chon. *Social Work Education: A Bibliography*. Metuchen, N.J.: Scarecrow Press, 1978.

A comprehensive bibliography with approximately three thousand references from 1960–1976 with selected references prior to 1960. The classification scheme includes seventeen general subject sections. Two sections that refer specifically to field instruction are "Field Instruction at the Graduate Level" and "Undergraduate Social Welfare Education."

Manis, Francis. *Field Practice in Social Work Education; Perspectives from an International Base*. Fullerton, Ca.: Sultana Press, 1972.

This small text is based on the author's ten plus years as a resident social work educator/trainer in Burma, Kenya, Iran, and the Philippines and on his experience as a social work educator in associate, bachelor, and master's programs in the United States. The varied perspectives presented on field instruction which derived from his international experience have considerable applicability to generalist-based field instruction in U.S. schools of social work at all levels. Addendums in the text provide guidelines for assessing this applicability. Strong suggestions are made for: (1) concurrent placements; (2) continuity of settings over extended periods of time; (3) student responsibility for learning; (4) student participation in analysis and evaluation of their own work; (5) cross-cultural learning; (6) use of ex-students as supervisors. The conceptualizations and practical applications should benefit students, faculty, and administrators involved with field instruction.

Manis, Francis. *Openness in Social Work Field Instruction: Stance and Form Guidelines*. Goleta, Ca: Kimberly Press, 1979.

This recent text continues and expands on the authors's previously published concern with student responsibility for learning. A research-based, six-stage model for developing and carrying out teaching-learning contracts between field instructors and students is provided. A set of guidelines are suggested to facilitate openness in field instructor-student relationships, professional growth for the field instructor, mutuality between instructor and student, and to facilitate the orientation and training of field students and instructors.

Towle, Charlotte. *The Learner in Education for the Professions as Seen in Education for Social Work*. Chicago: University of Chicago Press, 1954.

A classic presentation on social work education from a psychoanalytic perspective. Chapter 5, "Educational Principles and Process," and Chapter 11, "Faculty Collaboration and the Instructor's Preparation," are particularly pertinent to field instruction. Chapter 5 focuses on "relationship" as a means to facilitate learning, and Chapter 6 provides an excellent discussion on orientation and support of new field instructors.

Wenzel, Kristen, ed. *Undergraduate Field Instruction Programs: Current Issues and Predictions.* New York: Council on Social Work Education, 1972.

Five of seven articles deal directly with issues facing educators involved with field instruction programs. Most of the articles are oriented to undergraduate social work education but have import for graduate social work education as well.

STRUCTURAL MODELS OF FIELD INSTRUCTION

Experimentation and innovation with the structure of field instruction is an ongoing and continuous process. The boundaries of this process are limited only, it would seem, by curriculum objectives for social work education. The literature on structural models primarily relates to substantial experimentation undertaken by several schools in the late 1960s and 1970s. These articles report those efforts and provide a thoughtful base for future experimentation and innovation.

The structural models are distinguished by concepts of time, auspice, problem, and target community. Margaret Schutz and Alice Selyan provide some theoretical and practical considerations for block and concurrent field instruction. University-based social service centers in Illinois and New Mexico are described by Donald Brieland and Hal Goldstein. Mary Baker writes a criticism of school-based training centers, questioning the appropriateness of usurping the agencies' responsibility to provide service. Various teaching-learning centers are described by Helen Cassidy, Walter Kindelsperger, Carol Meyer, Paul Abels, and Michael Austin (ed). Scott Briar provides a discussion on the nature and characteristics of teaching-training centers.

Abels, Paul. "New Settings for Group Work: On a Clear Day." In *Current Patterns in Graduate Social Work Education,* edited by Betty Lacy Jones. New York: Council on Social Work Education, 1969, pp. 45–50.

Describes new/old settings for social work with groups and suggests the increased use of training centers where casework, group-work, and community-organization field students can focus on common client problems.

Austin, Michael J.; Kelleher, Edward; and Smith, Philip L.; eds. *The Field Consortium: Manpower Development and Training in Social Welfare and Corrections.* Florida: State University System of Florida, 1972.

Project Somebody, a storefront operation in delinquency prevention staffed by three levels of social work students, is described in chapters 5, 7, and 8 as a model for a field consortium for training and service. Research and demonstration are discussed as primary strategies for both agency change and educational reform. The storefront project serves teens in a southern black community and is staffed by AA, BA, and MSW social work students. An initial arrangement whereby students worked in groups of three (one from each of the three levels) led to increased conceptualization around characteristics and abilities of students from each of the three levels. Students carried the major responsibility for planning, development, and implementation of the project including a variety of roles. According to the authors, this resulted in a deeper involvement and stronger identification with social work. The rejection of both black and white students by the community is also described.

Baker, Mary R. "Discussion of Integrating Practice Demands in Social Work Education." In *Current Patterns in Field Instruction in Graduate Social Work Education,* edited by Betty Lacy Jones. New York: Council on Social Work Education, 1969, pp. 41–44/also in *Social Casework* 49 (1968): 486–488.

The author questions the use of school-based training centers in view of the responsibility so-

cial work education has to train and educate for agency practice. "Is there an implication that agencies are so rigid they can no longer render appropriate service?"

Briar, Scott. "Teaching Center Design as a Function of Curriculum Objectives." In *Modes of Professional Education: Functions of Field Instruction in the Curriculum.* Tulane Studies in Social Welfare, vol. 11. New Orleans: School of Social Work, Tulane University, 1969, pp. 69–78.

The teaching center as a focal point for integration of knowledge and practice is suggested. An argument is made for the teaching center's responsibility for knowledge development as well as for professional education. Five characteristics discussed for such teaching centers are: a focus on change function in social work; faculty-shared responsibility for student practice; professional and collegial style; innovative and experiential practice actions; and continuous research, monitoring, and evaluation. Schools of social work are encouraged to develop resources and facilities to support the knowledge development.

Brieland, Donald. "Broadening of Knowledge Base Through a Social Service Center." In *Modes of Professional Education: Functions of Field Instruction in the Curriculum.* Tulane Studies in Social Welfare, vol. 11. New Orleans: School of Social Work, Tulane University, 1969, pp. 106–121; and "A Social Services Center for a Multi-Problem Community." In *Current Patterns in Field Instruction in Graduate Social Work Education,* edited by Betty Lacy Jones. New York: Council on Social Work Education, 1969, pp. 61–70; also in *Social Work Education Reporter* 15 (1967): 30–32, 41.

These two articles describe the development and construction of a university-owned and -controlled "teaching" social service center. A major school of social work and a dozen agencies collaborated to constitute a network of services for a multiproblem community. Students who participated in this experiential program were unanimous in their approval of having the same instructor for field and practice methods. Issues for possible research and interventive strategies are discussed.

Cassidy, Helen. "Role and Function of the Coordinator or Director of Field Instruction." In *Current Patterns in Field Instruction in Graduate Social Work Education,* edited by Betty Lacy Jones. New York: Council on Social Work Education, 1969, pp. 147–156.

See entry under "Administration of Field Instruction Programs for annotations.

Goldstein, Hal. "A Social Work Teaching-Learning Center." *Journal of Education for Social Work* 16 (1980): 72–79.

The development and first year operation of a teaching-learning service center at New Mexico State University is described. The center was staffed by three faculty and served sixteen practicum students. Two community social-service-agency components were an information and referral resource center and a volunteer placement bureau.

Kindelsperger, W.L., and Cassidy, Helen. *Social Work Training Centers: Tentative Analysis of the Structural and Learning Environment.* New Orleans: School of Social Work, Tulane University, 1966.

The authors define and present the training center as a potentially powerful model for social work education. Brief case descriptions of two training centers are given against a backdrop of current objectives and policies of field instruction. They then analyze the criteria and progress involved in the design, structure, and environment of training centers. In the introduction, Mark Hale and Kenneth Kindelsperger describe educational issues of breadth and diversity, individual agency apprenticeship influences, and field instruction imbalances between demand and resources for educational services.

Meyer, Carol. "Integrating Practice Demands in Social Work Education." In *Current Patterns in Field Instruction in Graduate Social Work Education,* edited by Betty Lacy Jones. New York: Council on Social Work Education, 1969, pp. 33–40/also in *Social Casework* 49 (1968): 481–488.

A hospital teaching center is described as an alternative to traditional placements where six or eight selected cases are assigned during an academic year. Second-year students provided case-

work, group work, and community service to the pediatric, allergy, neurology, obesity, and emergency clinics. Students also supervised nonprofessional volunteers and did program planning, caseload management, and research. An argument is made for generalist training although that term is not used in the article.

Schutz, Margaret L. "The Potential of Concurrent Field Instruction for Learning." In *Current Patterns in Field Instruction in Graduate Social Work Education,* edited by Betty Lacy Jones. New York: Council on Social Work Education, 1969, pp. 99–108.
    A plea is made for knowledge-guided practice which results from affective and cognitive learning that moves through a progression of knowing, understanding, and doing. Opportunities to promote learning for practice in concurrent field instruction are illustrated. Learning principles are well integrated in a discussion of the potential of concurrent field instruction.

Selyan, Alice A. "Learning Theories and Patterns in Block and Concurrent Field Instruction." in *Current Patterns in Field Instruction in Graduate Social Work Education,* edited by Betty Lacy Jones. New York: Council on Social Work Education, 1969, pp. 87–98.
    The block plan is distinguished from concurrent field instruction by considering the applicability of the concept of Gestalt to learning. The total environment within which the learning process occurs becomes an integral part of that process within a system of internship and not apprenticeship.

TEACHING-LEARNING APPROACHES

Individualized and weekly supervisory sessions between field instructors and students have been and continue to be the traditional approach to field teaching and learning. The use of student units in traditional agency placements and social-service teaching centers under school auspices has been the recent primary alternative to the more individualized approach. Marilyn Lammert and Jan Halen and Fredricka Mayers in their articles provide descriptive and analytical reports and experiences with group teaching/supervision. Varied approaches to individualized and group field teaching are represented by the authors annotated. Frank Raymond describes what is perhaps the most innovative approach with the use of school faculty as consultants to field students and *not* to agency-based field instructors.

Hale, Mark P. "Curriculum Models for Social Work Education," in *Modes of Professional Education: Functions in Field Learning in the Curriculum.* Tulane Studies in Social Welfare, vol. 11. New Orleans: School of Social Work, Tulane University, 1969, pp. 211–227.
    Three general models for the MSW degree programs are identified and analyzed in terms of inherent problems. The relationship between field and class learning is a primary focus in the analysis. Of the three models—work, practicum, and intern—the latter is favored by the author. The work or apprenticeship model is traditional while the practicum is more characteristic in teaching centers. The intern model clearly distinguishes between the agency's responsibility to provide work opportunities without curriculum restraints and the school's responsibility to teach practice knowledge in class and field prior to the internship.

Koegler, Ronald R.; Williamson, Enery Reyes; and Grossman, Corazon. "Individualized Educational Approach to Fieldwork in a Community Mental Health Center." *Journal of Education for Social Work* 12 (1976): 28–35.
    An individualized educational approach to internship education is proposed to facilitate student learning of general skills through the use of combined practice methods in field teaching centers. Examples are provided to illustrate the development of individual curriculum based on the matching of student and educational program goals and on the previous experience and educational level of the student.

Lammert, Marilyn, and Hagen, Jan. "A Model for Community-Oriented Field Experience." In *The Dynamics of Field Instruction: Learning through Doing*. New York: Council on Social Work Education, 1975, pp. 60–67.

The authors report on their experience with a community-based student field unit operated directly under the auspice of a graduate school of social work. Group supervision was provided by faculty in carrying out the learning and service goals of the student unit.

Mayers, Fredricka. "Differential Use of Group Teaching in First Year Fieldwork." *Social Service Review* 44 (1970): 63–74.

The value of group teaching/supervision in field instruction is emphasized over the more customary weekly individual supervisory sessions which the author suggests should only supplement the group supervision on an as-needed basis. Cognitive, affective, and work group models of group supervision are described along with their advantages and disadvantages and their interrelatedness. Varied adaptations of these three models based on group composition, learning phases, and practice-specific situations are suggested.

Mermelstein, Joanne, and Sundet, Paul. "A Teaching Model for Rural Field." In *Social Work in Rural Areas: Preparation and Practice*, edited by Ronald Green. Nashville, University of Tennessee, 1977, pp. 161–174.

The authors say that "rural America is not a wasteland of social work education populated by an occasional urban-transplanted oasis." They propose pre-field instruction preparation consistent with the environment to be served. Strengths and weaknesses of three field instruction models (apprenticeship, collegial, role demonstration) are contrasted and discussed.

Raymond, Frank B. "Consultation as a Mode of Field Instruction." *Journal of Sociology and Social Welfare* 3 (1976): 565–577.

Based on the advantages and disadvantages of the three models of field instruction described by Mark Hale, consultation to the field student by a faculty member is suggested as an experiential approach to field instruction. A case example of a placement with South Carolina's Commission on Narcotics and Controlled Substances is used as a backdrop for theoretical considerations of this consultation approach. Potentialities and cautions are explicated.

Wijnberg, Marion H., and Schwartz, March C. "Models of Student Supervision: The Apprentice, Growth, and Role Systems Models." *Journal of Education for Social Work* 13 (1977): 107–114.

Three models of student supervision are conceptualized as ideal types with greater attention paid to the development of the role systems model. Content is presented on the nature of communication, role expectations, and performance and control mechanisms as they relate to the role systems model.

UNIQUE CONCENTRATIONS

Education and training content for social work practice with individuals, families, and groups in varied agency settings is apparent in most field instruction literature. Less apparent is content related to social work practice responsive to public issues and the needs of organizations and communities. The annotations presented here are recent examples of the limited field instruction literature which addresses some of the unique or specialized areas of practice. A substantial amount of literature on social work education in general does exist on unique areas of practice and can be located in *Social Work Abstracts* and Hong-Chon Li's extensive bibliography on social work education.

Addiction, Alcohol and Drugs

Corrigan, E.M., and Anderson, S.C. "Training for Treatment of Alcoholism in Women." *Social Casework* 59 (1978): 42–50.

Based on a review of the literature, a structural approach for social work practice with alcoholics at Rutgers' Graduate School of Social Work is described. A brief section on field practicum in alcoholism settings concludes with a bias for multisite practicums over the use of student units.

Wilbur, Mary. "Training of Social Work Students in a Narcotics Treatment Center: An Impressionistic Study." *Drug Forum* 1 (1972): 417–425.

The author's experience as a field instructor supervising students working with addicts and their families in a psychiatric hospital is described. An open-ended questionnaire was used to interview sixteen field students and provides the basis for the impressionistic study. An enthusiastic challenge is made for greater attention to the role of social work intervention within the problem area of drug abuse.

Administration

Barbaro, Fred. "The Field Instruction Component in the Administration Concentration: Some Problems and Suggested Remedies." *Journal of Education for Social Work* 15 (1975): 5–11.

Problems in developing administrative placements are reviewed from the perspectives of the faculty, agency, and field instructor with attention paid to elements of time and socialization. Special arrangements are briefly presented to address problems raised including the development of a certificate program in administration for field instruction.

Carroll, Donald, and McCuan, Patrick. "A Specialized Role Function Approach to Field Instruction in Social Work Administration." In *The Dynamics of Field Instruction*. New York: Council on Social Work Education, 1975, pp. 1–9.

Within a historical framework, the authors build a case for a specialized-role-function approach to field instruction in social work administration as opposed to a generalist approach. Four specialized role functions (supervision, staff development and training, program development and analysis, and program management) are briefly presented along with a sample of student field assignments.

Ellis, J.A. "Skill Training for Social Welfare Management: Developing A Laboratory Model for Field Instruction." *Administration in Social Work* 2 (1978): 211–222.

The utility of varied field instruction models for management skill training and development are examined and compared with a conceptual model for field instruction in social work management. The design and implementation of a laboratory model based on the conceptual model is described along with suggestions that the laboratory can be used to either supplement or substitute for traditional field practicums.

Aging and the Aged

Saul, Shura. "Learning about Aging." *Social Work Education Reporter* 20 (1972): 73–74.

A graduate field instruction unit designed to train professionals to work with older people as individuals through their families and/or other groups, in residences and institutions, and in the community is described along with the organization of the program and student assignments.

Cultural Diversity

Benavides III, Eustolio; Lynch, Mary Martin; and Velásquez, Joan Swanson. "Toward A Culturally Relevant Field Work Model: The Community Learning Center Project." *Journal of Education for Social Work* 16 (1980): 55–62.

The community-learning-center project was designed to develop culturally relevant student competencies for minority and nonminority field students and to identify the experiences that contribute to the development of such competencies. A questionnaire was developed and used to ascertain whether and how field instruction had contributed to the acquisition of culturally relevant student competencies in three categories: internal-interpersonal, external-interactional, and culturally specific. Black, Hispanic, and Native American centers were involved in this project. Direct work with minority clientele and field seminars to facilitate the integration of multicultural content are the final recommendations.

Community

Bryant, Richard. "Teaching Practice Skills in Community Work." *Community Development Journal* 11 (1976): 10–16; *and* "Fieldwork Training in Community Work." *Community Development Journal* 9 (1974): 212–216.

These two articles provide an international perspective biased toward greater community control for the field-work training of community workers. Critical observations are made on Jack Rothman's and Wyatt Jones's report suggesting greater control of community learning opportunities by what the author refers to as "educationalists." The teaching of three related skill clusters (communication and engagement, organizational and planning, political and analytical) is promoted through the doing of community work, observation, and the use of recording. Conservative principles for the planning and development of community placements are suggested.

Campfens, Hubert, and Loach, Fred. "Political Placements in Social Work Education: The U.S. and Canada." *Journal of Education for Social Work* 13 (1977): 11–17.

The authors report on a survey of the use of political placements by graduate schools of social work. Weaknesses in existing practices are noted and criteria for the development of effective political placements are described including student and setting readiness, personality of the officials, and structure for supervision and consultation.

Lammert, Marilyn, and Hagen, Jan. "A Model for Community-Oriented Field Experience." In *The Dynamics of Field Instruction: Learning through Doing.* New York: Council on Social Work Education, 1975, pp. 60–67.

See entry under "Teaching-Learning Approaches" for annotation.

Rothman, Jack, and Jones, Wyatt. *A New Look at Field Instruction.* New York: Association Press, 1971.

The authors suggest that social work is at a level of professional development where ". . . skill and theory are given somewhat equal treatment." They report on a late-sixties community-organization-curriculum-development project and include content on the restructuring of traditional field instruction for social work education and training in community organization and social planning. The current scene, trends, developments, and problems are reviewed. Guiding principles, formats, and a scheme are suggested for implementing an integrated approach to field instruction. The scheme suggests a sequential development of three emphases: laboratory-observation, skills development lab, and practicum. Strategies for organizing objectives and learning experiences are presented in addition to some useful information on simulation games and programmed instruction.

Criminal Justice System

Austin, Michael J.; Kelleher, Edward; and Smith, Philip L.,eds. *The Field Consortium: Manpower Development and Training in Social Welfare and Corrections.* Florida: State University System of Florida, 1972.

See entry under "Structural Models of Field Instruction" for annotation.

Treger, H. "Social Work in the Police Agency: Implications for Education and Practice." *Journal of Education for Social Work* 12 (1976): 43–50.

A three-year action-research project which placed social work practitioners and students in community police departments is described. Critical issues and concerns considered include staff and student selection, attitudes toward the law and authority, confidentiality, motivation of reluctant clients, and sensitivity to the "pig-bleeding heart" perceptions.

Health and Medical Care

Meyer, Carol. "Integrating Practice Demands in Social Work Education." In *Current Patterns in Field Instruction in Graduate Social Work Education,* edited by Betty Lacy Jones. New York: Council on Social Work Education, 1969, pp. 33–40/also in *Social Casework* 49 (1968): 481–488.

   See entry under "Structural Models of Field Instruction" for annotation.

Snyder, G.W.; Kane, R.A.; and Conover, C.G. "Block Placements in Rural VA Hospitals: A Consortium Approach." *Social Work in Health Care* 3 (1978): 331–343.

   The authors describe a three-year project involving the placement of twenty-eight students through a consortium arrangement with two schools of social work and eight Veterans' Administration hospitals in four western states. Student, administrative, and research experiences are described along with their practice experience with individuals, groups, and communities. Comments are made regarding the impact of the project on students, hospitals, and social work schools.

Tendler, D., and Metzger, K. "Training in Prevention: An Educational Model for Social Work Students." *Social Work in Health Care* 4 (1978): 221–231.

   A report is given on the development of a field work model for preventive social work practice with families and children using a student unit in a public health setting. The three-year project focused on early intervention with concern for life-span development tasks and on interdisciplinary collaboration on behalf of families. The processes for student orientation, intervention, collaboration, and evaluation are elaborated upon with a prevention theme.

Industry

Akabas, Sheila H. "Fieldwork in Industrial Settings: Opportunities, Rewards, and Dilemmas." *Journal of Education for Social Work* 14 (1978): 13–19.

   The author presents the Columbia University School of Social Work's 1976–77 experience with the placement of thirty students in industrial settings with opportunities for learning in direct service, planning, administration, and/or research activities. Issues involved in site selection, contractual and structural arrangements identifying appropriate assignments, and selection of students are discussed.

International

Masi, Fidelia A. "International Field Placements." *Journal of Education for Social Work* 10 (1974): 55–59.

   The approaches and findings of a survey of potential international placements are reported. The author visited schools of social work in Italy, England, and Holland, observed various community development projects, and completed a survey of NASW members of the European chapter. An analysis of the survey is presented along with a list of eighteen unsolicited suggestions for international field placements.

Manis, Francis. *Field Practice in Social Work Education: Perspectives from an International Base.* Fullerton, Ca.: Sultana Press, 1972.

   See entry under "Significant Publications" for annotation.

Mental Health and Retardation

Cramer, Margeryfay. "Fieldwork Preparation for Entrance into Mental Retardation Practice." *Journal of Education for Social Work* 13 (1977): 37–43.

   Based on experience at a regional center for the mentally retarded, the author reviews basic social work concepts and principles as they relate to work with the mentally retarded. The students' background, orientation to the institution, emotional implications, and assignments are also considered. Concepts reviewed include case movement, normalization, social role, cultural-familial retardation, and self-determination.

Dawson, Bettie Guthrie. "Supervising the Undergraduate in a Psychiatric Setting." In *The Dynamics of Field Instruction*. New York: Council on Social Education, 1975, pp. 10–19.
See entry under "Instructional Processes and Techniques: General" for annotation.

Kramer, Sidney. "Developing a Field Placement Program." *Social Casework* 43 (1961): 456–460.
This report on the planning and development of a field-work placement at a state hospital for the mentally ill was prepared in response to the need for information on how schools and agencies develop suitable placements for student training. A plea is made that design informs even the simplest structure.

Watkins, Ted R. "The Comprehensive Community Mental Health Center as a Field Placement for Graduate Social Work Students." *Community Mental Health Journal* 11 (1975): 27–32.
A historical review of comprehensive community mental health centers and the implications for placement of social work students is provided. Recognition is given to the hazards of minimal procedural restraints and lack of clarity on staff roles, especially the indigenous paraprofessional role. Negative reactions to student social workers as well as the positive contributions of students are explored.

Rural

DeJong, Cornell. "Field Instruction for Undergraduate Social Work Education in Rural Areas." In *The Dynamics of Field Instruction*. New York: Council on Social Work Education, 1975, pp. 20–30.
Do social workers who practice in rural settings need special skills and knowledge not required for practice in urban settings? Issues and concerns raised by this question are discussed in a context that recognizes the unique characteristics of practice in rural settings. Changes in traditional teaching methods and organizational structure of field instruction are presented as necessary for the preparation of generalist practitioners. The author reflects on his experience in developing a field instruction program for Northern Michigan University in the Upper Peninsula.

Green, Ronald K., and Webster, Stephen A., eds. *Social Work in Rural Areas: Preparation and Practice*. Knoxville: University of Tennessee, 1977.
A collection of papers addresses contemporary issues in rural America, education for rural practice, and rural practice issues.

School Social Work

Hawkins, Mable. "Interdisciplinary Team Training: Social Work Students in Public School Field Placement Settings." In *The Dynamics of Field Instruction*. New York: Council on Social Work Education, 1975, pp. 40–49.
A nine-week seminar for professionals from an intercity secondary school in Pittsburgh to enhance professional interpersonal-relationship skills is reported on. University disciplines include social work, education, counselor education, and psychology. The seminar project was part of a field-experience program for graduate social work students. A recommendation is made that "interdisciplinary team teaching" be included in curriculum design for multidisciplinary training settings.

About the Contributors

E. CLIFFORD BRENNEN, D.S.W., a professor at San Diego State University, has also been a faculty member at the University of Montana and Virginia Commonwealth University. He is the co-author (with Morton Arkava) of *Competency Based Education for Social Work*, and has published articles in *Public Welfare* and the *Journal of Education for Social Work*. He has been a member of CSWE's board of directors and accreditation commission and the joint NASW-CSWE board.

HELEN CASSIDY, M.S.W., professor of social work and coordinator of field instruction at the Tulane University School of Social Work, has practiced primarily in medical and public health settings. She has worked in the United Kingdom under a Fulbright Award and in Spain as a United Nations representative. Her publications include *Social Work Training Centers: Tentative Analysis of the Structure of Learning Environment* (co-authored with Walter Kindelsperger), editorship of *Modes of Professional Education: Functions of Field Learning in the Curriculum*, and a book on new concepts in mental retardation. Professor Cassidy has been president of NASW, a board member of the American Public Health Association, and has served on two CSWE commissions.

DONALD E. CHAMBERS, D.S.W., professor of social welfare at the University of Kansas, has extensive experience in Catholic Charities and mental health agencies. His publications include articles in *Social Work, Child Welfare, The Journal of Social Policy*, and *Social Service Review*, and a book on social policy analysis.

KAY L. DEA, D.S.W., associate dean and professor at the University of Utah Graduate School of Social Work, has practiced in juvenile corrections, family counseling, and psychiatric social work. A past president of the Baccalaureate Program Directors' Association, he has been active in NASW and has served on several commissions in CSWE.

PHILLIP A. FELLIN, Ph.D., is dean of the School of Social Work at the University of Michigan. He has co-authored two books, *Social Program Evaluation: The Assessment of Social Research* and *Social Workers at Work: Exemplars of Social Research*. He is a past vice-president of CSWE and has chaired its Commission on Accreditation.

AASE GEORGE, M.S., professor emeritus and former director of field instruction at the University of Kansas, has also taught at Ohio State University. Her primary practice experience has been in the YWCA and family and children's service. She has been active in the Kansas-Missouri and Kansas chapters of NASW, the Kansas Society of Clinical Social Work, CSWE, and the Child Welfare League of America.

MARGARET SCHUTZ GORDON, M.S.W., professor and director of field practicum for the School of Social Welfare at the University of Kansas, has also taught at Washington University in St. Louis. Her publications have focused on social work education, and her research project (with William Gordon), *Field Instruction Research Project: Final Report*, is one of the few substantial contributions in that area. She has been president of the Kansas Chapter of NASW and has served on several committees of the national organization.

WILLIAM E. GORDON, Ph.D., professor emeritus of research in the George Warren Brown School of Social Work at Washington University, was trained as a biological scientist and moved into public welfare in a research capacity. He contributes regularly to the *Journal of Education for Social Work* and *Social Work*. Dr. Gordon has served on the board of CSWE and as second vice president of NASW.

MARAH GRIST, M.S.W., retired in 1969 from her post as associate professor at the University of Utah. Her practice was primarily in public welfare settings, emphasizing foster care provision and development of foster parent services and organizations.

LOWELL E. JENKINS, M.S.W., associate professor and former field instruction coordinator at Colorado State University, has served as an agency field instructor and as a faculty field instructor at the University of Kansas School of Social Welfare, where he later was assistant director of field instruction. A past president of the Kansas Chapter of NASW, he has served on local, state and national committees of that organization. He has been published in the *Journal of Education for Social Work*, *Social Work*, and *Social Casework*.

ELEANOR HANNON JUDAH, D.S.W., was associate professor of social work at the Catholic University of America, where she chaired the undergraduate program, until September 1979. A Fulbright scholar to England, Dr. Judah has published articles in *Social Casework*, the *Journal of Education for Social Work, Social Thought* and *Charities USA*. Currently, she is book review editor of *Social Thought* and is engaged in freelance writing, consultation, and service projects.

RICHARD G. MIMIAGA, M.S.W., assistant professor and coordinator of outreach education at Colorado State University, has practiced primarily in child welfare and community development. He has served as president of the New Mexico Chapter and secretary of the Colorado Chapter of NASW and on the editorial committee of the NASW *Practice Digest*.

RUTH C. MYLI, M.S.W., is an associate professor of social work at the University of Utah. Her practice experience is in child welfare, and her publications include teaching materials related to foster care and work with Native American teenagers. She is currently on leave, serving as a staff member for the Pacific Northwest Synod of the Lutheran Church of America.

ANN JACKSON PILCHER, M.S.W., is a lecturer in the Social Work Department at LaTrobe University in Australia. Formerly she was a professor in the School of Social Work at San Diego State University and director of staff development for the Wyoming Department of Welfare. She has been active in both American and Australian social work organizations. Her publications and research have focused on supervision, social work education, and ethical standards for practice.

JERRY L. RANDOLPH, D.S.W., associate professor in the College of Social Work at the University of South Carolina, has published a number of journal articles and book chapters. He is co-author (with James B. Taylor) of a book, *Community Worker*, and a research project (with John T. Gandy and Frank B. Raymond) entitled *Minding the Store: Research on the Social Work Deanship*.

ANDREW L. SELIG, M.S.W., Sc.D., is head of the Social Work Department at the John F. Kennedy Child Development Center and associate professor of psychiatry at the University of Colorado Health Sciences Center. He has also taught at Harvard and the University of British Columbia, and is active in health-related organizations in the U.S. and Canada.

CARL M. SHAFER, D.S.W., associate professor of social work at the University of Southern California, has practiced in psychiatric and family service agencies as well as private practice. He is a member of the Society for General Systems Research, a past president of the California Society for Clinical Social Work, and a former vice president of the National Federation of Societies for Clinical Social Work.

BRADFORD W. SHEAFOR, Ph.D., is professor and former director of the social work program at Colorado State University. He has also served as associate dean of the School of Social Welfare at the University of Kansas. He has published articles in the *Journal of Education for Social Work*, the *Journal of Gerontology* and the *Journal of Social Welfare*, and is co-author of a book (with Armando Morales), *Social Work: A Profession of Many Faces*. He has served CSWE as secretary and as a member of several commissions, and is the Curriculum Task Force chair of NASW's Social Work Job Validation Project.

MAX SIPORIN, D.S.W., professor of social work at the State University of New York at Albany, has also taught at the University of Kansas, Tulane University, and the University of Maryland. He has practiced in family, psychiatric and medical settings, and has written many articles for national publications as well as a book, *Introduction to Social Work Practice*.

RICHARD SPANO, PH.D., associate professor in the School of Social Welfare at the University of Kansas, has also been a field instructor and a continuing education teacher. His practice experience has been in the family, medical and mental health fields, with research on social work history and foster care. His writing includes a book entitled *The Rank and File Movement in Social Work*.

Index

287